THE BRILLIANT CAGE

THE BRILLIANT CAGE

JEM STONE

DEDICATION

This book is dedicated to my Mother and Father, who selflessly gave their all in life and who stayed true to their hearts and their principles. It is also dedicated to All those who are suffering from Dementia and Alzheimer's or who have family and friends who are. May God Bless Everyone.

I want to give special thanks to my twin daughter, Justine, who helped take my cover art vision and digitally create it, and to my daughter, Jade, for all her help with the clerical aspects of completing this book. Together we are the "Trine."

INTRODUCTION

I want you to know what a unique and special opportunity this is for me, to be able to tell you the story of my eighteen-year journey, with both Dementia and Alzheimer's. Never before has a patient with Alzheimer's been able to describe what it feels like, both physically, emotionally, spiritually, and mentally when afflicted with these memory-stealing diseases. The toll it takes on the patient and everyone around them is such a tragedy. Until new medical advancements bring a cure, millions upon millions, of folks of all ages, will continue to suffer in silence. It is our wish that we can bring you some answers, advice, and hope, to as many souls as possible. This book is a collaboration between myself, my husband Ken, and our oldest daughter Tracy, who now goes by the name, Jem. I developed the ability to channel beings from the Spirit realm and my daughter Jem also perfected that ability at a very young age. Through the strong Psychic connection, we have with Jem, we can share our stories with everyone, from the Divine Realm of God. We hope you like it and that you learn something from our combined experiences of dealing with Alzheimer's and the amazing supernatural. Many Blessings to you all. Mel, Ken, Jem.

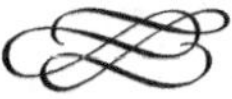

I passed away on the twenty-sixth of July of twenty-twenty, a few months after Ken, who died on May, twenty-third, of twenty-twenty. Covid killed me, not Alzheimer's. It was a blessing in disguise, as my physical health was good so I might have suffered for another ten years. Ken died of internal bleeding from complications of Hepatitis, after refusing life-saving surgery because he was tired of the daily grind and wanted to exit that life. We were both eighty-eight, years old and had been married for sixty-five years. We departed from the earthly plane just sixty-four, days apart. I had been hanging on, so he wouldn't be alone and he had been praying, I'd pass, so he wouldn't have to watch me slowly waste away. We were both ready to go and that's what we did. God knew our life plan and it went just the way it was designed to. It was a crushing blow for our four kids though, as due to Covid, they weren't allowed to visit us or be at our bedside when we were dying, so for that, we are truly sorry. Our funeral was held up for over a year, due to Covid restrictions on gatherings. Our cremains were finally laid to rest together, in September, of twenty twenty-one, in a military cemetery on Cape Cod, Massachusetts. All our loved ones were in attendance, which was very heart-warming. Ken and I had front-row seats to the funeral and the memorial service, one of the many perks of being in a Spirit form. They allow you to watch the goings on of your family and friends, once you are back home in the divine realm of Heaven. They understand how tightly connected you still are to those you love. Just because you leave your body and return home, it doesn't mean your Spirit cuts off all ties with the living. There are contracts between you and every soul that plays a part in your life. It's true, that after your soul exits the suit of flesh, it returns home to the Spiritual plane, also known as "Heaven". When you arrive there, you are greeted by all your Star family members and friends that have passed before you, as well as the Masters, Spirit Guides, Angels, and your Ancestors. Also, all the pets you have ever had, are waiting to cuddle with you and glory in your presence. If you have died from a long, lingering, illness, then you will be taken to a fancy hospital of sorts, where you will receive advanced healing treatments from the Holographic healing beds and the Master Healing Souls, as well as visitors that comfort and console you. All souls who died after a life of suffering from illness, abuse, neglect, or trauma, also need time to process, review and heal their auras and their spirit. Once you are healed, you are treated like the royalty each one of you truly is! No soul is left alone or rejected, especially if they have lived a life of faith in a Higher Power. A selfless life, full of unconditional love and kindness to all. Every soul that has lived a life filled with compassion and kindness, will be treated like heroes when they return home to the Kingdom of God. You are considered very brave to leave your celestial home, filled with God's Holiness, and enter a life that will be extremely challenging and difficult. A physical life on earth that is filled with many temptations like power, money, greed, envy, corruption, crime, rape, molestation, cruelty discrimination, murder, and slavery. Everyone must also deal with unpredictable weather and diseases, that's why it's extremely important to treat everyone and everything with absolute respect, caring and unconditional love. Do your part every day to be helpful to those in need and share your fortune with those less fortunate. To receive blessings, please remember to say thanks to God, Jesus, mother earth, and the universe for those blessings. That keeps the balance of positive energy flowing, so it will be repeated. Give and Take equals balance. If you always give gifts to someone who never says "Thank You", why would you keep giving them gifts? That's the way the universe works, balance is the key to everyone's happiness and success! Your subconscious wants to be able to return to Heaven and feel the powerful love of God and

Jesus once again. I couldn't speak about Dementia or Alzheimer's, while I was under their grip but now, I'm able to talk through my daughter Jem and hopefully, we can bring you some comfort and knowledge, to all those suffering the effects of this silent killer or who have loved ones that are inflicted with Dementia or Alzheimer's. We pray that all of you are spared these awful diseases and that a cure will come very soon.

God Bless You All and Thank You for being a part of our stories.

Melba, (aka) Moosie, Ken, Jem.

I knew that since my mother Vivian, had Dementia in her early eighties, I could carry that same gene. I just didn't know when or if it would appear. I watched my mother decline as her memory started to fade. She became paranoid, angry, and unpredictable. Dementia and Alzheimer's wasn't something I wanted but through each incarnation on earth, we each pick lessons to learn, as well as some that will help teach others. I was gifted with the ability to channel spirits, who would use my voice, to speak to our meditation group, "The Trine" on Wednesday nights. Each week, Ken and I would meet with three other, like-minded couples, for a thirty-minute, group meditation, then I would go into a trance state, allowing a positive Spirit from the Higher Realms to speak through me to our group. We recorded those sessions and someone also made notes. We took turns asking the speakers questions about our past lives and other mysteries of the universe. Our oldest daughter Jem was the only one of our four kids who had any interest in what we were doing. She started finding lost objects for her friends when she was seven and she could feel the energies of others, making her an Empath. Later, I taught her how to channel. Ken and I were more focused on researching our past lives, while Jem excels at Psychic readings and being a Medium, who talks with loved ones that have departed the earthly plane. She also speaks Telepathically, to benevolent beings, from other dimensions and to animals of every kind. Together, we hope to bring some enlightenment and information to anyone who has an open mind and who is willing to listen. Currently, while doctors and scientists are still puzzling over the human brain and its many mysteries, Dementia and Alzheimer's are affecting the minds of millions of people each year! Alzheimer's is the fifth leading cause of death in the USA today. Until there is a breakthrough of some kind or an advancement with a cure, Dementia and Alzheimer's will continue to ravage innocent minds. Before we start, I want to give you a heads-up, this book is based on real events, characters, dates, and real locations. We are an average American family that wants to share their experiences with what it's like, to have your wife, mother, and grandmother be afflicted by first, Dementia, then later Alzheimer's, for almost twenty years. Here are three family members, with separate views and opinions, on what they went through, dealing with the tragic effects of Dementia and Alzheimer's.

OLD TIMERS SYNDROME

Through my long experience with Dementia and Alzheimer's, I lived through every phase of those two diseases and their symptoms. Now that I'm in the Spirit Realm, I can share the truth with you, about what happens when you lose control over your mind, your body, and your sense of reality. How it feels to lose your sense of "Self ", as the diseases steal your ability to understand what is going on inside of you and around you. I am not trying to "Scare" anyone, I am trying to "Share" with everyone, my story from my perspective. Please keep an open mind, that's all we ask. Alzheimer's is such a tragic event. Those suffering from Dementia and Alzheimer's, cannot tell anyone how they are feeling or what they are going through because their mind starts to "skip", during its thought process but the person doesn't even realize something is amiss. Most people who recall forgetting little things like time and dates, just laughed it off as "Old Timer's" syndrome and made jokes about it. No one wants to think it can happen to them. Little do they know, that by the time you catch yourself going into a room and forgetting why you went in there, you "Might" already be in the early stages of Dementia. Now I am not saying that every time you forget something you should panic but keeping a journal isn't a bad idea, as it allows you and others to track your incidents. If you or a loved one is currently experiencing any signs of Dementia or Alzheimer's, please seek immediate help from a qualified specialist! Do Not put this off, as early detection gives you way more options. Better safe than sorry. I can tell you from my journey through both Dementia and Alzheimer's, that it was much harder on my husband Ken, and our four children than it was on me. We hope that by the three of us sharing our versions of our lives before and during Alzheimer's, we can shed some light on just how much these mind thieves steal from people just like you and me. We hope to bring you understanding and insight into what it's like for a family to battle these debilitating brain diseases.

TAKING YOU BACK

Let us take you back to nineteen sixty-eight, in West Newbury, Massachusetts. A large town that has way more cows than people. My husband Ken, short for Kenneth, and I bought a house built in the mid seventeen hundreds, situated on the main street that ran through town. The thirteen-room home consisted of four floors, complete with four fireplaces and at least ten layers of old, vintage, wallpaper, which took many hours to remove. The old place was in much need of some TLC, which came by way of Ken and I and our two oldest kids, Jim and Jem. Saturdays were work-around-the-house days and Sundays were for muse-ums, beach days, and Sunday dinners. After many months of hard work, the house became like an old friend and I believe it was proud of being fixed up and shown some love and respect. That place came with many charms and also some ghosts. Yes, I said Ghosts!

One night as I stood alone in the kitchen baking holiday cookies, l heard the wood floor creak in the walkway to my right. It only does that when you walk on it. When I turned to look, there stood a tiny girl about five years old, with her hair half up and tied with a ribbon, her hands clasped behind her back as she gazed up at me. She wore a dress with ruffles and stockings with tiny shoes. The clothing was from the early eighteen hundreds and when I smiled and said "Hello", she smiled back at me. I stepped back to open the oven door, removed the cookies placing them on the cooling rack. When I looked back, she was gone before I could offer her one. When we bought the house, the last owner gave us a few older pictures they had of the outside of the house. One picture was taken in the early eighteen hundreds, from across the street. In the photo, a woman was standing in front of the house with a little girl beside her, much like the ghost I had seen in our kitchen. The previous owners said that many years ago, during the depression, other owners sold candy and sweets from the house to neighbors and children. There were four levels to our home. The first floor had a kitchen, dining room, formal living room, den, and bathroom. A newer addition added on the back went the length of the house and gave us a lot of extra space. We used it as a den on one side and a large craft room on the other side. The craft room came with a vaulted ceiling and we built bookcases on the end wall that held craft supplies. There were tables and chairs for craft classes and we added a counter and cabinets, with a sink and a refrigerator. There was also a sewing area and card table. The second floor had three large bedrooms and the master suite was over the top of the extension in the rear. The large bathroom came with double sinks, a tub, a shower, and a washer and dryer. The attic was also fitted with two small bedrooms, one on each side and one in the front that looked down onto the street. We decided not to refurbish the top floor because it was a major restoration that would require redoing all the walls with insulation, drywall, new floors, and more. It hadn't been used in ages, so we decided to make it a storage space. We found old newspapers, antique items, and a rocking chair up there. The cellar had a dirt floor with a big furnace, which made scary noises when it was on. Jim and Jem made mounds of dirt in front of the old slate, tombstones, that belonged to those long departed and brought their new friends down to the cellar, to scare them at Halloween. There weren't any people buried down there (at least we hoped not). Having a dirt floor didn't help it to look very inviting. As the house went through many owners throughout the years, the original acreage that went more than a mile back behind the house to the Merrimack River, was sold off when an owner needed the cash or couldn't pay its property taxes. In the nineteen fifties, a contractor purchased the land beside and behind our house. He built a new neighborhood of small homes that were on a new, "L" shaped road, that went straight back behind us, with about six houses on each side, then it had a turn around on the right and went out to join an adjacent street on the left. There were about sixteen homes built back there in total. When the contractor built the road next to our house, they exhumed the bodies of the old family cemetery and put new headstones in the town cemetery for the bodies, and gave the old slate markers to the people living in the house at that time. Their last name was Carr and on one of the headstones, it said their child had died at six months old. Another one was engraved with a child's name who had passed away at age two. That was common for those times because health care back then was mostly home remedies in the seventeen and eighteen hundreds. Ken and I felt that since we were making period-correct upgrades to the old home, then maybe that would appease any woeful spirits roaming about but our two oldest kids, Jim and Jem felt very differently. They told us how the house creeped them out, especially at night. They didn't like being alone in the house either. They both reported hearing a rocking chair, rocking in the attic above the second floor, and hearing the sound of a baby crying, coming from up there. Ken and I had chalked it up to our kid's imagination until I met the little girl's resident ghost. Plus, kids do tend to attract ghosts because of their high energy and open minds. The first two years seemed to go okay and we were all busy with work and school and adjusting to life in a new town. While the kids were in school, I spent my days making wreaths and doing crafts. Sometimes I would be sewing or creating crafts to teach to the locals. Our property had two acres and came with three rows, one hundred feet each, of established asparagus. I planted rows of all kinds of veggies, gourds, and pumpkins that I canned. I also made my own jelly, out of hand-picked, crab apples, beach plums, and blackberries. If the two oldest kids were in the car with me and I spied a pile of pine cones under a tree, I'd pull over and make them get out and gather them up. This embarrassed them to no end! I made up for it with a treat of some kind and they loved the jelly I made from the things we picked together. Kids grow up fast and we wanted the older two to keep hanging out with us, even though it wasn't "Cool" to be seen with your folks after you were thirteen years old. All kids go through the "Pushing The Parents Away" phase as they get older. Once your child turns ten, they start asserting their wants and desires into the family dynamics, as they take hold of the reins, loosely at first. Neither Ken nor I had any siblings, so we didn't have any expectations of how sisters and brothers acted. We were strict when it came to making important decisions and we were honest with our kids and they were honest with us. Every parent wants their child to feel like they can go to them for help or advice. Ken and I were fair, and listened to our children's concerns and we did our best not to judge too harshly. When it came to exploring each new neighborhood, our whole family looked forward to the trips to unexplored places that surrounded Boston. From the malls to museums, the concerts to the beaches and to plays in the city, it was a very sweet and organic way of life while living in West

Newbury. I even bought our milk from a local dairy, which came in old glass bottles, which you brought back to exchange when you wanted more milk. Thanks to our amazing new neighbors and the country's surroundings, our whole family thrived during our six years there. A "Davis" family record for living in the same house in the same town. A lot of it had to do with the seventies being a much simpler style of life, more carefree and lighter. People all over the world were moving to vibes of peace, love, and kindness. Respect and compassion were the norms of society, as was the "live and let live" mentality. Humanity was like one giant, living, quilt of caring, that blanketed mother earth. Our souls were like one mind, one heart, and one thought. It was such a thrilling time to be young, involved, and committed to changing things for the better. It was a movement based on exploring every-thing, through an eyes-wide-open lens. Love thy brother and help thy neighbor, themes were every-where. Peace signs and yellow smiley faces, adorned tied-dyed Tee shirts, stickers, and posters. The "Forrest Gump " movie mirror's our story too. Forrest Gump's story took place in Alabama, our adventures were twenty hours away, up north in Massachusetts, where folks were kind and had respect for others and helped each other out. The whole country was facing the war in Vietnam, segregation, and fighting pollution. The Cuban missile crisis was front page news in the fifties but now folks were coming together to help make a difference in America, by standing up to government policies, regulations, and antiquated ideals. Peaceful demonstrations dotted the countryside and the cities. Jesus clubs, Buddhist groups, Hindu followers and New Age believers sprang up everywhere. Young folks wanted answers to the meaning of Life, why are we here on planet earth. We were tired of wars and we were challenging the Establishment and its policies. Meanwhile, Americans were grooving along to folk songs and rock music, full of harmony and peace. It was one of the happiest times in all our lives. As much as we loved living in New England, it was unfortunately, so steeped in deep traditions, that the locals were very uptight. Even Vermont had a growth spurt when hippies and young people moved there to live a free and creative lifestyle. New Englanders were downright superstitious, especially in the early seventies. After all, Salem Massachusetts was only thirty minutes south of us and that's where they had the witch trials and burned them at the stake. Living in a town of only a few thousand people tends to be gossipy and small-minded but the flip side to that is, that your neighbors became your extended families, who had your back, like you had theirs and everyone watched everyone's kids. It was a spider's web of support close by, that gave us all a solid level of comfort and ease. Most folks back then didn't even lock their back door! In nineteen seventy, almost everyone in our circle of friends was conservative and not very liberal at all. I'm in no way suggesting folks walked around with an iron poker shoved down the back of their pants but they were more cautious in nature. I suppose we should keep in mind that New England was full of tight-knit communities that were built by generations of families, moving to a certain area and staying there and their children stayed there too. That tradition continues throughout the North East. Ken and I were in our mid-thirties and we were well-educated. Ken held a master's degree in education and I had my teaching degree. We met at Teachers' College in Castleton, Vermont. Ken was born in Vermont and I hailed from Maine. During our summer breaks from the University, I got our friend's jobs, working at the pier in Old Orchard, beach Maine. There were five guys and four to five girls, who either worked the rides, the games-of-chance, or they were waiters or waitresses. My mother Vivian, knew everyone from O.O.B., as she was the safety commissioner, so we were all set for seasonal employment. We worked hard and played around between work shifts. It was during those short college breaks that we made lasting memories of those special summertimes. After graduation, Ken and I decided to get married on June eighteenth, nineteen fifty, five. The draft was still in effect, as the Korean War had ended, but the Cuban missile crisis and the war in VietNam were still a threat, so Ken enlisted in the Army. They stationed him in Fort Lee, Virginia after he finished his basic training, then we packed up and headed south. This was in the mid-nineteen fifties, and to all the Southerners, the war was still raging between the North and the South. Southerners hated people from the North and they didn't even try to hide their disdain from us. Boy, we were in for a real treat! After we got settled in, I wanted to work so we could afford to live off base. Most women at that time were stay-at-home moms, who cooked and cleaned. When Ken saw a post on a bulletin board, that they were looking to hire a secretary, he told me about it and I wanted to apply. I graduated high school two years early, due to a double-grade promotion and I was the Dean's secretary in college at sixteen years old. Ken spoke to his supervisor who let on that I wouldn't get hired but he admitted that he had to, at least let me take the civil service exam. I scored the highest grade in the history of the Civil Service Exam, given by the Army, at that time. Because my score was so high, I got the job and that put a lot of noses out of joint, I'll tell ya, especially because I was a woman and from the north! After a few years, Ken received his master's degree and started working as a federal employee for "Civil Defense". With that promotion came a transfer, up to Maynard Massachusetts, and off we went! We lived a little over a year in Acton Massachusetts, as it was close to his new job but we yearned for an older house, closer to the coast. That's how we found West Newbury and that big wonderful old haunted house. We were ecstatic to be back in New England again. We weren't quite the "Adams Family" but in West Newbury, we stuck out, especially when Ken bought a nineteen sixty-three Volkswagen, Beatle, (Punch Buggy) in bright yellow! He brought home an overhead projector from work and painted "Snoopy" outlines on the side doors in black.

Snoopy was the dog's name in the Charles Shultz cartoon, Peanut's. One door had Snoopy on his skateboard, the other door had him on "his" dog house. Sometimes, when Ken got home early from work, he'd drive onto the back lawn and down the hill to the house, just to make the kids laugh. I think you get the picture. We were young and creative with a good sense of humor, loving life!

Back in nineteen sixty-nine, Ken and I decided that instead of going on a lot of vacations, it would be much better to buy a cottage in Old Orchard Beach, Maine. We both loved going there and it was only an hour and ten minutes to get there from our house. This way we could have family and friends come up to stay and it would also be wonderful to hold family reunions there. When you drive north on the beach road from the pier, it comes to a neighborhood called Pine Point. It's a very sweet and peaceful neighborhood of mostly year-round locals. It butts up against the rock jetty and a channel into the marsh. My mother grew up there and our kids loved that area too. We drove up and down the little streets hoping to see a for sale sign. As luck would have it, we found a big, two-story cottage that sat on three-quarters of an acre, located behind a big paved parking lot that beachgoers used. It was right on the beach before you turned left to go into the Pine Point neighborhood. It wasn't winterized but everything about it was perfect! It had a big den, a large kitchen, and a screened-in front porch that ran the entire length of the front of the house. The second floor had two big front bedrooms, a smaller bedroom, and one bigger bedroom along the back. The only bathroom was at the top of the stairs on the second floor. The cottage had great energy and the view was spectacular. There was even a small workshop, shed near the back where the two older kids used to make stuff to float in the tidal pools. At the time, real estate prices were cheap, so we bought it right then and there. We paid sixty-nine thousand dollars, as it was such a good deal. Because the owner knew Vivian, my mother, he was happy we were the buyers. It helps to have connections. Vivian was thrilled as we all spent a lot more time seeing her and Gean. She was Dementia free in those wonderful years. Every summer we went up there on the weekends rain or shine and we all had a blast! Jim won a twelve-foot Styrofoam sailboat. He and Jem took it out on the ocean even though they didn't know how to sail and had a lot of fun just goofing off in it. Everyone loved beachcombing best of all. Finding sand dollars, seashells, starfish, sea glass, and driftwood. It was by far the best investment we had ever made, as it gave us many years of fun and adventures! Our whole family grew very close because of that special cottage and through those sweet memories, we all shared that carefree time in our lives. When Jim and Jem were able to drive, they took their friends up there to hang out and they would visit Vivian and Gean, while they were there. Ken and I had our friends come up there too and we played cards, games and we did puzzles when we weren't sunning ourselves or beach combing. Everyone loved to drive the loop by the pier and get pizza and french fries with vinegar. I would grind up the fresh Quahog clams the kids would dig up when the tide went out and make tasty clam fritters. We all have such fond memories of that Pine Point retreat! We finally sold it when we moved from Newburyport to Virginia. We got back three times what we paid for it. Jem was up there in twenty twenty-one and took pictures of it, as it's all been completely winterized and upgraded. I'm sure their family loves it as much as we did!

THE CRAFT CENTER

It was while I was over in Newburyport, shopping one day, that I was overcome with a crazy desire to open a craft supply store! Back then, the only place to buy craft supplies was a forty-five-minute ride, each way, over and back to a major city. I went home and spoke to Ken about the idea and he knew that once I had a notion to do something, he might as well save his breath and just go with it, so he agreed and we sat down to make a list of what needed to be done. We would need a store to rent, tables, peg board, a cash register, a business name and tax ID number. We bought display shelves, a sales desk and a showcase. We had a local artist make our outdoor sign. I found out there was a huge wholesaler for craft supplies in Woburn, Massachusetts along with the Boston whole-sale only flower mart, where we could purchase stock to sell. Two months later, we cut the ribbon in front of our new store located on State Street, in downtown Newburyport, named, "The Craft Center". I was meeting all kinds of new people and before long, I was joining the Chamber of Commerce and was asked to be on the committee for their annual, two-week, summer celebration called, "Yankee Homecoming". The celebration had many daily events such as various contests, sidewalk sales, bands, and concerts in the parks where food and dessert stands kept all the hungry crowds happy. A big parade as the finale ended a very prosperous event! Those fourteen days brought even more tourists to the bustling, smallest, city in the state of Massachusetts. Everyone dressed up in attire from the seventeen and eighteen hundreds which lent a vibe of authenticity to the festivities. It was an exciting time to be immersed, not only in running the store but to also be part of a large network of artists and customers, who appreciated what we were selling. Through our craft store, I met a lady named Lynn Random. She was a local potter and we just cliqued! Lynn and I shared many things in common. Ken and I went to dinner with her and her husband, Gig. Both men became instant friends, as the four of us shared a very strong, Spiritual connection. A few weeks later, we went on to meet some of their friends and families, which ultimately, led to us forming our Wednesday night, meditation group, consisting of four couples that shared our feelings and experiences of a Spiritual nature, that were sacred unto us. The eight of us took turns going to each other's houses and once a month we met at our home. First, we would do a twenty-minute group meditation and for the first few months we used an Ouija board, to ask the spirit realm questions and we took turns taking notes of the questions and answers, as records of their replies. After a few months, we realized that only lower-level spirits and trickster spirits were working through the board, so we all started reading books on channeling and we began to try various other methods of deeper meditation to help us break through to a more powerful level of entities of a higher vibrational frequency. It didn't take very long before I was able to enter a trance-like state and let a spirit speak directly to the group. It was decided that we should start taping the sessions along with taking notes as a backup. Ken would sit next to me and make sure I would be able to come out of the trance after each session. We grew very close to these souls we called friends. It was so special to each of us, to be a part of this group that believed in the same ideals, spiritual beliefs, and principles as we did. At that time, what we were doing was considered very controversial and carried a stigma, as some locals might have considered us to be witches or devil worshipers, out of ignorance of what we were doing. Our group of souls were searching for "Enlightenment" and seeking truthful knowledge about where we came from, why we were here, and where we were going. We felt so strongly about there being more to a physical life, than just working nine to five till you retire and die. We were young intellectuals, wanting answers to life's secrets and where we fit into it all.

The Universe was knocking and our group was answering the door!

Neither Ken nor I, ever had any negative intentions while meditating. We and our group of friends, were all loving, positive, and caring people, trying to get closer to God and the white light Source of "All That Is". We were exploring the act of expanding our consciousness and learning to harness our abilities, connecting with a higher power and frequency of love and light. When folks get together, their combined frequencies of positivity, unconditional love and their powers of white light can heal, calm, protect, and project that healing light onto other people or groups of people and situations. All positive white light energy of your Spirit contains magical powers of creativity and healing. Once you meditate and picture yourself drawing in the collective energies of compassion, faith, hope and unconditional love, that positive power of earth's energy will open up to you and everything in your life will start happening for you on a deeper level and with more frequency. Lots of little and some big coincidences will occur all the time. Everything just seems to flow with little to "No effort" on your part. You have raised up your own soul's frequency, so now you are hooked into the Universal Matrix of "All That Is". It's that powerful electromagnetic energy field of the earth that can heal and protect you. Here is a simple way to start connecting with your inner self, your subconscious mind. Try it like this in the morning before you get out of bed. Lay there relaxed, eyes closed. Now, slowly breathe in through your nose till your lungs feel full, then pause for ten seconds, slowly releasing that breath from your mouth until you feel your diaphragm squeeze in, then count to five before breathing in again and repeat that process two more times, for a total of three times. After a few weeks of breathing in slowly and slowly releasing your breath, you should start to notice that your mind and body pick up this exercise fast and it signals your Angels and your Spirit Guides that you are wanting to communicate with them. We refer to this technique as, "Dialing the Divine". Try sitting quietly for ten minutes with your eyes closed after your breathing technique. With eyes closed, look straight into your inner field of vision, your "third eye" should allow you to see images or scenes inside your mind's eye. It's located on the center of your forehead between your eyebrows. The "Pineal" gland, with practice, can reveal insights, leads, and clues to your journey of enlightenment, while you're incarnated on "Earth School". It was the early seventies era but we weren't in California, we were in New England. We asked our oldest kids not to tell anyone about what we were doing, so their friend's parents wouldn't stop their kids from playing with our kids. We weren't being dramatic, we were being protective, as it didn't take much for some of the old timers to make a ruckus over anything they didn't understand. If they found out we were meditating with candles at night in a group, they would have labeled us as Devil worshippers. Luckily, no one ever accused us or our group of anything at all, in the ten years we met once a week. Those friendships were on another level and brought the eight of us even closer together, something Ken and I had never had before. Our Spirit Guide's were delightful and they were a real font of information and comfort because they wanted us to be doing exactly what we were doing, so they made sure we were safe. They told us many things, about our past lives and who we were, and what we had done during those lifetimes. It was a truly unique and humbling experience for us all. Our group was more focused on questions about the universe and our past lives and not on predicting future events or fortune-telling. The eight of us were on a Spiritual voyage, made up of the secret knowledge of our ancient ancestors. During each meditation session at our house, Jem would sneak down the stairs and sit on the steps just out of sight, so she could listen to me channel a Spirit Guide. She was twelve then and very curious about what we were doing. Looking back, it was unusual for eight adults to sit in the dark with candles and meditate. One night, the guest Spirit I had channeled through me, spoke to her, and the group of us was surprised, as we didn't even know she was there. We were all amused and didn't mind the interruption. She came down and sat on the landing facing the group. The Spirit told her about a few of her past lives. In a past life she was a girl in Athens Greece, and she would run foot races with the boys. In another life, she was a Native American girl who raced ponies with the boys. The guide then asked her if she had any questions, to which she stated, she knew the house had ghosts but she asked the Spirit Guide if there was any way they could make sure she couldn't see them. The spirit said that could be arranged. She went on to tell us, that there was a ghost living in her closet and that one night, right after she got into bed, she heard her closet door creak open, then two footsteps next to her bed just before someone sat down at the edge of her bed as the sheets got tight over her feet. She said that she was so terrified she might have passed out because she woke up in the morning, remembering the event but not anything after the ghost sat down. The eight of us were stunned! This was the first time Ken and I had ever heard of the ghost in her closet. We became worried for her safety because not all ghosts are harmless. She told everyone that she dreamt of her closet door being open and as she stood looking down, the closet floor was replaced with a pit of "Hellish flame's" burning down below. Later that week both Jem and her older brother

Jim sat down with us and admitted they had found the Ouija board and had used it a few times after school until it started spelling out swear words and saying demonic things to them. They said they barely had to put their pinkies on it and it would fly from letter to letter. Ken and I were shocked by this unexpected information, as it had never occurred to us that either one of them would do anything like that. It really hit home, that a lot was going on that we weren't aware of or could control, especially while we were both at work. When dealing with anything supernatural or in the Spirit realm, it is necessary to protect yourself by putting white light energy all around you, to ward off dark or evil entities and also to keep negative beings from gaining control over your emotions or mind. This is extremely essential for young minds and souls, who aren't strong enough emotionally to protect themselves. Children become vulnerable targets for those poltergeists and low-level trickster spirits that have evil intentions. Their young minds and souls are wide open to receive and they are innocent, that's how children learn so quickly. Ken and I have always been open and honest with all four of our children, telling them the ground rules and the consequences if they break the rules, so besides the usual shenanigans, our kids were kind, respectful, hard-working, and loving. Luckily, near the end of our first year, the store was doing well enough that we hired a young woman to work a few hours here and there, so I could be more involved at home and make sure everyone was safe. I also had extra time to take on more duties at the Chamber of Commerce, which led to me becoming the first woman Vice President of the organization in Newburyport, Massachusetts. It was those challenges that spurred me on and gave my life zest and real purpose. I was spending more time in Newburyport, so Ken and I began looking for buildings that would allow us to live above our store. More and more, trendy stores were opening near our craft shop and property prices were soaring. In nineteen, seventy-five, we bought a large building on the waterfront, at the mouth of the Merrimack River in Newburyport. It was two buildings that were joined together like the letter "T." The street front was a beautiful two-story, brick building that we renovated into a lovely store on the first floor and a stylish apartment with a bedroom loft that had a curved wrought iron staircase, on the second floor. Both levels would bring in additional income, making it a wise decision. The two-story, wooden building was approximately ninety-five feet in length and went the long way, toward the river in the back. With the help of a local contractor, we designed a store on the first level, complete with a classroom, bathroom, shelves, and a sales counter for our retail craft store. Upstairs, we had a storage room that adjoined the front brick building on the street. We then added a den with a bedroom for Jem on the left and a loft bedroom above for Jim. The main house had three more bedrooms. Our master bedroom had a walk-in closet and a full bathroom. The opposite wall had two bedrooms, one for Dean and the other for Doreen. The four kids shared a large bathroom with a washer and dryer. The kitchen was across from the stairs that led down to the door and our store. The large combination, living and dining room had an open floor plan with a vaulted ceiling and wooden beams. My baby grand piano was on the living room side, along with couches and a dining room table, and a hutch was on the other side. We had glass windows and sliding doors that looked out over a large deck, with the view of the mouth of the river where it met the Atlantic Ocean. It was such an amazing vista all year round as the river was full of boats coming and going and there was a dock behind our house owned by fishermen, who pulled up their boats in the afternoon, filled with fresh fish, and auctioned off their catch to restaurant owners and dealers in tuna. On the right of our building, was a popular seafood restaurant named, "The Starboard Galley" and next to them was the very first, "National Coast Guard" station in America. Many a day we were entertained by their boats doing drills, of their amazing life-saving skills. The mouth of the Merrimack River is very treacherous to navigate. The Atlantic Ocean has strong, cross-currents that converge at opposing angles, putting it on the list of the top ten hardest ports in the world to enter. Thank God the Coast Guard is located so close. Our best friends, Gig and Lynn Random had their beautiful sailboat moored right behind our home. Unfortunately, during a bad nor'easter storm, the strong winds and currents pulled their sloop free of its mooring and it ended up in the marsh, where it sustained so much damage that they had to sell what was left of it as salvage. Nature is beautiful but it can also be fierce. We made it through the great blizzard of seventy-eight, when it snowed so hard and so much that it blocked all the storm drains, so when the salt water came up over the sea walls, it flooded many homes and businesses. Those are the risks people take when they live near a river or an ocean or any body of water, you must take the good with the bad. All in all, living over our store were some of the very best years of our lives in that we were in our early forties' and Jim had graduated high school and Jem was a senior. The twins were eleven and had made friends at the new school in Newburyport. We loved walking uptown after dinner, stopping to speak to friends and peek in the store windows. Oftentimes, we met friends for dinner, as there were wonderful restaurants to choose from within walking distance from our place. It was a stress-free time, strolling around with the tourists and stopping for ice cream. Life in the mid-seventies was rich with prosperity and Newburyport was on fire with popularity as new faces were moving in daily while commerce was thriving.

BOMB SHELTER

Everything was splendid for the first five years. Living closer to our friends meant we were able to spend a lot more quality time with them and continue our Trine meditation sessions. It wasn't until late in nineteen seventy-nine, that things started to shift in our area. Big box stores started to open up on the outskirts of town and soon we began to feel the financial squeeze. Folks were going to Kmart and other larger stores, to purchase their craft supplies, which left us trying to figure out our next move. There was no way we could compete with their low prices, so sadly after ten years in business, we decided to cut our losses and close the store. We listed our properties with a local realtor and held large sales to sell off the unsold inventory. Since real estate on the waterfront was very desirable, we received multiple offers and closed a deal within weeks of its listing and started packing. As luck would have it, Ken's job offered him a promotion to a GS16, which is the highest one can go before having to be politically nominated. The promotion came with a move near Washington D.C., the nation's capital, so we packed up and headed to a house we chose in Fairfax, Virginia. The house had perks, like an easier commute for Ken, who had been driving close to two hours each way, to his job in Maynard, Massachusetts. In Maynard, he worked in an underground building that was a Post-World War Two bomb shelter. That bunker was one of many command centers in case of a nuclear war or a national emergency, like a bombing, earthquake, or tornado. His official title was, "Regional Training Advisor" for Civil Defense. His territory was the Eastern Seaboard and Puerto Rico. Essentially, he was responsible for meeting with each city's police, fire station, town hall, and city officials to educate them about evacuation plans and what critical measures they should take, in case of a natural disaster or a war. The Federal organization is now called FEMA, an acronym for, Federal Emergency Management Agency. Ken had high-security clearance and was very well respected in his field. He had written many training manuals and other government materials that helped a lot of cities and towns put together solid evacuation plans and drills in the event of a disaster. His signature alone carried weight and he aided all those below him in rank to get their promotions when they worked hard and deserved it. He was also offered a position in an Ivy League college, as a professor but turned it down because he loved his job and its benefits. When we sold our buildings and moved, it was with a heavy heart, as we would be leaving our two oldest kids, our best friends, and my mother Vivian. Jim enlisted in the Air Force and was stationed in Germany. He was one of the first soldiers they sent to Desert Storm, the first big battle in the Middle East. Jem had graduated from high school, then jewelry school in Boston, and was making a great income from being a jeweler and a bartender. She found a nice apartment and was doing repair work for several local jewelry stores and bartending too. We were so happy they were both doing well on their own. Saying goodbye to our Trine group was hard for us, even though we knew we could visit whenever we wanted to but life just keeps you so busy that before you know it, a year goes by in what seems like a minute. Those six friends had become family to us and there were a lot of tears all around. The Spirit Guides had named our group, "The Trine", saying that we were like eight slices of a pie. The crane bird held great significance to the Masters who shared their knowledge with us. Our daughter Jem, hand carved from wax, a triangle with a crane bird engraved in it and she had them cast into sterling silver pendants, one for each person in the group. She put initials on the back of each person's pendant. One nice thing about Virginia was, the winters were way less harsh, so Ken and I had more free time, especially outdoors. I took a course and became a travel agent, landing a job working at a very big corporation, which got us great discounts for our journeys. He and I had only gone on one vacation, back in the mid-seventies, to Puerto Rico for his job then we stayed an extra week for some much-needed alone time. We also purchased two time-shares, one in Hilton Head and one in Nags Head in the Carolinas. Since we didn't play golf, we put both of our two-week stays into a pot, which allows you to trade your location for another two weeks in a different state or country. We were very fortunate in that we used our trades to see Europe and our oldest son, Jim, and his family who lived in Germany. While overseas, we went to Scotland, Ireland, England, and France. Back home in the good-ol-USA, we did a road trip across America that let us take in the beauty of many other states we had never seen. Years later, we had two big family reunions, one in Williamsburg, Virginia, and one in Daytona, Florida. We sold those timeshares when we could no longer travel after I started showing signs of Dementia. I had always been great with directions, making me our navigator but with my memory slipping, Ken found it too hard to take our trips on the road, as he couldn't watch me and look for the street signs and road markers while driving. The twins, Dean and Doreen, were sixteen and in tenth grade, when we moved back to Virginia. They had a very hard time leaving their friends and starting at a new high school for the last two years. Frequent moves are difficult on families, especially when your kids become teenagers and have to move around a lot, something we had done many times since we were married. Our kids were at different stages in their lives and the six-year difference between the first two and the twins made it stressful for them all to keep changing schools, neighborhoods, and houses. We met many wonderful people in all those places and kept in touch, right up until Ken was in his late eighties. He was so great at writing letters, cards, and postcards, to folks everywhere. I appreciated his commitment to staying in contact with all our family, friends, and the people we met on our trips to Europe and across the United States. I know, the wife usually does that sort of thing but through our entire relationship, he was the glue that held our family together. He was a wonderful father and a good listener to everyone he knew. So many people were drawn to his congeniality and friendly spirit. During our second term in Virginia, we went to Germany to visit our son Jim who was stationed there while he was fighting in, The Gulf War and in Afghanistan. He introduced us to a local group in Germany that held events called, "Volksmarches", where people got together and went on hikes for five to fifteen miles. Back then we were in our early fifties and we had no problem hiking. We loved it so much that we found members of that same club in Virginia, and went on many hikes with them for several years. We met lots of kindhearted souls and shared great stories between us. We finally stopped going on those hikes as the length of the walks was becoming too much for me. I told Ken to go himself because I knew he loved them but he was too much of a gentleman to leave me at home alone, even though I insisted he go. The truth was, he couldn't enjoy himself if he was worried about my safety and well-being. After watching our life stories while back home in the spirit realm, I see the times I held him back from doing the things he loved and I've made amends for that. Ken has also made amends to me, for not being romantic, as I craved romantic gestures like flowers, candy, and cards but it simply wasn't his style. We were always there for each other when it counted and that's really what life is about. We were loyal to each other and had mutual respect and love for each other. Being married takes work, as both people need to give and take and make sacrifices when needed. The rewards are always worth it!

As Ken's twenty-five years of working for FEMA was coming up soon, we were thinking hard about what we would do next, since the twins were now out of high school. Doreen chose college and Dean went to motorcycle mechanic school, meaning we could move back up near our friends again or move anywhere we wanted to. We didn't need such a big house anymore either, so after much deliberation, we decided to build a house on the land Ken's parents had left him. It was a small parcel that sat right on "Lake Memphremagog" in Newport, Vermont, three miles from the Canadian border. Ken was an only child, as was I, and since all our family and close friends were from Vermont, Maine, New Hampshire, and Massachusetts, it just made more sense to choose a place closer to those we love. We finally settled on building a tongue and groove, wooden home on Ken's land. It was a small lot of lake frontage. The house sat on top of a gently sloping hill, about thirty feet up from the lake. The lake itself was over twenty-one miles long and went way up into Canada and was over a mile deep in some places. We designed a three-story home, with three bedrooms and two baths. The home would be all wood, inside and out, and come complete with a Pellet stove and modern appliances. The first floor was a two-car garage on the back by the driveway and a den with windows in the front, that looked out onto the lake. A small half bath was in the hall before you went upstairs. The second story was the main living area with an open loft ceiling in the den and dining room section and our kitchen ran against the right-side wall, with our master suite and bathroom near the back. The third floor had two bedrooms, one on each side, and a full bathroom in the middle. It was quite a living experience being on the lake. The view was similar to watching a huge, big-screen TV with the nature channel on all the time. The waterfront windows were full of the changing seasons, as well as the rotating activities on the lake. The lake itself was teaming with such diversity of wildlife that it kept us entertained day and night, all year round. The winters were long and frozen, the spring wet and muddy, the summers warm and wild and the fall was a riot of colors and smells everywhere one looked. I spent my time reading, sewing scarves for local kids, and cooking. Ken spent his time mowing, shoveling snow, reading, and chopping wood. Jem's twin daughters, Jade and Justine kept us busy for two weeks every summer. She would drive the four hours up from New Hampshire, and stay for a few days, then she would leave and come back fourteen days later to get them. We had so much fun taking them to "Ben and Jerry's" ice cream in Stowe, Vermont, and to museums and antique stores. Ken would bring them out on the lake in a small row boat to fish and in the winter Jem and the girls would try to skate on the ice. Jim's three kids would come up there and visit for a few days too. My husband and I decided to get a booth in a huge old, wooden barn that had been converted into an antique mall that held many vendors. We set up a nice display of antiques and collectibles. Making trips up there twice a month, to replace what was sold and fix up the displays. We also sold the vintage and antique items that Vivian, my mother gave us, so she would have some extra income. Those day trips got us out of the house and we made decent money from the tourists that skied at "Jay Peak" mountain in Stowe. We had a lovely younger couple on the land to our right, who had lived in Newport all their lives, making them valuable neighbors. They were a font of local information, as they knew all the repairmen and whom to go to for this and that. They had trouble conceiving, so they adopted an adorable little two-year-old, then three years later she was pregnant with twins. I could relate! Though we were older than they were, we still enjoyed cookouts and game nights. Country folks are the very best because they are focused on their families and friends and they always look out for each other. It was nice having them next door. The local grocery store was located a few miles away on the other side of the lake. The "Pick and Shovel" was a unique blend of food, hardware, and pet supplies. It was a one-stop shop for goodies and gossip. Yup, folks found out the skinny from a trip to the P and S. Who was dating whom, who had died, who was born, who was cheating on their mate, nothing was sacred when it came to dishing the dirt. We weren't into that sort of thing but the locals would serve it up whether you asked for it or not, so we just went with it. The town sported a few restaurants like the "Miss Newport Diner ", which had great food and prices. There was a laundromat, dry cleaners, a few banks, and various other small stores that catered to both tourists and locals. A huge celebration was held when "The Dollar Tree" opened. Everyone was thrilled with the unique concept of each item costing only one dollar, making it an overnight sensation. Above all else, the most important tourist draw to the Lake Memphremagog area was the legend of the sea monster, with tales that dated back hundreds of years from Native American folklore. Sightings were a yearly occurrence and everyone was camera ready when near the lake, hoping for a money shot of the huge and elusive creature. Ken and I kept our eyes open but most of our glances turned out to be old logs or branches and debris. The locals had named her "Memphre" and the chamber of commerce asked our daughter, Jem, to design a line of postcards and some "Tee" shirt logos of the monster, which she enjoyed doing. The designs were of a very sweet, vintage postcard theme with Memphre swimming in the lake. All in all, our time spent on the lake was filled with lots of peaceful and wonderful memories because of its remote wilderness lifestyle. I like to think of the experience as a time of inner growth and a Spiritual retreat, after many years of working hectic schedules and all the other things that a busy life entails. We had great conversations and our connection to the wildlife was something we both treasured. Reconnecting with our northern family and friends was very special to us all. Almost like returning to our childhood roots. If we had been younger, we might have opted to stay in that hideaway longer. I look back now and wonder, if us living up there, so secluded and off the grid, with all that quietness, may have accelerated my Dementia and Alzheimer's. We had no social life or daily contact with other people. We went from living a very busy social life in Virginia, to being alone with each other, ninety-five percent of the time. We would go weeks without seeing anyone else. We won't know if it made a difference because I kept busy reading, sewing, and cooking and Ken was busy too, with the yard and writing as well as reading. He and I seemed to be existing in a place where time stood still, inside a snow globe of our own making. Perhaps the contrast between the hustle and bustle of life in Washington D.C., to a secluded life on a lake, was a bit extreme in contrast. After a few years, "Hicksville" started to lose its luster. It became dull, tedious, and lonely. If we had moved back to Newburyport, would we have been happier, living closer to our friends and kids? Would keeping busy physically and mentally, have made a difference in our lives or slowed the progression of my Dementia? I can't say for sure, however, I do believe that exercising your brain and staying active with a mentally stimulating regimen, does make a difference. When you keep your mind in a constant state of agility and engagement, just like when you keep your body toned and fit, I do believe you can fend off Dementia for a while longer. After all, your brain is a muscle, so it too needs exercise and conditioning. It surely can't hurt! Even doing those brain teasers and staying involved with friends and functions, like walking and exercising, boosts your serotonin levels and helps you remain happier and healthier. Anything you enjoy doing, don't stop, unless you must but don't hurt yourself. With all the new technologies available now, there are many ways to stay connected to friends, families, and online activities that help engage your mind. Even if you live alone or in a remote location, use your smartphones and computers to stay connected and in touch with others to avoid depression or loneliness. Form buddy situations, that way you can check up on each other and help others or get help when you need it. Many people feel less lonely due to the internet and that reduces fear, anxiety, and depression.

Jem and I had many Mother-Daughter talks about life and one of our topics was whether we would ever move to Florida when we retired and become "Snow Birds." A local Floridian term for those who winter in Florida and summer back, wherever they're from up north, experiencing the best of both seasons. We both laughed and agreed, that lifestyle wasn't for us, so when Jem told us in the spring of nineteen, ninety-five, that she was selling her tattoo studio in Portsmouth, New Hampshire, and moving to Florida, we were floored! She had found a job tattooing in a shop in Sarasota, Florida on the west coast of the state. Ken and I drove down to Portsmouth, New Hampshire, so we could help her and her twins move, by taking turns driving the moving truck and her car. It was also a way for us to check out the area they were moving to. She was busy loading up the moving truck, when a hurricane blew through the city of Portsmouth, giving her a wet and windy send-off from Mother Nature and showing her, she had made the right decision. When we all arrived safely in Sarasota, Ken and I decided to stay in a hotel for a few days to check out the area. We had never spent any time in that state and we wanted to get a feel for the area, it's weather, and the lay of the land. After a few days, we said our goodbyes and flew to Boston, where we drove a rental car up to Newbury-port, to Lynn and Gig's house. It was so wonderful to see all our friends and enjoy a Trine meditation session. After a week with them, we set out in our van for our home on the lake. On the four-hour drive back to our nest, we both felt that familiar nudge of discontent with our secluded spot on the lake. When we got home, we started looking at maps and checking out North Central Florida, for places to retire. At first, we considered keeping the Newport house and becoming snow-birds but, in the end, we knew we would worry about the house, the weather, and break-ins. We decided it was better to just sell it and keep one property, then we would be free of that burden. Ken's cousin Joe and his wife Kay, have a second home located in ZephyrHills, Florida and his other cousin Phill and his wife Dortia have a place in Leesburg, Florida. We would have family, thirty minutes away if we chose Lakeland, Florida. It was situated right between Orlando to the east and Tampa, Saint Pete, on the west and both were off of route four. Jem and our twin granddaughters were one and a half hours away south in Sarasota, making this perfect for us. Not only does Florida have great hospitals and doctors, but they also have year-round sunny, warm weather and you don't have to shovel snow or de-ice your car and windshield, which is a huge bonus. Sure, it gets hot in the summers but truthfully where doesn't it get hot in July and August? It was thirty-five minutes to Disney World, Sea World, Epcot and Universal in Orlando. Whenever family or friends came down, we could pop over to the theme parks and their many attractions. That would come in handy when the grandkids visited. Hospitals are first-rate there, as well as many senior living homes in the Lakeland area. All those benefits helped seal the deal, so we contacted a real estate agency and had them scout out three-bedroom homes for us in our price range. Two weeks after we hired the agent, we got a call that they found a place. It was a brand-new build in a gated golf club community. We checked out the pictures they sent and booked a flight to go down and check it out. We rented a car at the Tampa airport and drove thirty-five minutes to Lake Land and found our way to the "Sandpiper" golf club property. We were off of the very first street that enters from the side entrance. After you turn into the entranceway, you take the very first left onto Petrel Circle, a road that forms a big loop. There were twelve homes along the road, on the outside, and on the center circle, there were four houses, all brand-new builds. We chose the second one on the inside corner, which had a big corner lot with poured concrete, curbing dividers for the landscaping, all around the house. That way the lawn guys wouldn't mow over your flowers and such. The big, two-car garage had enough room for shelving units to hold our holiday decorations and lawn tools. When you walk inside from the garage into the house, there is a washer and dryer in the entryway, then a door to the kitchen. The kitchen was big and was part of the open floor plan. The dining room, living room, and formal dining room were also included in the open floor plan. The ten-by-twenty-foot screened-in Lanai offered a full view of the beautiful backyard and made the house look huge. There were two bedrooms and a bathroom on one side and a master suite with a bedroom, full bath, and walk-in closets on the other side. It suited our needs to a "T ". We made an offer that day and the seller accepted. Before you turned into the Sandpiper property, there was a strip mall right across the street, with a major grocery store, a pharmacy, plus other stores in the complex. A McDonald's was also in the plaza along with two banks. The Sandpiper property itself, had a very large golf course, a gym, a clubhouse, and a large swimming pool. There were many other amenities as well on offer. Our lakefront home sold to the second looker, who paid full ask. Our Spirit's felt lighter, as we packed up our thing's, no more ice and snow, only sunshine and sandy beaches! We moved into the Lake Land, Florida house in the early spring of nineteen, ninety-six, less than a year after Jem and the twins moved to Sarasota. That's how we came to live on a golf course when neither of us play golf!

TRASH TO TREASURES

Both Ken and I were blessed with good health. He had two hernia operations, they put the mesh in the second one. At age forty, I had all my upper teeth removed for dentures when we lived in West Newbury because bad teeth were hereditary in my family. Back in the fifties and sixties, the government put fluoride in everyone's drinking water, which we now know, causes tooth decay and other dental problems as well as cancer. Other than the occasional cold or flu, we were both hardy people that went on evening walks and swam in the pool. The clubhouse held monthly meetings, which I took turns hosting with several other members. It was a lot of fun. Ken helped volunteer with their recycling program and I helped make and sell baked goods, for the twice-yearly yard sales that were permitted. "Trash to Treasures", was a spring and fall event, in that every house was allowed to have a yard sale in front of their home two times each year. Ken volunteered to help the clubhouse sell off the donations, to raise money for local charities. Trash-to-Treasures was a huge draw for people because there were hundreds of homes having garage sales at the same time. It was a fun weekend event. Our neighbors on the circle soon became like family and we watched several of their homes during the summers, while our snowbird neighbors were back up north. I helped Ken put in two Koi ponds, in our backyard and also a privacy hedge. When the TV show, "The Sopranos" was on, we all met at a neighbor's house to watch it together and then dish about each episode. If someone needed a ride to drop off their car to be repaired or a ride to a doctor's appointment, we were the first to offer to help out. It wasn't unusual for us to have the keys to five houses at once, to check on. Some homes had Koi ponds too and Ken would feed their fish and keep the filters clean while the folks were away. Now our life was busy, social, and a lot of fun, due to our location and the weather. I lost twenty-five pounds after the first year, due to all the walking and swimming. After two years, Ken and I decided we wanted to go to cemeteries in Polk County and go from marker to marker, writing down who was buried there. It was our mission to remember those departed, by making complete maps and a key that told who was buried where. We started by going to the local cemeteries, where we would spend all day there, mapping out the rows of headstones from the back to the front. First, we spoke with the caretaker of the grounds and garnered as much intel from him as we could, about who was buried where. Oftentimes, when a person from up north moves to Florida and then dies, no one knows where they were buried. Especially people that have smaller families that aren't that close. It was our passion to record history. We wanted to make books about the local cemeteries in our area, so that people can go to the nearby library and look up where their grandparents or family members were laid to rest. We ended up doing eleven books in total and we donated copies of the books to each local library and town hall. It was a massive undertaking, that took almost four years, of every day crawling around, row after row of graves, in each cemetery but we are very proud of our contribution and our effort as a whole. Not very many people care but it's something that means a lot to us and it was worth our time and energy.

STRANGER TO YOURSELF

Everything I've told you about so far and even the first three years living in Florida was spent Dementia free. We were both sixty-five, in nineteen, ninety-nine, and after that, I started having very small lapses of memory, from time to time. Everyone back then called them, "Senior Moments" and by my late sixties, they became more frequent and lasted a bit longer. I didn't tell Ken because I didn't want him to worry and I was praying they were just a fleeting thing. When they started to become apparent and noticeable, I knew he would catch on fast. I was praying it was just part of the aging process but as things progressed, I knew something wasn't right. When I was sixty-seven, Ken could tell, I was having a hard time remembering all the cooking ingredients, as well as the oven temps and the duration of cooking times for each item. Pulling off a meal I had constructed a thousand times before, became an intricate affair and it showed in the finished taste of whatever meal I cooked. My sleeping patterns began to alter after that, so by my early seventies, I was waking up in the middle of the night and wandering around the house in the semi-darkness, touching things and exploring, as if I was in some foreign place, not inside my own home. I would come to, just standing in the kitchen, in the dark, and wonder why I was in there and not in bed. It really scared me, as I was also losing my hearing. That was my worst fear, to be deaf, separated by sound, cut off from the world of hearing, and plunged into a silence full of emptiness. Jem had once asked me years ago if I had to choose between being blind or deaf which would I choose. I said I would rather be blind and be able to hear music, voices, and sounds, she said she would rather be deaf than blind. She's an artist, so I get that. No one wants to have to make that choice but sometimes, life does the choosing for you. I had some hearing aids made but they weren't very good quality back in the mid nineties. I didn't wear them very often, which aggravated Ken to no end. Sometimes I'd put them down somewhere and forget where they were. Asking my husband if he had seen them would have raised an alarm, so that was not an option. Not being able to hear, made me feel left out of everything. I was tired of asking people to repeat what they said and I felt embarrassed to be excluded from conversations. I began avoiding the phone because of the echo and reverberation from the hearing aids, especially when I was eating. I just couldn't stand the sound of my own chewing being amplified in my head. It was so annoying! Because I couldn't hear what was being said, I refused to talk on the phone, which left my four kids feeling hurt and abandoned. It was as if I was a ball of yarn that was slowly unraveling and losing shape. I lay awake each night looking up at the ceiling, waiting for daylight because time had slowed down, almost stopped and I was at a loss over what to do. That might have been my reaction to it being so quiet and dark. I can say that it was like sitting alone in a row boat, in the middle of a lake, with thick fog all around you and no shore in sight. A feeling of total isolation and loneliness. It was the emptiest feeling of all, to stand there like a social outcast, just because you can't hear or understand their conversations.

GODZILLA

I loved playing the piano and singing when I was younger, though I had not done it in years, it has always been a very special memory for me. Ken bought me a baby grand piano after the twins were toddlers and I treasured that special prize. I would play and sing when we had neighbors over and around the holidays. We sold the piano before moving to Vermont but I often thought about it with longing. I remember getting up one night and walking around the house, looking for it, so I could play a song but I felt very confused as to why it wasn't there. I stood there in the dark, in the living room, and turned 'round and round again, hoping it was right behind me, only to discover it wasn't there. Those kinds of small memory slips started to become a part of my days, nights, and weeks. When you first start to forget things, you aren't alarmed, but as they became more frequent and lasted several minutes, it felt like I was living in winter all the time, where things were barren, with emptiness and coldness to everything. You're there in your physical body but your mind truly has a will of its own and it kicks you out of the driver's seat and takes control over your body and it functions, as if you're a stranger to yourself. Now you are unable to make concrete decisions because you can't trust your own grip on reality. The very lines of reality become blurred and you become afraid of everything because you have lost control over yourself. I tried holding onto my reality as I knew it, but it was like walking on shifting sands, with constantly moving thoughts coming in and out of focus within my mind. It felt like there were no more logical compartments inside my brain, where my thoughts were separated automatically into categories like, what's currently taking place, what things must I get done today, what were my responsibilities that day, etcetera. It was absolutely terrifying to not be able to direct my thoughts in my mind, not to mention putting any of it into coherent sentences. Compare it to throwing all your feelings, memories, experiences, thoughts, idea's, traumas, hopes, dreams, passions and convictions into a big laundry bag, shaking it all up hard, then try to find what you need at that moment to communicate it properly to someone. Every facet of my being, all eighty-plus years of my journey full of experiences, wisdom and memories were now lost to me in a matter of months. Frustration, helplessness, fear and anger were my new full time unwelcomed companions.

There were times when I'd have a few minutes of familiarity before it was just a whisper of smoke dissolving away. You can't trust yourself anymore. Signals from the brain to the body get crossed so often that you feel as if you might have to use the bathroom, only to sit down and nothing happens. All of these small things become huge when it's happening to you and you try to control them but your body and mind aren't speaking to each other, as if they are on strike, leaving you feeling angry and frustrated because you feel helpless and confused. Now you are slowly turning to your husband for help, with silly little things and it's embarrassing and degrading. That was the hardest thing for me, as I had always been a formidable woman that was tough, independent, and intelligent. I was a loving person that was capable of doing many things on my own and I was used to leading the charge, whether at home or in business. I was creative and hardworking, so this affected everything and it was a total game changer, in that Ken would now have to start taking over my household tasks, like cleaning, shopping, laundry, and cooking. It seemed like that list grew with each passing week. Soon he was driving us both everywhere and he had to watch me at the grocery store or I would walk up to a stranger's cart and I'd just start pushing it down the aisle, which embarrassed Ken. In my state of mind, my own feet were taking me places and I had no choice but to follow. It's kind of like letting go of the steering wheel and letting the car go where it may. In other words, like an accident just waiting to happen!

Had I lived alone, I can see how this could end badly. I went from small slips of memory, into longer spells that lasted ten to fifteen minutes each. In a matter of eight months, those longer spells meant that I needed constant supervision, as I might just wander outside, which is exactly what I did. One day, Ken was in the den that we had converted into an office for our computer desk and a couch for overnight guests. The desk chair has a view of our street at the front of the house. It's a corner room and Ken's refuge when he gets any free time to write. Ken was busy on his computer when he noticed someone walking by outside on the street, he did a double take when he realized it was me! He ran outside and stopped me and brought me back inside. If he hadn't seen me, I could have walked in front of a car or fallen and broken a hip. It shook him up and Jem suggested that he put a safety lock up high, on the inside of each door but he didn't want to do that because he was in the denial phase in the first few years. We both were. He avoided neighbors and took me with him on errands, so I wouldn't be alone. I believe they all had an idea that something wasn't right because I was always so outgoing and friendly and we were very close to all of them. I'm sure they had their suspicions but were too kind to come right out and ask. Some were only there for the winter, so they weren't around from March through November. Ken was getting no rest now because he knew I had Dementia but couldn't bring himself to approach the subject because I was having more spells that became unpredictable and he just couldn't find a proper time to discuss it. If he mentioned I should see a doctor, I would clam up and get angry, as I only went when it was necessary. Most men of our generation were used to their wives cooking the meals, cleaning the house, and handling the details of social engagements, plus doing the Christmas shopping and decorating the home for the holidays. Ken and I shared all the household duties, right up until our late sixties. As I became more affected by Dementia, he had no choice but to take over anything I couldn't handle. Showering was probably the worst task, all the way around for both of us. It wasn't normal for him to have to fight with me to take a shower and I wasn't trying to be difficult but I just didn't understand why he was being so pushy about it. My mind had lost its grasp of time and days, so I became suspicious of him when he tried to force me to shower, causing me to become stubborn and angry, which aggravated the heck out of him. In my defense, losing all concepts of time and how it related to our daily lives and schedules, made things much more difficult for both of us. When he had to take me with him, he would have to start telling me an hour early, so he would have time, if I didn't want to go, to convince me to go with him because he couldn't just grab me and drag me along. By the time I was sixty-nine, I started going through strange flashback phases that would last anywhere from two to three weeks or two to five months. In one such phase, I kept insisting that "Jeff Gordon", the NASCAR driver, who was winning all the races back then, was my husband and not him. In our garage, there were posters, signs, hats, and other paraphernalia of Jeff Gordon, who was my favorite driver. We also watched the races together on TV during the racing season. Ken knew I liked Jeff Gordon but he was hurt that I kept telling him he wasn't my husband. He knew the truth but after many years of marriage, it still stung. After all, he was doing double duty, every day, all day, without a break and he was doing his best to keep us both going while he was feeling overwhelmed and drained. He was in his office one day and he had put the TV on a movie channel that had classic movies for me, so he could work on his book. He was enjoying the solitude when I let out a scream that had him running into the living room in a panic. I was freaking out so much and crying that he couldn't figure out what was going on until I calmed down enough. I pointed at the TV saying; "A monster is attacking the city we need to hide!" He turned to see "Godzilla" destroying Japan, in a movie and quickly put two and two together. It took him a while to convince me we weren't under attack before I calmed down. We both laugh about it now, watching it from the afterlife but back then, to me it was real and terrifying in my mind. From then on, he made sure to keep only the PBS station or the local weather and news stations on. Another time I saw the president on TV and I insisted that I had eaten dinner with him, which wasn't true at all. I believe it's because your mind tries to latch on to a scenario you see on TV as a way of feeling anchored to something or someone. It's an act of "association", so the mind feels grounded, and it relaxes you because you feel a part of the current event. When you unconsciously begin to blend fantasy with reality, your conscious self tries so hard to find its normal place in life but it's like trying to navigate the ocean in the dark, an endless feeling of uncertainty. Ken had to make so many sacrifices in his life when Dementia hijacked my brain.

GOD'S ONLY SON

It was as if I was living beyond time, free of stress and worry, free of life's constrictions and rules, as I had just mentally checked out. That's how it appeared from Ken's point of view. To him, I was oblivious to the structure of everyday life and its boundaries. I was inhabiting a human body of flesh but my mind was living timeless, as we do when we are back home in our celestial forms, as white light beings. To my husband, I was the lucky one that didn't have to concern herself with what to cook for dinner, what to wear to the store, what pill to take, and when. However inside, I could feel his frustration and his worry, and anguish. I was just powerless to help him out and it left me feeling worthless because I had no way to tell him that I understood what he was feeling. I had lost the power to control myself or help with chores but I could read his thoughts since we had been together for so very many years, that I knew him inside and out. I hated that I was useless and that caused sudden bursts of angry fits, like throwing things and yelling, something he nor I ever did. We never fought during our marriage, we talked things out between us and moved on. There were times in the very first few years with Dementia when I felt like I was still "Me" but trapped way down inside myself and when I tried to talk or scream, nothing came out. It was beyond frustrating, to not be able to communicate when you're an intelligent being. Finally, after a few years, you give up trying because it hurts your heart and there comes a point when you have to accept, you'll never be yourself again, no matter how hard you try. When you realize deep inside yourself that you aren't going to improve, that each passing month and year you'll just become even more of a burden to those you love, it's the hardest truth to accept. Just when I was feeling like all was lost, I started to astral travel in my sleep. I would doze off for a nap and as soon as I fell asleep, I would be back home in the Spirit Realm. My body would still be sleeping but my spirit would project its consciousness to the Heavenly realm and I would visit my mother Vivian and many other family members that had already passed away before me. I would be greeted by beautiful Angels and they would take me to see my family and friends. I would also be greeted by all the pets I had ever owned, while in my many lifetimes on earth. My Spirit Guides and a few Angels had many wonderful conversations with me about my situation, in my current life. They would comfort me and tell me they loved me and how proud they were that I was doing such a good job of being a human with Dementia. All the while huge, gorgeous Angels hovered around me, consoling me, while my mother and my father, (whom I had never met while on earth), spoke gentle words of love and encouragement to me. I sat petting my toy Poodle, Nicky, whom I had for fourteen years before she was attacked by a boxer dog and killed. I felt such empathy and love, that it filled my heart and it gave me the strength to return to my earthly body and continue my journey with Dementia. It was during those naps and while sleeping at night, that I returned home every time, to reunite with all those wonderful beings who gave me comfort and those amazing healing vibrations. I had located a door to Heaven and I was no longer useless or depressed. That's what got me through my eighteen-year ordeal with first Dementia then Alzheimer's. That, and Ken's selfless sacrifice and his love and devotion to me. I'm not the only one who did this, every person who has either of those terrible diseases does the very same thing. Every soul who has led a good life of compassion, non judgment and love for others, is taken to the house of God/Jesus/Source and treated like royalty, while their bodies lay sleeping. They are shown love and compassion in great measure, so they do not feel abandoned or alone. It's God's way of showing you he loves and cares about you. I sat by pools of the clearest water I have ever seen and they fed me wonderful meals of every delicacy and flavor. While in the Divine realm, my mind was clear and I could speak to my loved ones, about how I was feeling while on earth. I shared my concerns and they answered my questions and gave me tremendous amounts of unconditional love and sympathy. Without that outlet, I would have had no way of knowing what was happening to me and my family. They told me how long I had chosen to live but said I could choose to exit at any time if I felt I'd had enough. I told them I would finish what I started and wait for Ken, so we could leave together. I attended parties and gatherings, dressed up in beautiful clothes, and enjoyed many conversations with my grandparents and other ancestors, long departed. On each visit to that Divine Realm, I appeared as the thrifty-year-old "Me," looking young and feeling vibrant. I visited the hall of "Akashic" records and looked up the lives of Ken and also of our four children. Those books contain the detailed history of each person's incarnations on earth and the lessons planned, for each life, as well as all their accomplishments, while in that life. Each soul has their own volume that contains all of the thousands of lifetimes you've spent on planet earth. Younger souls have thinner volumes and older souls have thicker books of records. Many Psychics and remote viewers visit this hall of records, through deep meditation to assure accurate readings for their clients. Though each life in the planning stage allows for the choice of Free Will, after the soul crosses over after their death, some corrections may be made to the final edit of the details of that particular lifetime, if there were variations from the original blueprint, of that soul's incarnation goals and contracts. On many of my visits, I sat with Jesus Christ himself. "He" and I spoke of his time on earth, as in a past life I was one of his closest followers, while he was on planet earth. I had followed Jesus, from the very beginning of his journey, to teach people about Christianity. At that time, I was very worried for him and begged him to run away from the soldiers, who were seeking him out to crucify him. I was angry that he didn't hide and I cried so hard when they crucified him. I had no idea at that time of God's plan for him to rise again or what amazing miracles he was truly capable of. I told him how wonderful he is and how great it was to speak with him again. We also talked about the events that were currently taking place, back on earth. Jesus talked about what transpired while he was living that human life and he explained why he let the soldiers take him, as it was all a part of a bigger event that would gain him billions of followers of Christianity over thousands of years. I just knew that when Jesus spoke, a sense of calm and compassion flowed from his very presence and that I was under his spell, as my soul felt a deep affinity with his words and actions, during those supernatural months he and I spent together on earth. Even now, I realize what a special gift and blessing that life was for me, to be right next to "God's Only Son", while he was in the flesh. What a tremendous opportunity I was given and how rare that life was. To have a front-row seat and witness "His" Awakening of

Humanity to "His" movement of Christianity. How blessed was I, to stand near Jesus, as he selflessly performed miracles on the sick and suffering, while passing on his beliefs, from needy soul to needy soul. I have no words, for the enormity of what that meant for humanity during those traumatic and uncertain times in human history. It was beyond words and beyond amazing. That lifetime was extremely rocky and it tipped from euphoria to fear, daily with the wonderment of "His" Holy presence and the unpredictability of those tumultuous times. I had been gifted with the highest honor in existence and I'm forever grateful to God for that gift! Jesus shared his amazing healing light with me and I felt high on life just being with him. Those visits energized me tremendously and helped me to survive for so many years without my memories or my ability to control my mind and body.

During those first three years when I was lucid most of the time and only going into short spells of forgetfulness, Ken prayed that my condition wouldn't worsen. He spoke to me a few times, about me taking a competency test at the doctor's. Being born in the depression era, my mother Vivian, though a nurse herself, didn't go to doctors unless she had to. Her fear of doctors was passed down to me and I passed it down to my children. It was a generational thing. You got up and went to school or work and you only stayed home if you were deathly sick. People were just a lot tougher and harder back then. Much to my husband's disappointment, I refused to take the test, partly because I didn't trust doctors and partly because if I was diagnosed as having Dementia or Alzheimer's, that would make it all too real. I was terrified that the test would confirm that I had lost my motor skills and reasonable thinking process and I flat out refused to go, which tied Ken's hands as he couldn't force me. I was foolishly living in denial and my pride and ego were being stubborn. Doctors will not prescribe any drugs without that test, so we were at a stalemate. If I had gone earlier and started taking medication right away, I might have prolonged my slide into Alzheimer's or at least slowed it down. Poor Ken was trying so hard to keep it all together but he was slowly losing his grip on control. Our kids told him he needed a break because the daily grind was not only wearing him down physically but emotionally as well as Spiritually. They said that the kind of daily care I required was just too much for him at eighty years old and his depression over what we were going through was very overwhelming. Trying to get me to take medication and my daily care like, showers and brushing my teeth, were something a nurse should be doing. Ken had considered hiring an at-home nurse but decided that he would still have no peace, or time alone if we continued to live together. He had done everything for both of us for those first ten years. He took me to doctor appointments, and the hairdressers, and helped me get dressed, fed, and undressed, which took up eighty percent of each day as he had to prepare three meals a day, then try to corral me to sit down and eat it and clean up afterwards. He was dealing with an eighty-year-old baby that was cranky and difficult. That would wear anyone down, especially twenty-four hours a day. He could no longer take a nap or write, as I was liable to walk off down the street or turn on the stove and possibly burn myself or set the house on fire. He didn't visit our neighbors or invite anyone over, so he was virtually a prisoner in our home. Though I couldn't help my behavior, I could feel his frustration and desperation growing by the day but I was dead set on not facing the horror of my dire situation. Finally, one day he caught me when I was lucid and as he explained in a calm voice that he just wanted us to try a medication to see if it would help me, I relented and agreed to the test, so he took me right then before I could change my mind. I sat down with our doctor and he asked me a lot of questions and told me to remember a few words, then after more questions he asked me if I remembered the words, which I didn't. I was used to passing every test I had ever taken with the highest score, so to fail the most important test of my life was a crushing blow to both of us. Okay, well now that I knew I had Dementia, at least we could try some medications to help slow its progression. I was given a pill for my Dementia and an antidepressant medication. Those two pills were wonderful in the very beginning because I no longer had fits of rage or threw things in anger. I was calm but not sedated. I could go through a day and night without that fear of darkness, loneliness, or anxiety, which helped tremendously. I started sleeping through the night but I still had bouts of forgetfulness and I repeated the same questions over and over during the day. I felt much less fazed by those spells and sat quietly watching TV, instead of wandering around the house, which Ken appreciated.

As to whether the medications were helping my mind, I really can't say because I wasn't in full control of my faculties. I was much more cooperative and compliant when Ken was feeding me and bathing me, and dressing me. I wasn't a zombie, but I just went with the daily program and did much less complaining or making a fuss. Those little things were of such great importance to Ken and he started to relax a little more because I was also taking naps which gave him computer time and he made phone calls to family and friends. He was even writing a book, something that was on his bucket list. I went willingly to run errands with him and to appointments and I rode in the car, without trying to open the doors while he was driving. The years went by with little change, except my spells of forgetfulness lasted longer and longer until finally Ken took our kid's advice and started looking around for nursing homes for me. A great factor in moving to Florida is that it's famous for being a retirement state, as they have many hospitals and assisted living places, and good quality nursing homes. We both turned eighty and our kids were adamant that he needed to have me cared for by professionals, so he could get some enjoyment out of whatever years he had left. He had been my hero at home but it was time for him to have some of life's adventures himself. By that time, I was a full-time victim of what was now considered Alzheimer's. Being zoned out seventy percent of the time, I was also experiencing episodes and phases of what I call "Past Events" trauma, like talking as if I were five years old and constantly asking where my Daddy was and when he was coming home. Then I carried around a baby doll and hugged it and spoke to it in whispers. At first, Ken was unsettled by my child-like performances but he eventually gave in to them and bought me new baby dolls and stuffed animals. After much research and investigating, he chose a nursing home five miles from our house that was a four-star facility. His attorney advised him to take my name off our house and he set me up on Social Security Medicare, that way the state wouldn't take our paid-for home. He then had Jem fly in from Los Angeles, to help him pack up our antiques and collectibles. Ken sold the house and bought a two-bedroom apartment, in an assisted living complex, that had a huge dining room, a pool, and a gym as well as a hospital wing if you became ill. This beautiful place was only one mile away from my nursing home, so he would be able to drive over every day and feed me lunch while he visited. Now that Ken lived alone, in his new apartment near me, he started meeting friends in the evening at dinner. He had a social life of sorts and less stressful days because he no longer had so much on his plate. All that came with a price and that was feeling as though he had abandoned his wife in a storage facility and left her all alone there with strangers. Since I wasn't capable of defending myself, he felt awful about putting me there, when I didn't even understand what was going on. It was like dropping your child off, on the steps of a church and driving away. The heavy guilt of giving up on someone you loved and lived with, for almost sixty years. There are no words for those kinds of empty feelings of guilt. It's all-consuming in the beginning. Going home after each visit, to a new and empty apartment, that holds every memory you have in your heart, in the pictures on the wall and in the bed you both shared your hopes and dreams in. I know it took tremendous strength to bring me there and drive away. He must have felt like he left his best friend, who needed more care than he was able to give, at a strange place when they couldn't understand why you took them there and then went away. I can't even imagine how horrible that must have been for him in the beginning. When you leave your soulmate all alone with strangers because you just can't do it another day. It's agonizingly painful, when you drop off a dog, let alone your wife of fifty-seven years. The woman you married and had four kids with, the woman that stood by your side, through thick and thin, who was your partner and your twin flame. I'm so very proud of Ken, for doing the right thing and I love him for coming every day for two hours, to sit with me, hold my hand and feed me lunch with tenderness and love. We were so spiritually connected, that I loved him for making the hard choices that saved us both. I harbor zero anger or blame because he did what needed to be done when the time came. We love each other unconditionally.

SEEING THE TWINS

The busy nursing home that was my new residence, was a coed facility that had a special wing, just for Alzheimer's and Dementia patients. Each room has two beds in it and a bathroom, plus two closets for clothes. Men are in separate rooms from women but they are all free to wander around the halls, sitting room, cafeteria, and living rooms. Aggression is not tolerated and any patients exhibiting signs of that, are given drugs to calm them down for the safety of all the residents and the caregivers. Visitors are allowed at all hours after nine am, until nine pm, as long as you aren't disturbing any other patients. There are two seating times for each meal, breakfast, lunch, and dinner. Those that are capable of feeding themselves, go first and an hour later, the second seating is for those too advanced and not capable of feeding themselves. Because there are at least twenty patients in the second seating and only three workers at that time, available to help feed them, many go without aid and therefore get very little to eat. If Ken had not come to feed me every lunch, I would have wasted away faster. You can't blame the staff, as they were employees and were doing the very best they could while understaffed. The nursing home had a rule, that after they take a new patient in, you cannot visit them for two weeks, something Ken didn't remember until the day he brought me there or he chose to forget. They told him that it was a rule for two reasons. The first rule-Patients are confused and don't know where they are or why they are there, so if they see a family member, they cry and beg to go home with them and it's too traumatic for both parties. The second rule-It takes about two weeks, for the patient to get adjusted to being there and learning a whole new way of life. For them to adjust to the new medications. They feel it's best if they are immersed in their new environment, without visitors coming and going. I can't say how Ken took this news but I will tell you, that suddenly being in an unfamiliar place and being hustled from nurse to nurse and put in a strange bedroom, that both confusion and fear reared up from my inner self, even when I was medicated. I had upper dentures that were taken from me, along with my hearing aids. That was extremely frightening and very traumatic for me. Who were these people and why was I here? Why were they pushing pills at me and changing my clothes? People I didn't know were undressing me and putting a diaper on me. I must have shown the horror on my face because I was given a pill and it put me to sleep. That same night, I went straight to my heavenly home and I was immediately surrounded by Angels who calmed me down and explained what was going on back on earth. They told me that I needed medical care, that Ken wasn't qualified to give me, so he had no choice but to surrender me to professional nurses and doctors for both our safety. Just hearing that, I felt instantly calm and safe. Being told Ken hadn't abandoned me, relieved my worries and fear. I didn't feel betrayed or unloved. These huge Angels were filling me in on what was going on, so I wasn't scared or lost. It was a huge relief that they made sure I knew I was still loved and needed by my family. Everyone wanted me to feel safe and to get proper nursing care. After hours of being consoled, I woke up the next day, with more curiosity than fear and tried my best to be a good patient by saying, "Thank You" when I remembered to. Even though everything and everyone was so new and noisy, the calming medications helped me to not freak out, they took the edge off. I still cried at times, from the confusion of it all. My intelligent mind was watching everything and making mental notes. Though I was quiet, inside my mind was humming, with all the hustle and bustle of the daily machinations of life inside a huge nursing home. There were over eight hundred patients in this big complex! I wasn't used to the noises or smells of the cafeteria and all the other patients, some of whom sang, screamed or cried off and on all day, and into the night. It was sensory overload because our home was carpeted and quiet with just Ken and I. Those first two weeks were a blur of events, that all blended like a weekend at Disney World if you went on every ride. It was one giant ball of confusion and chaos. After the two-week quarantine went by, I received my very first visit from Ken. Through the haze of my new medications, I couldn't remember his name but I recognized him right away and knew he was someone very important in my life. His hands were shaking and so were mine as he came up and hugged me. We hadn't hugged in years but I could smell his cologne and it brought tears to my eyes. I stepped back and searched his face for memories but when he smiled, I relaxed and we held hands as he guided me down a quieter hall, where we stopped and just took each other's measure, as you do on a first date. That's what this was, a first date with my husband at my new residence. Our eyes spoke volumes, as we just stared at each other through wet lashes and the conversation was wordless and sweet. When we had said what needed to be said with our eyes, we heard the bell ring for my lunch and we went into the dining room, hand in hand. He took my food tray from the caregiver and began getting everything cut up, so I wouldn't choke on it. He loaded up the spoon, handed it to me and I ate it without tasting it, happy to be there with this man I loved. He was my Angel, my rock, who was there for me when I needed him the most. This tall, handsome, selfless man whom I had shared my love and my life with. His sacrifices taught me what real love is about.

My spirits were lifted each day when he walked through that door and we often sat on the couch and fell asleep holding hands like teenagers. Sometimes, I would catch a glimpse of sadness in his eyes and I knew it was hard for him to see me in there and to leave me each day, like opening up a wound, over and over but he always came again without fail. That act of love held me together, through each day in that place alone. He brought me baby dolls to cuddle with and stuffed animals that made me laugh. He also bought me clothes and hung them up with my name written in Sharpie ink, so they would be brought back after laundry day but most times they would disappear or other ladies' clothes would end up in my closet that didn't fit, which made Ken mad. He would be so disappointed when expensive clothes he bought for me would be gone right away, as he wasn't sure if the staff was stealing them or just other patients. They had a big room, that they corralled everyone into after lunch and they hired singers, performers, and such, to entertain folks but most wandered away from boredom. I wasn't fond of the loud sounds, so I preferred to walk up and down the halls all day long. Sometimes, Ken would take me for a walk around the grounds when it was cool. We would sit in the gazebo and watch the birds and lizards play. We were both hanging on as best we could while living separate lives, something we never planned on. If the roles had been reversed, I'd like to think, I would have taken the same great care of him, as he did for me. We both became accustomed to the lunch routine and he was often surprised by how much I ate, as the food was ground up like dog food, so patients like me, without teeth, wouldn't choke. He had filled out a list of foods I liked and didn't like when he enrolled me there, so when I would accidentally be served something he knew I didn't like, he would be surprised when I gummed it right up! He would get upset with the kitchen workers but in all honesty, it all tasted the same, as my brain didn't seem to control my taste buds. Things I never liked became good because I didn't eat much at breakfast or dinner, when left alone to feed myself. I could eat the bread myself and other finger foods. Some of the advanced patients lost the ability to remember how to chew food and swallow, so they died much sooner than those who could still eat. Using the spoon when I was alone didn't work out too well, so Ken's feeding me became my main meal of each day. After a few years, I didn't feel hunger pains but I do remember being thirsty, as they only gave us drinks at meal times, so Ken made sure I drank a lot and he had the nurses give me two "Ensure" drinks a day. When Jem flew out from L.A., she always stayed at the house for a few weeks at a time, helping Ken finish converting the two Koi ponds into a Zen rock garden, requiring much less maintenance for him. When he sold the house, it helped as a selling point because the backyard was absolutely beautiful, thanks to all their hard work. Every day, she would come with Ken and help feed me and bring me treats and gifts. I knew she was someone important to me in my life, so I tried to talk to her but it came out like a whisper. She would make the baby dolls dance and sing, like puppets and make me laugh. I'm very grateful to her for her time and energy in helping both her father and me when she came. When her twin daughters, Jade and Justine, flew out to see me, I cried the moment they stepped into the room. I was so very delighted to see them that I couldn't hold back the tears, as it had been a few years since I last saw them. Ken was shocked by my sudden burst of emotions, as I never did that. They were our first grandchildren, so we were very close to them since birth. They both worked for a big production company in Los Angeles, making it hard to get time off. They were our secret favorites because I had given birth to twins myself, so when Jem found out she was having twins, it made it very special to us. She had been a tremendous help, during her teenage years to our whole family by babysitting the twins and coming home every day after school and cooking, cleaning, and doing laundry for six people, while being an honor student and also being on the track team, art committee, gymnastics, and many other sports and school activities. Looking back now, I don't know how she found the time to do all the things she did, while in high school and taking care of everyone at home. I also had visits from my twins but my oldest son was overseas in the Air Force, so he didn't have much free time to get back home to see us. Everyone had such busy lives and jobs that kept them going. That happens with families that move around a lot like we did. Our oldest son's two boys are Marines and they were posted in far-off places. We all loved each other, so we understood that seeing them was hit or miss.

LIMITLESS SOUL

When I first got to the nursing home, I was five foot, seven inches, tall, and about twenty-five pounds overweight but after the first three years, I lost weight from being there. I was never a person that was concerned by my looks, as I was more about being my natural self but not having my dentures or hearing aids, it gave me a sunken and aged look. When Jem came to visit, she brought her smartphone and she would sit next to me and hold the phone up sideways, with the camera pointing at us. It was the very first time I had seen myself in more than five years. I was amazed by the image of an old, shrunken, woman staring back at me and I was quite captivated by whom I saw in that reflection. I looked like I was a person from a lost tribe that hadn't seen anyone from the outside world in many years. It was so strange, to see yourself many years later and I was so taken with my appearance, that

I just sat and smiled at the face smiling back at me. I approved of the nobility and strength and fortitude in her gaze. I also saw through that hologram and into my own, true, soul's identity because my spiritual connection to my inner self had become fused with my higher consciousness. I was amused by my jaunty smile and cool demeanor. In other words, I was now truly connected to all parts of myself and l was one with myself, I was whole. That gave me a new kind of reassurance and inner confidence. I felt more grounded and tethered to this new reality. This helped me when I was in my body awake, making lots of observations of all the little going on and I felt like I was in on the joke, that this gig was temporary and I would soon go home with Ken to Heaven and share all that I had been taught. My looks didn't faze me, as I was able to gaze right through that vestige and see myself, for who I truly was, behind reality's veil. I was aligned, through my mind, body, inner child, and my limitless soul. Now I felt powerful because I knew myself, for who and what I truly was and I was proud of all that. Very few people get to that level of understanding, about the true nature of their "Self", while they are in an incarnation on earth. People nowadays are afraid to look deep inside themselves and to make contact with their shadow selves. We all have many facets to our being, some good and some dark. Without really knowing what you value, and what you truly believe in, you won't get the full picture of who and what you're capable of doing and becoming. Due to society's constant demands of how folks should look and what they should think and how they should feel, folks are too busy just paying the bills and surviving, so there's no time to reflect on life's values and principles. They don't even know where to start on their voyage of "Self Discovery", so they put it off. Eventually, you will feel lost and adrift because you don't have a strong foundation to lean on. Without some kind of belief-based ideology, your soul won't feel complete or in synchronization as you go through your life. By the time you're twenty years old you should know what you stand for, what your truth's are and have some inkling of where to start on your Spiritual journey. Currently, everyone's trying to fit in and feel accepted and liked, especially now, with social media and its powerful global influence. Everyone craves to be admired, to be thought of as hip and cool. No one wants to be left out or ridiculed. It means so much more, during these current times, than it ever did before in the history of humanity! The absolute need, to conform and to fit in, it's almost a matter of life and death. It's so sad to watch from the other side, to see how youngsters are being bullied and how tremendously critical humans have become these days towards their fellow man and woman. Youngsters are in a battle every day, to be loved and accepted by their peers, with such constant negativity and pressure, from advertising, the internet and the establishment, pushing their agendas onto every soul, in today's confusing and desperate times. It made me glad that I had already lived through all of those kinds of pressures and critiques. I was happy that my husband and I were on the last part of our journey together and I felt safe and snug, having lived through so much, that he and I were above all that noise and bother of society's critical gaze. I had been in this nursing home for six years now, and I was still fascinated by the never-ending dramas unfolding all around me every day. Ken and I had enjoyed living with just each other and our simple daily routines before I moved into the nursing home, so we harbored no ill will between each other, as we had led very rich and for-filling lives, right up until Dementia and Alzheimer's robbed us, of a normal husband/wife relationship, while in our seventies. So far, I had outlived five roommates, as they had all died from Alzheimer-related issues. Some were older than me but most were younger, which I found surprising. One day, a fifty-eight-year-old lady, who was from Puerto Rico, moved into my room. When I first saw her, I noticed how pretty and well-spoken she was. She was carrying a nice purse and was highly functioning and talkative. Though I couldn't speak out loud by that time, I smiled at her and nodded, so she wouldn't think I was being rude. Her brother and his wife had brought her there and after the two weeks had passed, they returned to visit. She was quieter than when they came to drop her off, due to her new medications and she sat with them in the living room and asked them when she was going home. Jem happened to be visiting at that same time and she and the woman spoke about clothes and fashion. She was the youngest patient in our wing of the facility. Jem was fifty-four, during that visit so she was only four years younger than my roommate, which shook her up. In a matter of just a few weeks, she had declined from being a happy and outgoing flirty woman to being withdrawn and quiet and I heard her crying herself to sleep most nights. Jem and Ken both spoke about how sad it was, to see her change so dramatically in only a few weeks. We couldn't tell if it was the medications or if she was just depressed about being abandoned in the nursing home, surrounded by other patients all with varying degrees of mental clarity. It was almost as if the nursing home's environment had sucked the "Normal" out of her, as her decline was so sharp and swift. I'm in no way being critical of her family's decision but out of all the other patients I saw come and go, she stuck out as someone that wasn't very afflicted when she came in, yet her condition degraded so fast, that she died before she was even there a year. It was so heartbreaking to watch, poor thing, she just gave up and gave in.

GROUNDHOGS DAY

Every year an outbreak of "Scabies" would hit the nursing home and we would all be forced to stay in our rooms for up to two weeks. They are tiny Mites, that burrow under your skin and spread an itchy, painful, rash all over you. They spread very fast through the nursing home because of all the patients being in constant contact with each other. Also, the nurses are with the patients helping them every day so they can catch it too. One year, Ken got infected by them, so he couldn't come to see me. This stressed him out, as he knew I needed him at lunchtime but his doctor misdiagnosed him, so by the time he found out that he had them, he had been infected all over his body. The poor man was itchy and miserable because they are very hard to get rid of. They got in the furniture at his apartment and he had trouble putting the cream medications on his back, so he had to have everything washed a few times and his whole place sterilized. He suffered for over six weeks before he finally got rid of them! Those were some of the hazards of visiting me daily. It's common knowledge that Alzheimer's usually kills its host in a matter of two to five years, leaving me mystified that I was outliving all these other ladies. Even though I had no recollection of time or days, when you are placed in a group nursing home environment, the facility keeps each day structured the same. I didn't concern myself with the time or date. With each new day and whatever unfolds, it's the same as any other day. Like the movie, "GroundHogs Day", I wake up, and have breakfast, then Ken comes at noon time and we sit and visit until lunchtime, then he feeds me and we sit on the couch for an hour, until I fall asleep. After dinner folks just sit in the living room watching the big TV, followed by bedtime. Each day seemed like the last and losing your memories, makes it all seem like one continual period. Without the night and day, it would have felt endless. I was holding on, so Ken wouldn't be alone because I knew that if I was gone, without his daily visits to see me, he wouldn't have much in life to look forward to. He had three, good guy friends and two lady friends that he hung out with. The men ate together at their table and two of his lady friends met him for lunch twice a month. Ken helped one of his friends, who was temporarily in the hospital wing where they both lived. As soon as Ken would leave me at two in the afternoon, he'd go help his friend Bill. First, he'd go get his mail, then he would go back to Bill's hospital room and open the mail, help him go through it, then he would write out the checks and get stamps to mail it all off. Ken was just that kind of guy, helping others and expecting nothing in return. When Bill died two years later, Ken met with his family from out of state and brought them up to speed on all of Bill's affairs. He took it hard when Bill passed, as they had become very close, almost like brothers. It also gave Ken a purpose besides caring for me. He had made a lot of friends over his lifetime but Bill was the first guy friend that wasn't married, so they were like two bachelors hanging out. They came from similar backgrounds and they had tons in common. Ken had always wanted a guy friend whom he could just hang out with. We had couples that were good friends but if they were married, then he and the wife would always be together. I suppose when you are in your eighties, having an ear to bend or someone you can trust to talk to, really means a lot. Perhaps, Ken and I planned to exit our lives together, so whoever got sick first, would have to hold on until the other one was ready to cross over. In the end that's exactly how it happened.

CHRYSANTHEMUM

Some folks would nap in their rooms or watch TV but I loved walking up and down the halls all day long. I went through that stage for almost six years, until one day while walking down the hall, I slid to the floor. The nurses ran some tests, to make sure I hadn't broken any bones but I seemed fine. I wasn't in pain but I believe that because I didn't eat very much, my body just gave out. Six months later when it happened again, the director met with Ken and the head nurse and they all agreed I was very lucky I hadn't broken my hip and they decided I should get a wheelchair. It was the right choice at that time, and even though the one thing I loved doing was taken away from me, it was done with the best of intentions. Ken had a nice tray ordered, so I could sit up and eat from my wheelchair and also put my drinks on it or my favorite stuffed animal pals. It took weeks of trying to get the hang of the chair and to get it to move around because I had no coordination, or upper body strength to push the wheels so I gave up. Sadly, I would be pushed down a hall or somewhere outside and I was unable to move from that spot without assistance, I often remained there for hours. Jem and Ken felt bad for me when I lost my strength to walk safely around the halls but after being in the chair for six months, I had forgotten what it felt like to walk. If I had had my complete sanity, I would have felt like I was in a prison, being in that big, noisy place with all those strangers, being bossed around and kept inside. Luckily for me, my mind was operating independently from my body and I was powerless to exert control over either one! In its own way, it was a blessing, being in my own world, or I may have gone mad from the endless repetition, day after day. One thing that I can say for sure, is that in the beginning stages of Alzheimer's, I did feel hunger, anxiety, headaches, fear, toothaches, pain, and stomach aches. Fear and anger were controlled by the strong drugs which helped a lot. I was taking a cholesterol medication, as well as a blood pressure pill and one for nerves and depression. After my second year in the nursing home, I very rarely spoke. I made hand gestures and pantomimed little acts to communicate my thoughts. After four years, as a resident of the Dementia ward, almost all feelings of anxiety and fear had dissipated like a fog that lifted up and away, revealing sunny skies and a beautiful outlook. I loved being a keen observer of the goings on around me. The halls were teaming with men and women talking, laughing, shouting and crying, while nurses tended to the needs of everyone. I believe that my being in such a big and busy care facility allowed me to be engaged around the clock with everyone's life dramas. From the sweet and kind caregivers to the daily occurrences and situations of my fellow patients, I was never bored and I wasn't lonely. I was very fortunate that the staff was comprised of kind, friendly, compassionate, and loving ladies from many different countries. They all went out of their way to help everyone as much as they possibly could. Never did Ken nor I, ever see a worker yell at a patient or abuse them in any way. That was a source of great comfort for my family. By now, I was just about deaf, so I sat in my chair and watched the goings on, almost like a soap opera on TV. I could also gauge the vibrations of each room or read the expressions on people's faces, which allowed me to get a nurse to push me to another room if trouble was brewing between the patients. There were two gray haired ladies in their early seventies, who shared a room and they could talk and feed themselves, as well as understand what was going on each day. They were there in twenty-twelve when I first became a patient at the nursing home. They would tell the staff if someone was being mean to other residents or stealing items from a patient's room. They were way savvier than all the other patients and they were both there for seven years before one of them died. It was very hard on the one that survived because they had become like sisters, who did everything together. It was the two of them against the world. I guess that's how it was with Ken and I, as we had been married for sixty-three years. Near the end, in the last two years of my living in that nursing home, I could tell that Ken had become weary of life itself and with the daily grind of feeding me each day. He became more vocal about the little things, like the food the workers were putting on my tray, that were not supposed to be fed to me. He wrote an angry letter to the man in charge, bitching about things he saw as sloppy performance and that only made the workers mad, so they wouldn't put gravy on my food or they left out the pudding I loved. His heart was in the right place but taking out his frustration on the help, only made it worse for me. I am just telling the story and I'm in no way blaming him for his actions because he was defending me and he felt helpless and depressed, watching me slowly waste away. Neither one of us ever wanted to be put on life support or have feeding tubes, so unfortunately that put a lot of strain on him, to have to stand by and not be able to do anything. If I hadn't had him to feed me a good meal once a day, I'm sure I would have died a few years sooner. Sometimes, he thought that by him feeding me lunch, he was only dragging out the inevitable, so he was having a crisis of consciousness. Of course, I was completely unaware of all the horrible things he was dealing with, which I'm sure must have been excruciating to live through. That's why I call him my Angel, as he was doing his best to see that I got great care and that I was being treated well, all the while he was barely hanging on to his own life. To me, those are the earmarks of real Love and Devotion and I'm so very proud of his sacrifices and his strength. I also want to tell you, that every two weeks, since I first lived in the nursing home, Ken bought big boxes of sweets and candies from Sam's Club, for all the staff and they appreciated him for it. During my eight-year stay at the nursing home, while Jem was showing me some pictures of flowers she had taken with her phone, I said the word, "Chrysanthemum" out loud and startled her. She was so delighted that I had not only remembered the name of the flower but that I said it loud enough that it was in a normal tone. The nurses told both Ken and Jem that I always said, "Thank You" after they showered me, even though I would cry every time. It's true, I did cry every time I had to shower, as I felt violated and very uncomfortable having strangers touch my naked body, against my will. Even in my condition, it took at least six years to not feel as scared and uncomfortable when standing naked in a huge, cold room while being touched by strangers. No one had seen me naked except for my husband or an occasional doctor, in eighty-five years. Again, it's a generational thing, for folks my age. Once while Jem was visiting, she saw me come out of the shower room crying, so she jumped off the bench and came over to me. She had only seen me cry twice in my life, so she was worried about me and she could tell that I was cold from my wet hair, so she took off her coat and wrapped it around me in a loving way, telling me I would be all right. Since she was my oldest daughter by six years, she and I had a lot in common. Not only was she also a mother of twins, she too loved to cook, sew and was crafty and artistic. The most special thing we shared was our Psychic abilities, in that we both could Channel Spirit's from the higher realms and let them speak through us. It was a strong link between the two of us. She would look into my eyes and send me telepathic messages, while we sat at the nursing home. I could give her a look and she knew exactly what I meant. We were happy just to sit together and enjoy each other's company. She brought her long-haired Chihuahua, "Chewy" when she drove out from L.A. She had him in a baby stroller, so I got to sit and pet him and I loved him so much. He had the sweetest temperament, especially for a Chihuahua. He was calm and never barked or growled. One time while she was staying with us at our house, in my very early dementia days, she was running his bath water in the guest bathroom, when she came into the big living room looking for him. Well, he had heard the water running and had run to the chair I was sitting in and was hiding behind it, so when she asked if I had seen him, I pointed down next to my chair and then felt bad I had ratted him out! But he loved to have his long fur blown dry, so he was never fussy. He was the best little dog I ever knew. Jem never went anywhere without him since he was a puppy unless it was necessary, he even rode on her Harley motorcycle, in a little pack where he was strapped in a pack in front of her. In twenty-fourteen, she drove out from L.A., so she could visit us and help Ken drain our two Koi ponds of water. First, they cut out big squares of the plastic bottom so they could drain the water after it rained. They went about filling the deep plastic liners with cement blocks. Next, they used a fake Astroturf, turned upside down, to cover the tops before filling it all over with white rocks and other decorative stones, to make a "Zen" meditation garden. She returned a year later and together, they redid all the details and the landscaping, along with painting all of the concrete curbing. It was such a wonderful transformation that I got to see after I left that life.

RICH IN SPIRIT

Neither Ken nor I ever cared about material things. Being very old souls, we were deeply rooted in our spirituality and were more focused on our inner selves and being genuine. We had decided early on that we would put our energy into family and friends, instead of fancy cars and trinkets, even though Ken's career was very lucrative. "A life rich in spirit beats a life rich in paper"! To choose Love and Light over Darkness and Decay is to lead a life with God and Jesus as your copilots and to bask in the goodness and love of every moment spent on earth, feeling truly blessed. Knowing your true identity as a child of God/Jesus/Source, allows you to show others how to find their path to "His" Holiness. To be illuminated is to truly shine from within your Spirit. It means your Mind, Body, and Spirit are now, "One". To be a beacon for other soul's is to help them connect to their inner selves, which is a beautiful reflection of God. While on earth, it is each star child's main mission, to reunite with their true-life path and to gain the knowledge of their own innate abilities, their skills, and their powers, they brought with them at birth. Once you let go of your ego and operate your life, tuned into your subconscious energies, then everything is possible for you. When you finally know yourself, your shadow self, and your subconscious self, it's beyond powerful because you truly "See" yourself inside and out. It is every soul's dream to unite themselves with every facet of their being. When they have no more secrets from themselves within their conscious and their subconscious, that's called, "enlightenment". Also, when a human is filled with "Christ Consciousness", there is no room in their heart for anger, fear, greed, jealousy, or hate. That's how you are when you are in your natural state back home in the Spirit realm. You exist in a constant state of Holy, Benevolence and Joy. While in the nursing home, I came and went several times per day and night. The misery of my condition was nonexistent beyond the veil and all my earthly problems seemed more like a part I was playing, like an acting job I did part-time. During naps and sleeping at night, I went home to be with my Spirit family and relax or go to parties with friends. Upon waking in my bed alone, I was back to playing my part, as a victim of Alzheimer's once again. This may sound confusing but it's the reality of all people with Dementia and Alzheimer's. Much like, when you go to your jobs or schools during the day, then you go home afterward to your homes and apartments to eat and relax, watch some TV and hang out with family and friends. You are yourself during the day but when you go to sleep at night, you dream or astral travel, to other places and visit other souls and other realms and dimensions. You may even return to some of your past life incarnations and memories or visit future lifetimes, while you sleep. Just because your body is resting, that doesn't mean your mind is resting. Your brain continues to work out your problems, seeking solutions and it's busy caring for you and your stressful situations. Before you go to sleep, ask out loud for your brain to please help you find a solution for something specific, then when you wake up in the morning, lay in bed a few minutes, thinking about that problem and see if a solution pops into your mind. Examine your dreams, to see if your answer is in there. It may take some practice, but soon you will find problems aren't that hard to solve, when you condition your brain to work on them while you sleep. You may come up with lots of out-of-the-box ideas and solutions while you sleep! Please ask for only one problem solution, each night, so you don't confuse or overwork yourself. Always thank and praise your mind, when it delivers a solution because showing gratitude is the fastest way to get results. If your boss only puts pressure on you, without telling you when you do a good job, you will lose interest in working harder or expending extra energy, so you will want to quit that job because you aren't being valued and appreciated.

Thankfulness is one of the primary functions of Universal Law. There's an old saying that I love, "People will do more for praise than they will for a raise"! Even when you pray, remember to Thank, God/Jesus/Source, The Angels, Spirit Guides, and the Ascended Master's, and All those "Seen" and "Unseen", who work tirelessly behind the Veil to care for all the Soul's currently incarnated on Mother Earth. Give Thanks to Mother Earth, the Universe, and "All That Is" too! Thank all of your ancestors, as well as your animal totem Spirits. It takes a very big team of Highly Enlightened souls to watch over, save, and assist, over seven billion humans! They deserve our love and respect for their selfless duties of tending to the masses. We wouldn't even be here without their Galactic guidance and love. Countless lives are saved every day, by Guardian Angels and other benevolent beings, who are also doing their best to battle the demonic forces that are trying to seize control of planet earth. You can all help, by simply putting out positive, loving, compassionate, and healing vibrations, each day as much as possible. Even if things are scary and unsure, that's the time to send out a thought of gratitude for something you are grateful for or for some blessings you received. Tiny Sparks, when all put together have the power to harness the frequency of "Oneness and Unconditional Love". That frequency has the power to banish negativity, pain, anxiety, depression, poverty, crime, corruption, evil dark forces, and demonic entities. "Light" chases away the Dark and goodness triumphs over evil!

I'm simply trying to say that the human suit is just a temporary gig, for some, longer than for others. Each life was pre-planned, so the length of each incarnation varies, not only by the plan but by each human's ability to use free will. Even your original plan has more than one exit, so use your time on earth wisely. Choose to do the right thing and I promise you that many blessings will find their way to you. All of us in Spirit are Cheering you on, you are not alone! You are loved!

PUFFER FISH

Meanwhile, back in LakeLand, Florida, life for Ken and me was just a monotonous repeat of the day before. At least Now he could go to dinner or a movie with one of his new friends or write. His quality of life had increased sharply after he moved into his apartment. I was so happy for him! During the waking hours, each patient does their best to get through the day. Being a part of a large group of folks, that are all going through the same thing you are, helps you to not feel so alone. I had spent ten years at home with Ken, unable to interact with him in my normal way, so suddenly being with so many people who were suffering the same effects as I was, helped me pass the time by observing absolutely everything. Humans historically have always formed tribes, clans, clubs, villages, churches, groups, sects, and other types of social situations, to feel safer and more connected. It's through the sharing of information and bonding with others, that people learn and teach each other, which can be life-saving. Loners are a breed unto themselves and without social support, they must fend for themselves and navigate a life that is often harder, as they have no one to bounce ideas off of, and in cases of emergencies, their chances for survival are meek at best. While in the nursing home, I kept to myself because my hearing was almost completely gone, so it was harder to communicate with my fellow patients. After seven years of being in there and now confined to my wheelchair or bed, I felt even more excluded from everything and everyone around me. My spirit felt young and I was healthy, except for not getting enough to eat. I was just existing. Ken was doing okay in his living quarters and helping his friends and he too was healthy and doing his one-mile walks each morning. It seemed like everyone around us was passing away, while we were soldiering on, at eighty-seven years old. Once a person's mind has been compromised by Dementia or Alzheimer's, you are freed of doubt and worry, over money, jobs, obligations, relationships, and all other issues of daily life because God erases them from your mind and your memory bank. The medications help calm and soothe you, so there is zero stress or anxiety. It is a blessing that people with Dementia and Alzheimer's suffer no worries or fear because they aren't capable of doing anything to help themselves in any capacity, anyway. The downside is, that it's much, much harder on the families, friends, and caregivers of the inflicted because their hands are tied with no cure available or any way to stop their progression. Much like Cancer, the loved ones are heartbroken and destroyed, while sitting helplessly on the sidelines, praying for a miracle that may never come. Being a caretaker of a person with Alzheimer's takes tremendous inner strength, stamina, and energy. It's often a dirty, stressful, and thankless job and those who do this with compassion and love, are in very high favor, with God/Jesus/Source and "All That Is." When a loving caregiver passes over, there is a huge celebration for them and you might be surprised to know that some of them are truly "Real Angels!" They are what some call, "Earth Angels", Angels that take a human form to help humanity. That's why it is important to treat everyone and everything kindly and with respect. You never know, that homeless person might be a real Angel, testing your soul's aptitude and kindness. Being humble is one of the first steps toward reaching your true self. Egos are over-inflated. When a soul is insecure, it puffs up, like the Puffer fish does, while a truly blessed and Spiritual soul, will not need an ego, as they have obtained its connection to it's subconscious self and know it's worth and value are based on it's love of its soul. Once connected, they are raised up in frequency and light, making them feel all the conscious energies that interconnect everyone and everything, in all of the Universe's, in all of the galaxies and all the realms and all of the dimensions and multiverses! Looking back now on my life in that incarnation, I can honestly say that it was those glorious trips back home to the higher realm of the spiritual plane, while my physical body was sleeping, that kept me alive for as long as I was. Thanks to Ken, I had someone who loved me, fed me lunch every day, and held my hand, so I could draw on his strength, love, and compassion. It was also due to the fact that earlier in life, I had made a Spiritual connection to my inner being and unlocked my powers and the abilities of my "Star Seed", through meditation and by channeling those entities beyond time. I lived my life following the rule of balance, in every phase of my life while in the flesh. It was through Ken and my relationship, with that higher power, that we connected to everything and everyone, throughout the universe. Being humble, grateful, and compassionate, enabled us to see there was a source of love and knowledge that went far beyond our simple lives while living on earth. Being open to accepting the fact that we were mere specs, in the fabric of nature and our surroundings, and knowing the enormity of how truly magnificent the goings on, behind the veil, truly is. The "Oneness" of the matrix and the higher frequencies of energies, mixed with its complete involvement, in the entirety of all things. What we learned by communicating with supreme beings from much higher dimensions and realms, allowed us access to things beyond our wildest imagination. Once you enter that sacred space, you are taught by Master beings how the game of life is truly played, making it impossible to unlearn those lessons, as they leave an everlasting impression upon your soul.

Once you have peaked behind the curtain of "OZ", you will never step backward to the antiquated beliefs you were taught in the past. It propels one to bring others into the inner realm of light and higher learning. Since Ken and I were both teachers, that's exactly what we did throughout our lives. We never forced people to believe as we did, instead, we shared our vast knowledge with all those willing to learn and who were open to discovering their inner selves, their innate powers, and their true-life path in this physical incarnation. Those Masters, often referred to as the co-founding beings of the Christ consciousness, are directly under Jesus in Heavenly status. "All That Is", is a phrase that encompasses the entirety, of all the universes, all the dimensions, all the multiverses, all of the electromagnetic energies and plasma there is and there will ever be. "All That Is", is made up entirely of supremely intelligent, conscious matter. It is a divinely compassionate, loving, and powerful element, that was used in forming all the planets, stars, galaxies, nebulae, and all the dimensions. "It" created the supreme entity known as God. "All That Is" gave God, the most potent power along with the most powerful abilities throughout the universe, and "It" gave God the freedom to create "His" legions of Angels, Masters, and many other highly evolved entities, who were made from the Christ Consciousness. God was shown how to use "His" powers, so he could then create "His" entire kingdom to house all the divine beings, in a very high vibrational frequency of a very high dimension, where no one can enter unless they are found worthy and deserving by God himself. Next, God, All That is, the Masters and the Angels, worked together to set up codes, rules, and regulations for the governing of all beings great and small. God is the king of the Spiritually Divine, Heavenly Realm and "He" is the supreme ruler over the morality of the behavior of All the white light entities called, Soul's. Whether they are at home with God or incarnated on one of his many planets, what God says or rules, goes, it's the law. Period. "All That Is' ' and God are a team. Upon establishing God's Divine Team and Code of Conduct, "He" then created man, woman, animals, sea life, and everything that exists throughout the galaxies and dimensions, along with the realms and multiverses. Science is "God's App", which he uses to create all beings in the divine matrix that inhabit all the planets and stars. Just like science is man's tool to create new and improved technologies. God has supremely advanced technologies to create, heal, govern, and rule in the Heavenly realm. They are so very far beyond what's available on earth, that there is no way to convey their entirety with your current understanding of the concept of God and of the Spiritual energies of "All that is". Each relies on the other, like a symbiotic relationship. Think of the heavenly realm, as one big non-profit organization. "All That Is", is the "Source" that created the divine Souls and God is the CEO, in that "He" is responsible for the fate and welfare of everything in existence. God is also tasked with handling the "Morality" of All beings throughout all the universes, realms, dimensions, the multiverse and timelines. Jesus is his COO, "He" acts as Counsel for all the many diverse planets, their occupants and their concerns. Jesus has his own division of Ascended Masters along with his family's of Intergalactic and Interstellar benevolent Beings of Light. Together they are working very hard behind the scenes to help humanity on planet earth, wake up to the reality and truth of what's really happening all across the globe! Corruption is so rampant in every part of the government now that the Divine Realm called for, "All Hands On Deck"!! They have advisors, aids, and cabinet members, to help monitor all the billions of people and to make sure everything runs smoothly. Angels act as the go-betweens for human beings, as they are responsible for working directly with all of humanity. Perhaps some of you will argue that God is the creator of everything because "All That Is" doesn't have a body. "All That Is" is the term for the "Source" of all the electromagnetic matter and energies of pure divine consciousnesses, that there is and will ever be. "All That Is" needs God to be the most powerful entity in the entirety of all space, time, dimensions and multiverses throughout all the galaxies. Without that highly evolved electromagnetic energy, there would be nothing for God to use as the material for any of his creations. A jeweler designs and creates jewelry but without metals, there would be no jewelry. "All That Is", is the element and God is the being "He" put in charge of all the creations, who were made using the matrix of the divine conscious matter.

God uses that same matter to comfort and care for all of the benevolent beings of light. It's the divine matrix of pure consciousness that makes up everything throughout the galaxies. It's a living and healing form of various light frequencies that supports and sustains all life. In the higher dimensions, there is no such thing as "Ego", as highly evolved Light Being's don't compete to be better than others, as they are all made up of the same energies and they are filled with loving light and compassion. Each Being of Light has many powers, skills, and abilities. They can instantly manifest whatever their hearts desire, so they have no need to compete. Abundance is also every Soul's birthright. That's why in the higher dimensions, love, compassion and joy are so abundant. When you can obtain anything you want or need, it erases all need to struggle or stress over those silly things that only exist in the third dimensional reality. Negativity does not exist in the higher dimensions and low-level entities cannot exist in the light. Darkness has no power over a lightbulb. Until you realize just how powerful each one of you is right now or what things you're truly capable of doing and becoming, your room will remain dark! Your Soul is filled with brilliant white light consciousness that you can use once you relax and let your subconscious be your guide. Fear is a low frequency emotion that holds you back from uniting your outer and inner consciousness and becoming truly Enlightened!

The deeper Alzheimer's dragged me into memory loss, the closer I came to my true state of being. Those rejuvenating visits I had with God/Jesus/Source made it easier for me to continue playing my role as a patient in a nursing home, back on earth. Having watched our life story many times over, I can see how hard it was for Ken, to reverse our roles and become my caretaker. Being in our late sixties and in good health, I understand his frustration with knowing there would be so many things we wouldn't ever be able to do again. If I hadn't had Dementia in my late sixties, say I didn't get it till I was almost eighty, Ken and I would have enjoyed those extra ten years. Because of my Dementia/Alzheimer's condition, there would be no more family get-togethers. Events like movie nights, going out to eat, site seeing, socializing and road trips were gone forever. We wouldn't be going antiquing and exploring. Now Ken would be the only one answering the questions when we watched "Jeopardy" and the only one answering the phone. There would be no more discussions on so many topics. Even after sixty-three years of marriage, we both still loved each other's company. Our whole relationship stopped being about just the two of us talking and being husband and wife, as it switched to patient and caregiver. Gone were his can-do wife and best friend. It was so hard to watch and see everything that he was robbed of because of my condition. He was never mean to me, just frustrated and very depressed, while our good years went by without us. Alzheimer's took away everything we were as a couple and as lovers. It was honestly so heart-breaking to view. Ken was a man leading two separate lives after I went into the nursing home. I was so grateful he sold our house and bought his two-bedroom apartment near me. He had met new friends whom he could go out to lunch and do activities with. My heart was happy to see he had some guy friends and that he was doing some fun things while I was not there. Being able to watch him on the big screen, while I was visiting Heaven in my sleep, allowed me to catch up on everything that had been happening around me and to those I loved, while I was incapacitated by Alzheimer's. I could see with my own eyes and hear with my ears what Ken, Jem, and the other three kids were going through, while I wasn't there. I felt sad when they were sad and happy when they were happy and I understood they were all handling things in their own way. I could tell they were worried about Ken and me. It was comforting watching my husband visiting his cousins at Thanksgiving and knowing he had some good times with family and friends. I understood how busy the kids were, with their lives and knew they felt bad for me and their father. It made me feel loved and appreciated when they were working hard to raise money and awareness for Alzheimer's research. It was so heartwarming to know they hadn't forsaken me. Just watching what they were up to, helped me to feel less lonely and depressed. If I had any questions, I could ask the Angels or my Spirit Guides. They made tremendous efforts to calm me or relieve my angst and worry. It's impossible to describe just how important watching those videos are to every person with Dementia or Alzheimer's, as we spend each day helpless and trapped in feelings of frustration and fear, we are powerless to speak from our voice, intellect, or persona. While we sleep, we are transported back home to the Spiritual Realm, where we appear very normal and like our thirty-year-old selves, as we relax, converse with others, and catch up on all we have missed. Every human has these abilities, no matter what race, religion, or country you are from, when you get to the Celestial realm, you are a very powerful being. The second you get there you instantly recall how amazing you are and what miracles you are capable of! It's a very empowering event because while you are still living that incarnation on earth, you are shown everything when you cross over in your sleep. After all, when you return to your body upon waking, you are incapable of telling anyone what you just saw or did due to Dementia or Alzheimer's. You are granted total access, while you have those memory-stealing diseases so that you won't suffer from fear, worry, anxiety, or depression. The trips to heaven, help strengthen your soul's ability, to stay anchored and tethered inside the corrupted mindset of the patient. Otherwise, the brain would confuse the body's many functions, so much and so fast, that it would be easier, for the soul to make a faster exit from the body, instead of following through with your life's plan. A soul chooses Alzheimer's, so it can learn a lesson and also teach a lesson but if every soul vacated the body right after getting Dementia or Alzheimer's, then there wouldn't be enough time for the soul to learn from the experience. Suffering, is part of the human life cycle, that every soul uses to learn from. If each life, was all fun and had no hardships, then what lessons would be learned or taught? Through adversity comes revelations. You learn more from your enemies than from your friends. Think back on your own lives, what lessons did you learn the most from? What teachings did you fall back on as you grew older? Who taught you the most valuable lessons? People come into our lives and teach us things, then depart. We can seek guidance from friends, family, partners, teachers, coaches, churches, and professionals. If you can, volunteer to help young people, who would appreciate your wisdom and sage advice. Sometimes just being a good listener, helps get others through rough times. A kind word, a hug, a shoulder to cry on, each is a great act of kindness. No act is too small. God appreciates all your positive efforts!

It's interesting that some things in your life, things you love, are like a sturdy cord that runs in and out of your life, right up until your passing. Even all of our kids are collectors of some kind of antique or vintage trinkets. I believe it's nice to hold onto special things from your past that you love. They become keys that unlock the doors to your happy place and allow you to step back in time, to revisit those sweet memories. I missed out on so many things, during almost twenty years with Dementia and Alzheimer's. Not just family and friends' events and gatherings but also, all the pleasurable memories I could have made with those I love. I can't tell you how surprising it was, to review my life and see all the new advancements made in technology and all the amazing gadgets, as well as all the medical progress. Way before I had been affected by Dementia, Ken and I both agreed, to not be resuscitated or kept alive on machines. We both were organ donors and wanted to donate our brains for Alzheimer's research in the event either one of us had the disease. Because I died of Covid-19, they were unable to use my brain, which was such a shame. One of the perks, of returning home to your natural state of being, is that you get to also look at your children's lives on the screen, so you can go back to when they were born and see things from their perspective. This allows you to learn how your actions and treatment of each child have influenced or altered that child's life, positively or negatively. If you have done your very best as a parent, then it is a pleasurable experience, however, if you were cruel or harmful as a parent, it's going to be a heartbreaking experience to relive. Please be aware that for every action, there is an equal and opposite reaction. Sometimes a parent can bend over backward and do their level best, to raise their children properly but that child can go on in life to do horrible things. In that case, you can't blame yourself. Other times, even if a child has a horrendous upbringing, they can become kind and loving adults. The outcomes are affected by free will, karma, outside influences, and choices, good and bad. Each soul is on earth to complete a mission and return home. When you go through life being kind and compassionate, I promise you that you are earning good karmic points. If you are living a life of evil and negativity, then your fate won't have a happy ending. One of the many benefits of returning to your natural state as a spiritual being is that after the celebration and the welcome home parties, you get to watch a movie about your life spent on earth during your incarnation. You also may choose to watch your children, family members, and friends you knew, in that physical life span, to see how you affected others and how their actions affected you. It allows one to honestly see, if you treated them kindly or if you didn't treat them as well as you could have. It's a way to know if your actions helped or hindered them. Most parents try their best and strive to give their kids a better life than they had when they were kids, however sometimes when you give children everything they want, they don't learn the value of earning their own money by doing chores, so they lead a spoiled life. When they are older and must enter the workforce, they aren't prepared for a job where they are required to work hard for a paycheck, then they get angry and expect everything to be handed to them. You are doing a disservice to children when you spoil them because they aren't prepared for the harsh realities of life on their own and many will falter. Finding the balance, where a child learns rules that guide them and protect them they will learn to appreciate things in life. It's the key to helping your children respect themselves and others and it makes them more self-reliant and efficient. Leading by example is a very important tool and being kind, considerate, and compassionate are the most important lessons that you can pass on to those you love. People are judged by their actions, making it imperative to instill these values in your kids, as well as to practice them yourselves. When humans seek the true meaning of life, the answer is to live each day with appreciation, kindness, gratefulness, compassion, and love. Even in the worst of times, look for something small to be grateful for. By helping others, you help yourselves. Choose Love over hate, be kind, not mean, help others who are in need, and treat all things the way you expect to be treated and you will be rewarded with unbelievable glory and blessings beyond your wildest dreams! Help animals that are hurt or hungry and you will feel a glow within yourself, that comes from the feeling of doing a kindness, no matter how large or small. No act of love and compassion is too small, as they are what connects you, to the supreme ruler, God/Jesus/Source. When you perform kind-hearted feats of any size, you send out beams of holy, white light, straight up to heaven and if every person does this each day, you can literally, light up the energy of the earth, so that it raises the collective frequency that enlightens all of mankind and every living thing on your planet. I suppose Ken and I, got great comfort, being surrounded through our years by all the objects in our home, that were handed down through generations with loving hands, that held special memories of our ancestors, long departed. Both he and I shared a love of Genealogy. It wasn't rare to find us whispering about this or that, dead family member's history, as we learned about their lives. Maybe because we were only children, that made us curious about who they were and what their life was like. We saved all the old letters, postcards, and objects that were passed down from distant relatives, who were connected to, or a part of our family. While living in West Newbury, in the "Haunted House", we would drive to larger cities, in hopes that their archives would hold more information than our small local library or town hall. When we started this quest, back in early nineteen seventy-one, we were light years ahead of the now popular websites that analyze your DNA and tell you your family history. Come to think of it, we started buying homes and fixing them up and selling them at a profit in the sixties, so we were ahead of our time as house flippers! Ken was really into following his family tree, as he had many names of past relatives from his mother and father. He discovered that one of his father's relatives, George Soule, came over on the "Mayflower" ship, as an indentured servant and settled in New England! Some of his other relatives had served in the war against the British and one ancestor threw tea, in the "Boston Tea Party". At least two other members of his father's family fought against slavery in the South. There may have been some folks in New England that endorsed slavery but no one that was related to the Davis family ever was. His family had farms in Vermont that raised milk cows, chickens, pigs and made maple syrup. His other relatives were furniture makers, photographers, and just hard-working people that believed in freedom for all. Many sympathizers in the North ran underground railway systems for smuggling black people, out of the South, to escape slavery and to live better lives. When we had researched as many family members as possible, we sent our research data to Washington, DC to, "The Sons Of The American Revolution", to be verified. Weeks later we received their seal of authenticity with a letter stating we and our four children could also join, which is a real honor if you are into that historical stuff. When we got settled in our home in LakeLand, Florida, Ken and I decided that we wanted to make a book of each large cemetery, beginning with our own Polk Country first. We started by speaking to a groundskeeper at a nearby cemetery and asked if he had a map or plot plan, with the names of those buried there. Every person we met, while writing ten total cemetery books, would show us what written papers they had but many were missing the full names and dates. Some had no such list or paperwork at all. We would start early in the morning, walking up and down, row after row, trying to make sense of it all. Each cemetery was huge and it took us weeks, months, and years to make detailed maps and keys that had accurate names and dates, of who was buried there and when. That was a huge undertaking at the time, though we were in our early sixties and good health. We had picnics under the shade of a tree or sat on a viewer's bench here and there. I used tracing paper and a pencil, to rub over the oldest and most worn of the gravestones. In between rain showers, we went from headstones to flat markers, then to fancy mausoleums. Ken read the names off the stones and I kept meticulous records. It was a labor of love and it would be the last thing of that nature we would ever do together. We donated a book to each town's library, as well as their court of records department and a copy was given to the person in charge of each cemetery. Polk County is one of the largest counties in central Florida. Many times, when families aren't too close and the elders retire to Florida, the grandkids have no idea where to find their family's grave sites. Now at least, there are some records to look at, that we hope will help people find their relative's final resting place. We pray in some small way, that we have left a legacy that will live on for future generations. That's just the kind of thing that made us tick. Whether it's restoring an old building or preserving things from the past, that's where you'd find us, loving every minute of it!

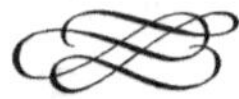

It was early May, of twenty-twenty, when I left my body and traveled home to heaven to visit with my Spirit families. It was while I was sitting by a large fountain, speaking with my Mother Vivian, when I felt a strange feeling, a disturbance in the energy force surrounding me. It's hard to put into words but it was as if I heard Ken's voice, calling my name. I stood up and looked around confused. Vivian asked me what was the matter. I told her I wasn't sure, and I started walking, as if on autopilot, so she followed me. We were met by one of my Spirit Guides, who told us to follow him. He brought us into one of the viewing rooms where we watch ourselves and others back on earth. He had us sit down on a comfy sofa, while he waved his hand over the control panel for the big screen. An image of a hospital room came on the screen and it took a full minute before I realized I was looking at my beloved husband Ken, hooked up to wires and machines! My sweet hero looked so small and fragile that it took my breath away. I asked my Spirit Guide what was wrong with him. In a gentle voice, he told me that Ken was having internal bleeding caused by complications from Hepatitis. Nothing was making sense, I couldn't find a way to process this information, even though my mind was clear while I was in the Celestial Realm. Vivian took the reins and inquired as to the severity of Ken's condition. "He needs life-saving surgery, however, he doesn't want to go through with that at age eighty-eight, because he can't watch you suffer anymore", said my Guide. The Spirit Guide left to give us some privacy. My thoughts were so scattered. I had no way to help my husband or even go visit him because of my Alzheimer's and I couldn't comfort him in any way. What would I do without him? Poor Ken was now suffering and alone. I went and spoke to my Guide again and asked what I should do. He replied, "Ken is worn out, mentally, physically, and spiritually and he has chosen to let go of his life in the flesh. He has asked that we convey his love and devotion to you. Do not feel sad or bad about him departing this life, it isn't your fault, he just wants to go home." I understood how he felt, as I too, yearned to be back home full-time and done with this life of blood and bone. Now that I knew he wouldn't be coming back to see me, I suddenly felt so alone, it was almost suffocating. I decided I wouldn't eat or drink much of anything, speeding up my death. Now I would go straight to the viewing room, as soon as I fell asleep. Each night I went back to the Spirit realm and I spent the entire time watching Ken in his hospital bed back on earth. Angels and Guides surrounded him, while he lay still, being fed with an IV. I sent him tons of strong white light and lots of Love to keep him safe and protected. I may not have been holding his hand physically but psychically, I was smothering him with love and light. My consciousness was visiting his consciousness and he knew I was concerned for him and he was worried about me. He was so weak and drained that it broke my heart. Weeks went by and he was doing worse every day. The hospital staff was trying to keep him as comfortable as possible, with pain medication and his sleeping pills. This was all happening in the early spring of twenty, twenty, as Covid-19 was terrorizing planet earth! At the time, I didn't know anything about it, as my focus was on Ken's health and well-being. When he passed away on May twenty-third, I wasn't sleeping at that time, I was awake and playing my role as an Alzheimer's patient in a nursing home. That night, as soon as I entered the dream state, I was transferred to the viewing room. I tapped the screen onto Ken's hospital room, but his bed was empty. I turned off the viewer and I was just about to walk out of the room when Archangel Michael appeared before me. He was so tall and glowing bluish white, that it was comforting just to stand next to him. He wrapped a wing around my shoulders, like the softest quilt. He whispered to me, that my beloved soul mate, had exited the earthly realm and had returned to the Divine Holiness of God. He went on to say that his soul's Aura was being treated for illness, pain, anxiety, depression, and life trauma but in a few days, I could go see him. I was sad, happy, excited, nervous, and crying and laughing all at the same time! I was releasing twenty years of suffering in silence, all at once. I was instantly surrounded by Angels, Guides, Masters, and Ancestors as we all celebrated Ken's long, wonderful life on planet earth! We planned big parties and celebrations for him when he was released from his healing sessions. I was beyond thrilled, he had crossed over and was finally free of that doll suit of flesh. Now I could see him and touch him and sit and talk with him when I came home to heaven, as my earthly body lay sleeping.

FINAL TRIP

Back in my nursing home, I could feel the strong vibrations of fear and worry, coming from the nurses and caregivers. The very air crackled with tension and anxiety. I could hear them whispering and I heard the word, "Covid", more than once. They were now in fear of coming to work because their jobs had them up close to so many patients. I don't blame them, as they had families at home waiting for them. If I couldn't return to Heaven when I slept, then I wouldn't have known Ken had died and that humanity was in a war against a silent and deadly killer! Seven weeks after Ken departed, I woke up with a cough, finding it hard to take a breath. The staff was all wearing masks and they reeked of fear. I was given some cough medicine but it didn't do anything to stop the cough. I felt hot from the inside like my body was burning up. They gave me something strong to put me to sleep. It was so strong that my consciousness was unable to leave my body to travel to the Heavenly realm. I came to, sometime the following morning but because of my high temperature, I was given an IV and strong drugs to bring down my temp. I fell in and out of conciseness, for a few days. Upon waking in my bed, it felt like someone was sitting on my chest, the pain was so intense. Doctors and nurses zoomed in and out of focus while they treated me. I was so drained after being sick for over a week, I was really out of it. I couldn't breathe and I felt like I was drowning in water from my lungs, it felt like I was choking on my saliva. The strong drugs kept my Spirit earthbound but just barely and I hadn't eaten in days. The IV they had me hooked up to give me fluids. I wasn't scared but I didn't understand what was happening to me. I had never been this sick before in my entire life. I don't remember how many more days I lay there in that condition but I do remember floating up and over my bed, gazing down at myself, as if I was watching a stranger. Looking down at the form lying below, I felt sorry for that sick and pitiful person, then I wished her well, as I rose up and out of that nursing home, in the arms of an Angel.

HEAVENLY REWARD

My eyes were heavy and I kept them closed. I felt so safe, secure, and loved, that I didn't want to wake up from this dream. Then a hand-picked-up mine and enfolded it in a familiar grasp, causing my eyes to pop open. Standing next to my holographic healing bed, was my handsome husband of sixty-five years, looking like he did on our wedding day when we were both twenty-five. I thought I must be dreaming! We both smiled hugely and he squeezed my hand while tears were streaming down our faces, as we laughed and cried. It was as if we had just won a bazillion dollar lottery, when in fact, we had won the universal reincarnation challenge called, "The Creation Game"! Together we had survived almost ninety years of living on planet earth and we had been compassionate, loving, and kind. Both Ken and I always volunteered to help others by being generous with our funds and by sharing our time and positive energy. There was so much we both wanted to talk about that we kept interrupting each other, then we'd start laughing about it! All that we had gone through, everything we had learned or taught, it was so overwhelming that we had to slow down a little, as both of us were still a tad weak from the whole ordeal. How do we describe all of our feelings, our many experiences, and all that we had shared and weathered, while we were humans? It's very restricting, to encase part of your powerful soul into a delicate flesh-and-bone frame. To endure pain, heartache, anger, and strife, as well as to experience love, joy, happiness, and compassion. To live through the tedious and mundane daily stresses of life as a human being while in a suit of flesh. It makes you appreciate returning to your natural state, as a powerful being of white light! We had endured as a couple and we stayed strong till the very end. Now we could celebrate a "life worth living" and share our adventures with our Star families and all our celestial souls we love and have missed so much! Ken and I are back home, the duo is together again and we are proud of all we have accomplished while on planet earth. Our souls have reconnected with the everything of, "All That Is". We are now vibrating at such a high frequency, that we are jubilant and joyful. It's like having your "best day ever", constantly! We attended "welcome home" parties and celebrations for us and for others like us, who had just returned home from their missions on earth. The celestial realm is full of sensational celestial parties to embrace the many returning souls. The beauty and the holy light of Jesus and God, flow through every molecule and fiber of our essence, as we sing and dance our way through the heavenly stars…

May God Bless You All!

May Balance Be Your Guide

Never give up, never give in!

Take care and Thanks for being you!

Together, Ken and I wish the very best for all you beautiful souls on planet earth! Mel

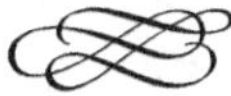

•KEN WITH A PEN•

When my wife Melba first started to show definite signs of Dementia, more than just forgetfulness, I felt a deep, sinking feeling in my chest. When a week had gone by with her asking the same questions over and over all day, I felt fear, anxiety, and anger that we would have to deal with this awful disease. Her mother, Vivian was best described as a tough, determined, hardscrabble woman who had lived through two world wars and the great depression, making her fiercely independent and firm. She was our introduction to how cruel this enemy of the brain could be to its innocent victims. Mel and I had tried very hard to get her to move in with us but she was a stubborn woman, who said we should move in with her. That made absolutely no sense because Vivian lived in a tiny house on twenty acres, on a prime piece of real estate in Old Orchard Beach, Maine but there weren't any extra bedrooms, and no way could we build a house on her land at the outage. With Vivian in the early stages of Dementia, she wouldn't be able to live alone and her long-time companion, Gean, had some health issues, so we couldn't expect her to care for Viv, even though they were both nurses. Vivian wasn't your typical eighty-something-year-old woman. She was five feet, ten inches tall and she wore pants, not dresses and she owned a shotgun to shoot over her garden to scare off the woodchucks. She never killed any animals, it was just a game of cat and mouse between two rivals over the veggies in the garden. Even Mel never knew her mother's real age because she got her driver's license back when it was just a paper card and no one looked up how old someone was, they took your word for it. Before you get too comfortable thinking you've got this granny figured out, she had a genius IQ and a very keen eye. From nineteen thirty-nine through nineteen forty-five, during the Second World War, many job fields opened up for women that had always been filled by men. Now, with no men around because they were off fighting overseas, they asked women to apply. Vivian was twenty-two years old when she was put to use by the United States War Department, as an airplane mechanic! She scored the highest on the test out of more than one hundred other women. She built and repaired airplanes that were used in the war against Japan. When the war ended six years later, Viv enrolled in nursing school and became a registered nurse, a skill where you could always find employment. She and

Gean both worked at a local Old Orchard Beach, Maine nursing home. Her special passion was being an avid gem and mineral collector. She and her nursing companion Gean drove all over the states and went to semi-precious stone mines like amethysts, beryl, quartz, tourmaline, and garnet, where they paid a few dollars to go into the shafts with their picks and dig up or chip off, the specimens. The duo went to New York to the Herkimer diamond mines, and they brought back quite a few very nice pieces. If she found a particularly nice gem, she would have a guy she knew cut facets and polish it. Behind her house, she had huge twenty to forty-pound pieces of pink quartz, clear quartz, and other varieties of minerals. Viv was intensely brilliant and her blue eyes would light up like a five-year-old, as she showed you the latest finds in her gem collection. Gean and Viv also loved antiquing and they each had a great set of eyes for spotting great quality and rare items. It was sort of a family joke about Viv being a magic woman. Mel told me tales about her mother being able to heal people using strange methods. Once when Jem was eleven years old, she showed Viv a wart she had on her finger. Vivian told her she would buy the wart from her for a penny. Well, she must have put some kind of medicine on the penny before she rubbed it on the wart because the wart disappeared in two days! She also had a playful and jovial side that came out when we brought our two oldest kids to meet her. They were amazed by her antics and the little trinkets she gave them. Viv had purchased a few acres of land on a main road to the beach, after the war, and her uncle Rex helped build four, one-bedroom cottages and a bigger house/office on the property. That way she and Gean could live year-round in the house and rent the cottages out in the summers for extra income. The cottages sat half a mile from the large pier, on one of the main roads to the beach. They were set back from the road on a horseshoe driveway. Viv and Gean kept them so clean you could eat off the floor. They rented the cabins out to tourists, especially to the French Canadians, who drove down every summer to ride the rides, walk on sugar sand beaches and ogle the bathing beauties. At night, folks would sit in their parked cars on the beach strip, eating ice cream and making fun of some of the strange clothing on the tourists. It was life on an American beach, wholesome, beautiful, and genteel in its simplicity. The pier was packed with people, arcades, games of chance, and Pier french fries served with vinegar. Boating, surfing, fishing, and swimming kept the whole place humming, while the salty sea spray and the cotton candy clouds made it a picture perfect day. The cabins were booked up a year in advance after a few summers, with solid regulars that were fine, respectful folks who were smart to book their reservations in advance. Both Viv and Gean kept their jobs at the nursing homes year-round, so they could save money.

MR. GIFFORD

When we first moved from Virginia in nineteen sixty-eight, to Acton Massachusetts, Vivian, and Gean called and asked if they could drive down for the day with one of their patients who was turning eighty. We decided that we would get ice cream and Mel would bake a cake, so we could celebrate his birthday. Jim and Jem were happy to blow up the balloons and tape up the party streamers. A party was a big deal back then and we were all excited to see Vivian and Gean. When they pulled into the driveway, we met them outside with hugs and handshakes, then we went in to sit down for a nice dinner of pot roast, mashed potatoes, veggies, rolls, and delicious gravy. The kids had fun entertaining Mr. Gifford and he blew out his candles while we all sang him "Happy Birthday". After we ate the cake, we walked outside and said our good-byes. The ladies helped get Mr. Gifford settled into the back seat and they got in front. We waved to the trio as the car drove away, headed back up to Maine. During the two-hour drive home, the ladies discussed how good the meal was and what a fun birthday party it was. Later that night I got a call from Vivian, saying that while they were talking in the front seat, they heard a loud sigh from Mr. Gifford, then he went silent. They pulled the car off the side of the highway into a rest area and they got out, opened the back doors, then felt for his pulse and checked his breath but he was gone. Since they were on a state highway, they drove straight to the hospital in Biddeford, Maine, and explained what happened. I told Vivian how shocked Mel and I were because it was only a few hours ago that he was eating birthday cake with us at our table! Mel and I had several conversations about that night and we believe that the whole day was part of a Divine plan and that we were supposed to celebrate Mr. Gifford's birthday and his last day on earth. We felt honored to have been a tiny part of it. That small act of kindness and compassion was pre-planned by a grand design. Mr. Gifford had been treated to a road trip and a celebration of his birthday and also a celebration of his life! He was surrounded by those who loved and cared about him, not alone in the nursing home, which was a blessing for sure. We had shared a fine meal and made him feel like he was a part of our family. Mr. Gifford had lived a wonderful life and we were so glad to be with him in his final hours. He left a lasting impression on each one of us. A few weeks later, Vivian received a call from a lawyer. He said he needed her to come to his office. He wouldn't say why, just to please come, which she did. Seems Mr. Gifford left his entire estate to Vivian! She sat there in shock because she had no idea when he had found the time to do this. It was twenty acres of prime land, on a corner spot that was on two main roads that intersect to the beach. There was a cute, one-bedroom house with a small kitchen, bathroom, and living room. The old barn attached to the side was for two cars and it had room for a workbench or two. This was such a boon for both ladies because they were advancing in age and they couldn't keep up with nursing and the cottages. She and Gean could picture the garage as a great place to store their car and their antique treasures. They could set up shelves like a store, for their side business of selling antiques and vintage knick-knacks at flea markets and roadside sales. The house was small but the place was secure in a nice quiet neighborhood where everyone knows your everything! Vivian sold the cottages and used some of the money to paint and do small upgrades to the house. Both ladies loved to garden, making fresh food a way of life and they could plant a much bigger garden behind the house. See how just one act of kindness can make the ripples get so big, they create Tsunamis of loving, positive power, and luck. That same power heals, saves, and loves you right back!

Vivian and Gean could now retire from nursing and just enjoy their lives, especially without cottages to clean. Mel's mother was doing great the first seven years and both of the ladies were pretty healthy. It wasn't until we moved from Virginia to Vermont on the lake, that we were able to drive down more often to visit Vivian and pick up some of her antiques that she wanted us to sell at our booth. After seeing her every other month, we started to notice she seemed lost in thought or worried about something but she was such a private person, we didn't feel right asking. After a year and a half of seeing her and dropping off her sales money while we visited, it became apparent that Viv had Dementia. In late November, we dropped by Vivian's to say "Hi" and to leave her inventory list of what had sold and for how much along with her check with the proceeds. Vivian started asking us where this piece was or where another item was. She was getting paranoid and thought we were taking her antiques and not paying her. Mel was hurt and trying not to get angry, as we were only helping her because we wanted to. Neither Mel nor I, ever took a commission or rent for the booth, not to mention the eight-hour, round trip, each visit. Before things got more heated, Gean took me aside, while Mel walked outside with Vivian to the garden. She told me that Vivian was always grumpy but that she was not only forgetting things but being downright nasty and mean to her. I wasn't shocked, as I had seen the changes getting more noticeable but it put us all in an uncomfortable situation for sure. We didn't expect Gean to stay with Viv if she was being abusive to her, so she made plans to head down to her family's home in Connecticut in the spring. That gave us three months to formulate a plan. I promised not to tell Vivian that Gean would be leaving, as that could affect Viv's behavior or it could become dangerous for the two of them. Viv was a big woman at five feet, ten inches, so if she walked off, it would be hard for Gean to corral her back into the house. I filled Mel in on the drive back home about the new turn of events. I could tell that she was sad and upset, especially, since they were never close as mother and daughter. We chewed on some ideas and figured since Vivian was so bull-headed, she wouldn't do well living up on a lake, far from the beach, so we would ask Gean to look around for a nursing home near them. Since she was a nurse, she could get the inside scoop about which ones were the best and then we would contact them. Six weeks after our last visit, we drove back down to Old Orchard Beach, to bring all of Vivian's items that hadn't sold. We felt it was better to tell her we closed the booth, that way we could end that transaction because it was too upsetting for both mother and daughter. As luck would have it, Vivian's mood was cheery and her eyes were bright. We all decided to go to lunch at a local seafood shack named, "Ken's Clams", a favorite with the locals. It was a crisp, cool spring day and Vivian seemed almost "Normal", in that she was clear-headed and mentally sharper than she had been in months. It was surprisingly nice. There's something that Melba left out of her version of her story because it's too painful to talk about. Mel just won't talk about it, Period, so I will fill you in. When Mel was sixteen and entering college, she needed a copy of her birth certificate for college, also her medical records and she needed a driver's license. Her mother gave her the birth certificate. On the certificate was her name as the baby, Vivian's name as the mother, and some man's name was written down as her father but Melba had never seen him, never heard of him, and never met him in her life. When I met Melba in college, we were a part of the "Brainiacs" club, it was just a handful of like-minded, intelligent, and geeky youngsters, who wanted to save the world. I was six feet tall, thin, and on the goofy side and she was five feet, seven inches tall and beautiful with high cheekbones and denim blue eyes. All of us kids lived at the dorms in college in Vermont but everyone went home on holidays and breaks. Mel mentioned her mother Vivian but never said anything about her father, so I let it go. Mel was born out of wedlock in nineteen thirty-four, at a time when you were considered a whore or a scarlet woman without morals if you had a child without being married. Back then, Mel was considered a bastard because she had no father. Her mother left Maine and stayed in Connecticut with her older brother Rex and his wife Rena until Melba was born, then she moved back to O.O.B. when Mel was six years old. Kids in school knew Mel had no father, so they made fun of her and bullied her. It didn't help that she was so much smarter than her classmates. This was because while she was a baby in Connecticut, she was around mostly Vivian, Rex, and Rena. Rex was Viv's only brother and his wife Rena was sweet and kind and always made her feel welcomed and safe. She was a great sister-in-law. If your child is only around adults, talking about grown-up things, then the baby will pick up those same words. Mel grew up only hearing adults speaking about subjects she didn't understand and without any other kids to play with, the result is a very well-spoken child with an advanced vocabulary. During our first few years together, we both had so much going on that I never brought up anything that had to do with her father because it would be like reopening an old wound. When Jim and Jem were nine and eight, I waited until Mel was in the kitchen making dinner and I took them into the den and told them never to ask their mother about where her father was. It felt so strange to say this to my kids about their mother because I had both of my parents at home while growing up. While living in Virginia when Jim and Jem were toddlers, my Dad and Mom drove down a few times a year and we also drove up to see them in Vermont. We would go fishing, nature walking, have cookouts, and go antiquing. Our two oldest kids knew their grandparents on my side but I figured since they were getting to be almost teenagers and nosier, I should talk to them before they started to wonder why Vivian wasn't with Mel's father or any man for that matter. Mel's anger towards her mother was barely disguised, when we brought our kids by to see her. She had just wanted a father like other kids had. She felt left out and alone. Watching her mother play with our kids, made Mel angry that her mother had never been like that with her. After our move to West Newbury from Acton in nineteen sixty-nine, Mel told me of her desire to find out who this man on her birth certificate was, so she could ask him why he didn't want her and why he had abandoned her. I agreed and since we love doing genealogy, it became a sacred quest for us, to help her heal from that traumatic experience and to live free of those negative emotions. To Mel's frustration, she kept hitting roadblocks in the search for her father. Vivian didn't help by staying so tight-lipped that even a car jack couldn't pry her lips open! There weren't any home computers back then, so finding a person relied on being a private eye and chasing the clues. Since Viv wasn't cooperating the case went cold for twenty years.

She and I were so busy with work, kids, and our many moves, which meant we had to put the hunt for her father on a back burner. Mel had raised herself, especially during her teen years. She made new friends in junior high school and played on the women's basketball team. She had become very popular by being not only beautiful but also kind and friendly. By the time she graduated high school, Mel was only sixteen years old. That's why having kids of her own was so important to her, it's all she ever dreamed of as a child was to have a father and a mother. She told me she wanted us to be great parents to our kids, to give them a loving environment with both of us present and involved in our children's lives...Okay, now you're all caught up. Getting back to our visit with Vivian on that day, Mel decided to ask her mother where the man on her birth certificate lived and if he was still alive. Since Viv was in rare form, it was now or never. She got Viv to sit at the kitchen table, then she sprung the question on her mother. Vivian's reply was, "What man?!" Who the heck are you talking about, man?!" Mel took her birth certificate out of her purse and handed it to Vivian, saying, "Here"! The look of total surprise that bloomed over Viv's face was as scarlet as the story. Mel became concerned when she saw how genuinely confused her mother looked, staring down at the paper on her lap. The room was silent. Gean and I were two players in this game but the Mother-Daughter stuff was strictly between them. After a minute, Vivian slowly raised her head to gaze at the daughter she didn't want and who now, didn't want her. The playing field had swapped sides, letting Viv feel a taste of what it's like to not be wanted by your own flesh and blood. "Gean, put on some coffee, this will take a while." I took a quick bathroom break and Gean got the coffee set up and then I sat back down on the chair next to my wife. I took her hand and was startled by how cold it was. I was praying that whatever the story was, my wife gets to hear all of it today and that she gets some closure, so she can heal from this trauma. As Vivian began to fill in the blanks of the story, it shook us to the very foundation of our souls! We were both "God Smacked"!

In the fall of nineteen thirty-three, Vivian was sixteen years old and she lived with her mother and father in Biddeford Maine, in a small home. Her father worked in the sawmill, as did most of the men in a working man's town. One afternoon in October, Vivian's mother asked her to go down to the railroad tracks behind the furniture manufacturing building and collect a basket full of kindling for the stove. Off Viv went down towards the tracks, holding a big basket on her arm. While she started filling her basket with small wooden scraps, she was approached by a man from the furniture building. The man told her he had some better pieces of wood and to follow him. Viv does as she was told and walks around the side of the warehouse behind the man. When they are out of sight, the man raped Vivian, then told her he knows who she is, who her family is, and if she ever tells a soul he will kill them all. Vivian was in shock, not only because of the violent rape but because she had never had any sexual education and she had never even kissed a boy, as she was still a virgin. After the man left, she put on her clothes and then made her way back home, putting the basket of wood by the stove, as she went into her room. Her mother was a few houses down taking care of an elderly neighbor till eight at night, giving her time to clean herself up and hide her bloody dress. Before eight o'clock, she left a note on the kitchen table, saying she had to be up early for a school test so she was going to bed. She barely slept, as awful nightmares mixed with shame and fear tossed her around with a fierce anger, unlike any she had ever known. She didn't know the name of the man that had stolen the most precious thing from her but she knew by his clothes, he wasn't a labor worker because he was clean-cut and his clothes were tailor-made. His hands weren't rough from a day spent chopping wood. Vivian decided to make it her mission to find out who he was, even though she was never going to tell anyone about this horror show. After three months went by, just as Viv was starting to feel a little more like her old self, she began to realize that the vow she had made to herself of keeping her secret safe, was now broken by the baby she had growing inside her. Panic and rage were cycling through her. She was afraid of what to do next. It was tragic enough to survive the rape but how can you want a baby from some creep that forced himself on you? Now her mother would know she was pregnant and she was starting to hyperventilate when suddenly, she had a dark thought, an idea that took shape in the form of revenge. It was going to take a few years but Vivian vowed to have that baby and then she would move right back to that town, bringing "His" child with her and live right there, where he would have to live his life looking at his kid and wondering if she would ever tell the police. That story would ruin his reputation and status among the businessmen and town folk. That plan helped Vivian keep her sanity through the next seven years of having to move away, being an unwed mother, being disgraced, then giving birth, and having to work to feed herself and her child. All the things that were stolen from her, her pride, her virginity, her home, and her freedom, drove her on through the years. The whole thing made her hate men and she became a hardened and tougher woman. She finally told her mother a week later, while they were home alone. Of course, her mom was devastated by this horrible news and shocked that her poor daughter had been living with this burden alone for three months. She asked Viv for as many details about the man as she could remember. Telling her husband now she decided, would only lead to trouble if her husband went looking for the guy. Also, she was afraid he wouldn't look at Vivian in the same way, even though it wasn't her fault, as she was the victim. She would cross that bridge later when she came to it. After she and Viv talked, she told her that she would make sure she was safe and protected. Viv went to bed feeling great relief that her mother was going to help her get through this. She slept the best she had in many weeks and it gave her inner strength to know she wasn't dealing with everything alone. Two weeks later her older brother Rex came by to visit and he brought Rina, his wife of two years with him. Vivian and her mother sat at the table with them, a family closing their ranks to protect Vivian's reputation. Together they devised a doable situation that worked for everyone. They decided Viv should move in with them in Connecticut, that way she could have the baby without the neighbors talking and gossiping about her being a single mother. Rina hadn't had a baby yet, so she could help Viv by taking her to the doctor and making sure she ate right. Rex was a very tall man with broad shoulders that were cut from years of hard work. He was glad his sister would be living with them, so he could keep her safe. Rex secretly wished he could get that creep alone and really mess him up but right now he knew Vivian needed him to lean on, so he tabled that thought but deep inside he was seething. Back in nineteen thirty-four, if a woman had a baby out of wedlock, she was considered a whore, a tramp, and spoiled goods but because of the wars going on overseas, a woman could move to a new town and tell folks her husband had died in the war. Better to lie than to live as an outcast and have the baby endure a life full of ridicule and hardships. Times were hard enough back then. They didn't have many options and Viv didn't want to stay in town because she might run into her high school friends who would be shocked and then the news would hit the gossip train and she would be ostracized by everyone in town. She also didn't want her parents to feel ashamed and embarrassed, so Vivian packed some clothes and some trinkets she loved and went to Connecticut that night with Rex and Rina, carrying a few bundles of her things and feeling very grateful, that after everything she had been through at least she had a family to help her. Her spirits were lifted once again. That's where Vivian stopped her story and Gean gave her a cup of coffee. The room felt crowded now that it was quiet, each soul deep in their thoughts. I looked at Mel and she had a shocked and amazed look on her face. I gently squeezed her hand just to reassure her. She stayed quiet for a few minutes while the rest of us drank our coffee. All her life, since she was six years old and had to move back to Maine, she had been mad at her mother, and sometimes she even hated her mother. Just to listen to her mother tell the story of how she was conceived through the violent act of rape, she must be feeling sideswiped by a truck. I know it was all she could do not to bolt from the room so she could cry alone. If I hadn't been there, she would have left, as she needed to process all that she had just learned. All those years of hating her mother for not treating her in a nurturing or loving way. Now Mel must be thinking, every time her mother looked at her, she was vividly reminded of that violent episode of being raped. No wonder Viv hated men. It all made sense now, her mother's anger and indifference to her. Her mother wasn't mad at her, she was angry at Mel's father for raping her and forcing her into motherhood at sixteen years old. To discover Vivian had been gutsy enough to move right back to the scene of the crime was downright shocking. What had her father thought when he heard Vivian was back and with a young girl in tow? I bet she could picture him sweating bullets, knowing his flesh and blood child and possible heir to his furniture stores was back and living in town. By that time the furniture company had several locations, so it was a big deal to be related to those in the higher class of society. Mel was living proof of the crime as well as irrefutable evidence. Maybe she figured it was Vivian's revenge for the pain and shame she had suffered but by doing so, she had inadvertently made her daughter suffer a life of ridicule and misery without a father. We both felt relief and sadness now that she finally knew the truth, thanks to Viv coming clean by sharing the details of what had transpired before her birth. If Vivian had never told her before Dementia and Alzheimer's claimed her memory entirely, the truth would have perished with her. For that, both of us were so grateful to Viv that she dared to set the record straight. Knowing she was a product of rape didn't make Mel feel better but it did save her time chasing down the man whose name was on her birth certificate. Who knows if the guy even knew that Viv used his name on the birth certificate, it was just her word. It was a blessing to hear the truth, just for peace of mind. Wow…you have to marvel at the twists and turns of life's plots. Maybe that's why Mel and I love researching our ancestors. When we dig up tidbits of information or dates and locations about their history, we feel a real kinship with them. New doors open and pathways from the past to the present lead us to connect the dots. Finding new leaves for the family tree and following all the tiny informational crumbs from source to source, fusing the past to the present. Life is a constant flow of energy and an evolution of cells and souls. Lots to be discovered.

AGE OF AQUARIUS

Being married to Mel was never dull. She was not only a genius, but she was also highly creative and multi-talented. During college, we and some of our classmates hung out together during summer breaks. Mel had connections in O.O.B., at the pier for the games, rides, and some of the restaurants that landed us all jobs for the summer. The girls rented two rooms in a hotel on the strip and the guys rented two rooms in the same place on the next floor up. We were earning money and having a blast. Those were sweet memories of an innocent era when life was beautiful and appreciated by all. Nothing was taken for granted. I think it was when we moved to West Newbury, Massachusetts that she and I felt an affinity with that old house. After all our earlier moves to apartments and houses, this time felt like a charm. The whole town was so country, it felt like you went back in time, especially if you were looking at over two hundred-year-old homes, without modern cars in the driveways. Most of New England is rich with historical examples of America's beginning attempts towards freedom and independence, especially along the coastal cities and towns. Everywhere you looked there were markers, statues, and plaques, explaining what historical events had occurred on that spot and in what year they had transpired. Newburyport was mostly comprised of very old Federalist, Georgian, Colonial, Saltbox, and brick homes and buildings. Some houses were built with a widow's walk on the roof. Legend has it that the wives would stand up at the glass windows and gaze out to sea, looking for their husband's ships to return to port. Many homes had ghosts of women still walking and waiting. It wasn't unusual to find homes built in the sixteen and seventeen hundreds. Our neighbors were kind and welcoming and our kids were happy there too. In the beginning, we put a lot of time, sweat, and money into the renovations but the results were just what we wanted. My wife outdid herself with the handmade decorations inside and out during the holidays, as Thanksgiving and Christmas were everyone's favorite. Mel and I were both only children and neither of us had mothers who were affectionate or nurturing, so now with our kids we looked forward to each season and added to the traditions we were creating together as a family of six. Nothing is prettier than the first snow of the season, especially on Christmas Eve. We were experiencing new things all the time through our children's eyes. It's always a lot of work but very worth it. When we opened the craft supply store, "The Craft Center" in Newburyport, it was a whole new world of running a retail store, something we had last done while in Virginia when we had an antique shop. Newburyport was fast becoming the "It" place to be and we were meeting new folks and learning the ropes of the wholesale world and the trade shows. Crafting was blowing up and everyone wanted to paint, make model cars, do stained glass, pottery, beading, and every other fad like macrame. Without realizing it, the two of us were slowly becoming hippies of some sort. Newbury-port, with its seaside charm, located on the mouth of the Merrimack river was luring folks from the cities that were looking to live the laid-back lifestyle of the seventies. Being the smallest city in the state, there were no skyscrapers, just stunning, old, exposed brick buildings with heavy, hand-cut, wooden beams and a huge dose of history. Young couples our age started snapping up property in broken-down neighborhoods and restoring them. The baby boomers had breathed new life into the area by renovating the lovely historic buildings, as it was long overdue for an upgrade and a fresh approach. The "Boomer's" also had more financial abundance and shopped locally in support of their neighbors and fellow store owners. That's also how we met the three other couples that we would bond with on a very deep Spiritual level and become the "Trine". This was all happening during the special astrological, "Age of Aquarius", a planetary alignment that was extra fortunate in peace and prosperity. Mel and my generation were opposed to war and conflict. We were children of parents that had been through two world wars, the Korean War, Vietnam, and the Cuban missile crisis, not to mention the Great Depression, Prohibition, and the Dust Bowl. Our generation wanted to stop pollution, end segregation, and implement new laws, restrictions, and taxes on big companies that were cutting down trees in the RedWood Forest and factories that were dumping their chemicals in the rivers, lakes, and oceans. Humanity was crying out for peace and kindness. It was a very prosperous era, due in part to the large number of new jobs being created, as exciting advancements and new technologies came onto the scene. Peaceful demonstrations and events like "Woodstock " were popping up across the country and you could feel the Love in the air. The "New Age" religions and spiritual groups drew many people together with the purpose of uniting folks to take part in ushering in new changes for the betterment of mankind and Mother Earth. People felt good about doing their part to make the world a better place. When we moved to Newburyport in seventy-five and lived over the store, those were some of the highlights of our lives. We had new friends, a successful store, and a busy social life and our kids were excited and healthy. It was the happiest we had ever been.

KARMIC WHEEL

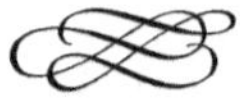

Mel and I were both active in our kids' lives and also in helping those in need. Many a winter we supported the local artists by letting them run a tab in our store, so they could make it through the harsh winters, till spring when things got busy again. It worked out well for Jem, as we traded art supplies for art lessons from some of the best artists in the area. We attended a Spiritualist church in Lynn, Massachusetts that had great guest speakers and also healing sessions. It was a perfect way to congregate with other like-minded people. It wasn't a local church but we went a few times a month. Looking back now, I regret not involving our kids in more Spiritual endeavors. With all our moving and starting over in new places, we just didn't have the extra time and neither of us had grown up in a religious home. Jem was the only one that went with us to hear the messages passed down from pastor

"Thom", who was an exceptional speaker and a Psychic Channeler like her mother. At the end of every service, he would give messages that came to him from Spirit for patrons of the services. One time when Jem went with us, Thom picked her out from the crowd and told her she was going to make a living with art and be famous for her colors. He didn't know her at all or that she was already an artist in many different mediums. Mel was sitting next to her and when Thom said, "This message is for the young lady in the plaid pants", both Mel and Jem looked around us to see whom he was talking to, when all of a sudden, Mel looked down and realized Jem had plaid pants on, so he was speaking to her! Jem was also surprised to be chosen, as it was a very large church with hundreds of people and he only gave out a handful of readings during each service. Our daughter became an accomplished Psychic that could channel Spirit Guides and other entities. She started giving readings for future events to clients. Together we made a great team and it made us closer as a family. Sharing information gained through channeling, we all learned vast amounts of information of the supernatural kind. Mel and I educated our kids with frequent trips to museums, historical places, art exhibits, and things of that nature. Perhaps the sixties and seventies were eras of great change and marked by many tremendous events, like the first man on the moon, the assassination of President John F. Kennedy, and Dr. Martin Luther King. The whole nation was trying to recover and rebuild the economy after the wars and the Great

Depression. And let's not forget about the Dust Bowl, which left the people in the heartland of America buried under dirt from terrible droughts. Thousands of people were out of work and homeless. Each generation must deal with great tragedies as well as great accomplishments and each one of you plays a part in the dramas that unfold around you during that incarnation. You are a part of someone's past, someone's present, and someone's future, all at the same time. Free will is your birthright, so use it wisely or you'll have to come back to correct what you didn't fix, while in that lifetime. It's the law of the Karmic Wheel that insists that what you do comes back to you. As you give, so shall you receive. Treat others as you want to be treated. Those three statements are the main elements needed when living a life in the flesh. Basic decency is rudimentary in your pursuit of enlightenment. You must treat all creatures big and small with compassion, love, and respect. If you use those three words to guide your actions while on earth, you will surely ace every test you set up for yourself. Be accepting of others and nonjudgmental of their choices. Worry about your journey and let others discover their truths without forcing your beliefs on others. Mel and I loved many things about other religions such as Buddhism, The Tao, The Christian Faith and the principles of Hindu teachings. Our Spiritual pursuits ranged from a little of this faith and a little of that faith. We were big fans of meditation and connecting with the Spirit Realm. This way we were receiving guidance and information directly from the source, instead of ground-up truth served up on Sunday mornings. We hold no animosity towards churches, temples, or synagogues, as we believe in free will and each soul should choose what faith speaks to them. The exception for us is, any Demonic interaction, as it is not aligned with God/Jesus/Source. We were not supporters of any evil, demonic, negativity, cult's or fear-based religious practices. When you live a life of kindness, compassion, and love, then it's not a deal breaker if you don't attend church every Sunday. God knows what's in your heart and mind. If you always come from a position of positivity and compassion, then you will never stray from your chosen path in each life you live. Energy from God/Jesus/Source is inside every human being, your body wouldn't be animated without a cotton ball size, chunk of your Spirit, put inside you to be the ignition of your vehicle, (body) while on planet earth. You can't fit your whole "Light Being" into a human body, it's way too powerful. The bright white light your being consists of would shine white light from every pore, your eyes, nose, mouth, and ears, so you'd look like a glowing body of light. Even clothes couldn't contain that much light. There is so much more to the whole affair, that's why I wrote a story, putting their teachings on paper so that it can activate others into being more positive and aware of the truth of your own powerful soul's journey in this life. We included it in this book and we hope you enjoy it.

LIFE IN THE FLESH

I guess once we started to speak to interstellar, intergalactic, and inter-dimensional beings and entities, we felt intensely close to God, Jesus, and the Angels. It was life-changing. During the ten years we were a part of the "Trine", the Masters in the Spirit realm, taught us many valuable things that we held sacred unto ourselves. We learned about reincarnation, the past lives we had lived, and the meaning of life itself. They showed us what the reality of life in the flesh entails and why souls choose to come back again and again, to participate in humanity's life cycles and to help others. Death is a release from the suit of flesh and the reward is to be reunited with all your family, friends, God, Jesus, the Angels, the Masters, and your Spirit Guides and Ancestors. To be united with "All That Is", the energy source of all things in the universe, is the greatest feeling of all. They are waiting for your return and there will be many parties and big celebrations when a soul returns to the Divine realm of God/Jesus/Source. Everyone feels jubilation and joy to see their soul family members back home and safe. Those lessons stayed with us all of our lives, so Moosie and I didn't fear death. Our Faith in our Spiritual families and the love and compassion we shared with our Spirit Guide's, gave us comfort that death is a reward for living a good life. Believing in reincarnation, in Life After Death, gave both of us inner strength and resolve to press on through the hard times and rejoice in the good times. Together, she and I felt a real true love that was bigger than the Universe. Getting information and tutelage from high-level beings of pure consciousness, had a way of grounding a person and one began to realize just how small and insignificant, a human being's life and dramas are! How fragile are the egos of Man, who would freak out if they knew the truth. Humanity has a bad habit of take, take, take with no regard for the repercussions or consequences. Those in power in the government would be shocked and humbled to know the truth, of how easily the truly great powers in the Heavenly realm could wipe out humanity entirely. Of course, if that had been their mission, they could have done it at any time. Just ask the Aztecs, Mayans, and Atlanteans. Beings from the celestial realm of God/Jesus/Source, can manipulate the weather on earth. Tornados, blizzards, earthquakes, hurricanes, tsunamis, avalanches, mud slides, great floods, droughts, volcanoes, asteroids, and other major catastrophes can be stopped or started by Highly Evolved beings from higher dimensions.

THE CHOOSING

You choose what lessons you want to learn before you are born. You sit in a planning room in Heaven, with your choice of Spirit Guides, Masters, Angles, and Oversouls while you and members of your "Star Family" plan out a whole big "TV Series" of sorts. Think of it like a very long-running, situation drama/comedy/romance, TV show, where each person you know plays a part in it. Some have top casting and some will be co-stars while others will be supporting actors, stand-ins, walk-ons, and some extras. Each one that wants to help can play a part in your script. You will have the leading role while you play yourself, and your mother and father will be your supporting actors, your siblings, and other extended family members as well as close friends will also be cast members. Some may only have walk-on parts while others play heroes or villains. No one is forced to join the cast, it's all volunteers or young souls entering a human life for the first time that starts in "The Creation Game." There are exceptions to this as highly evolved, ancient souls may choose to join in, especially if it's a huge role that could change the course of history. During the Renaissance period, all those artists, builders, and most of the scholars were ascended "Masters" who came down to introduce the fine arts to earthlings. Albert Einstein, Leonardo De Vinci, and Nicola Tesla were some of the "Master" beings from the Heavenly realm. Many school teachers choose that role so they can nurture young impressionable minds. Older souls that have completed many lives may therefore take on a mentor-like role in the flesh to teach and comfort other younger souls who are just starting out. Then other people that come into your life for shorter periods, like teachers, coaches, mentors, co-workers, and classmates have walk-on parts in your production. Backstage are your Spirit Guides, Angels, and Ancestors. They are your advisors who guide you. God/Jesus/Source is both the backer for the whole production and also the creative source of inspiration and power for the entire show. Earth is "His" stage, where each soul plays out their life dramas in their endeavors to obtain the rank of Adept. After many lifetimes and all the lessons have been learned, a soul can choose to step off the Karmic wheel rut and stay home and relax in the Kingdom of God/Jesus/Source. Every soul's goal is to reach Enlightenment. Once that level has been reached, you are free to do as you please and travel to other realms or planets. The

Spirit Guides told us that before a soul can travel to other dimensions and other planets, that soul must first pass all the levels and obtain Enlightenment, before being allowed to do as they please. To complete all the assignments, you must be aware of your behavior while in the flesh and you must always choose to be loving and compassionate over being mean and cruel or you will have to just keep coming back, again and again, to repeat the lesson before you can move forward. Moosie and I raised our kids on these principles but never insisted on who or what religion they should follow. In fact, with our oldest two, we set up rules that were not so strict that they felt controlled, as they were more like rules of safety and their responsibilities to be followed or else receive the punishment. By the time the twins were teenagers Moosie and I were a lot more lenient with them than our first two. I guess most parents lighten up after the older kids break them in. It also helped that the older two could handle things while we were working. When they got their driving licenses, they would help pick up or drop off the twins at places, which made our lives much easier. When Jem became very fluent in channeling, we were able to share things with her and her with us, on a much deeper plane of thought. Thus, creating a sacred bond with her about our beliefs. This is why we can enlighten everyone about Melba-aka-Moosie and my experiences with both Dementia and Alzheimer's.

SHOWER WARS

In the late nineteen nineties, Moosie was still doing great and her mind was sharp as a stiletto. It wasn't until around two thousand and one, that I started to notice her slipping gears a few times. At first, I would answer her question and then an hour later she would ask the same question again. Like any husband, the first couple of times per week of her doing that it didn't register but as the weeks went by and the same thing repeated more frequently, I had warning bells going off like crazy. My wife was super intelligent and capable of multitasking like a pro, so I started a mental journal to track the frequency of these events. Let me state at this time, I also had to almost force her to get her hearing checked. When the doctor told her she needed hearing aids she wasn't a very good patient, as she always forgot (probably on purpose), to use them. I was forever finding them in all sorts of places around the house. By two thousand and three, her condition had advanced to early Dementia and she was becoming withdrawn and uncooperative. During that same time frame that's when the shower wars began. Getting her dressed became a daily thing as well as me having to prepare our meals three times a day, something I dreaded. She was such an amazing cook and baker that she spoiled me, in that I never had to do more than fix myself toast, oatmeal, coffee, sandwiches, and heat leftovers up in the microwave. Now I was responsible for three meals a day for both of us, as well as all the grocery shopping and giving her the proper medications at the appropriate times. She wasn't always cooperative when it came to taking pills because neither one of us was on any daily medications, except her cholesterol pills, vitamins, and an occasional Tylenol, so she was very suspicious and wary of me when I gave her a pill to swallow. I worked a desk job for FEMA for twenty-five years and I hadn't had to worry about Moosie's health or her ability to handle the kids or the household, as we were both very healthy and hard-working. I commuted to my job in Maynard, Massachusetts from West Newbury and Newburyport, which was an over two hours drive each way, so by the time I got home dinner was on the table. It was like living with a superwoman for over fifty years and then almost suddenly, within five years of the onset of her Dementia, she had become not only partially deaf but mentally incapable of handling everything she had always excelled at. This meant so much on so many deeper levels than just her not being able to do some housework, as I had always helped with the vacuuming and the laundry many times during our marriage. It was the little things in our lives like watching Jeopardy and both of us answering the questions and having deep discussions about things going on in our community and our four kids and all our grandkids' lives. She would draw a blank when asked a simple question and not remember who our neighbors were. Any type of physical contact was out of the question and I even felt uncomfortable helping her wash in the shower but I couldn't leave her in there alone in case she scalded herself or fell. It became almost impossible to take her to a doctor, then talk about her as if she wasn't standing right next to me. I won't deny that I started to feel overwhelmed and like a stranger to my wife. Gone was the tough woman that had faced challenges with a strong mind and a defiant attitude. In her place was a woman-child that would laugh one minute and cry the next. Her emotions were on a roller coaster ride and unpredictable. It was emotionally crippling and so hard to handle, that I became bitter at times when I ran out of patients and I would become cross with her, then I'd feel so bad about my behavior that I'd want to break down and cry. Depression set in as she and all her many daily needs became all-consuming. I craved her nap times just so I could get a break and a few minutes of peace. Even when you love someone entirely, you don't know what it's like to have to go from being a husband to a father, for that same person in just a span of a few months. No one prepares you for taking complete, round-the-clock care of a sick person or someone with special needs. This is especially true for men of my generation, who had wives that cooked, cleaned, and took care of the household. You know it's not that person's fault but you can't help but feel trapped and cheated out of what should be the golden years of your life. I felt indentured and depressed by it all. When you take vows to love in sickness and in health, you never believe that the day will come when you must step up to the plate and do it, especially because both of us had good health.

COMFORT ZONE

Women are way more nurturing and compassionate than men as a whole and as mothers, they are selfless in their commitment and dedication to their mates as well as to their children. Statistically speaking, men die earlier than women do but, in my case, it's like my wife regressed to a child whom I had no idea of how to handle or care for. I was unprepared and way out of my comfort zone. I tried my level best to get through one day at a time and I taught myself, with some tips from Jem, how to take shortcuts when cooking and easier ways to throw a meal together. That helped a lot because every minute I could shave off was a minute for myself to regroup. I found easy and quick ways to cook some simple and healthy meals as neither of us ate fried food or takeout. I bought snacks and Ensures for Moosie which helped keep her hydrated and gave her much-needed protein.

This was essential as she had no concept of time, so I had to make sure she wasn't hungry between meals. While she napped in the afternoons, I turned my energies to my writing. I had several articles published in local newspapers and I became a dedicated advocate for Alzheimer's and participated in local marches and fundraisers. I started a blog and wrote short stories and poetry that helped me maintain my sanity. Those things allowed me to step out of my situation with Moosie and enter a private world, where I could express myself in my true form. By now, all our kids and neighbors knew of her condition and everyone was very sweet and supportive. They were compassionate and didn't try to interfere or stop by unannounced. Once the cat was out of the bag, I felt a huge weight was lifted off my shoulders and we were able to still have Thanksgiving and Christmas dinners for our whole family, thanks to Jem cooking everything and cleaning up. I can chuckle now about her saying Jeff Gordon was her husband but at the time, I was hurt and frustrated. Out of all the emotions I went through while caring for Moosie at our home, I was heartbroken for her and our kids and grandkids. She was such an integral part of our small family, that not having her be an active part of everything was so very sad. Moosie was an amazing grandmother to the grandkids, so to have that wiped away by Alzheimer's, was a hard pill to swallow. Praying for a cure that never comes, is the torture of the families who have loved ones, that are affected by these mind-hijacking diseases. Moosie and I had a rare opportunity in the very early onset of her Dementia when she said she wanted to donate her brain to Alzheimer's, with the hope it would help in the finding of a cure in the future. In the early stages of her Dementia, we went through a phase when she and I, took out a box of family photos and we both went around the house, placing pictures of our kids and their kids, on tables, chests, counters, and the fridge, in the hope it would help her recall their names and identities. I'm not sure if it helped, but I found it reassuring in a small way. Since the very first time we met, in teachers' college in Vermont, our relationship was based on the connection of our minds and our mutual thirst for knowledge.

Mel was engaged to one of my best friends in college and I was infatuated with her but felt she was out of my league, as she was five feet, seven inches tall and gorgeous, with strawberry, blonde hair, and high cheekbones. She played basketball and was the Deans secretary at our school. My friend that she was engaged to, was a rugged kind of guy and a good-looking jock. In an unexpected twist of fate, he broke off the engagement, confessing he was gay, something never done back in those days. Mel was shocked at first but we all stayed good friends and we never told anyone why he broke it off, just to protect him. One day during spring break, I had to drive a classmate with Epilepsy, to her family's home for the Easter holiday, so I asked Mel to go with me, and to my delight, she went! After we dropped our friend off, I had hours to talk with her on the ride to Old Orchard, beach Maine, and that's when things between us went from the friend zone to the couple zone. After college, at nineteen fifty-five, I enlisted in the Army and we were married, before I went into basic training. The Korean War was just coming to an end but they still had the draft. It was decided that we could get teaching jobs just about anywhere. My eyesight was not great, so when we were stationed in Fort Lee, Virginia, I was put to work writing training manuals for the Army because I had a college degree in education. During my enlistment, I got my master's degree while working on the base. Both Jim and Jem were born while I was in the Army. Jim was born on the base, in November of nineteen fifty-seven, and Jem was born in February of nineteen fifty, eight. Life was good to us, as I was able to climb the ranks of the federal government through my positions in Civil Defense, (Now known as FEMA), I would retire twenty-five years later as a GS16. Having a master's degree in education meant I could have been a high school principal or a college professor but the federal government had great benefits and retirement plans. While in college, I never dreamed of working for the federal government, so it just goes to show you how life will take you where you are supposed to be when you let God and your intuition guide you!

RUM RUNNERS

Before I passed away on May twenty-sixth, in the year twenty-twenty, I was a writer of many articles that were picked up by local newspapers and other publications. I sent copies of my work to my kids and grandkids, so I wrote an article about Moosie and my many moves and the houses we rented, bought, or built, as some interesting things occurred along the way in our first few years together in Virginia. When I turned eighty, I had both my ears pierced and Jem made me a fourteen-carat gold earring with a faceted emerald and a diamond that I wore in my left ear and a small, gold hoop in my right. While researching my family's genealogy, I came across a relative of my fathers, that had lived a few generations before I was born, and to my delight, I found his picture and in it, he was wearing two gold rings, one in each ear, giving him the look of a real character. Out of boredom and wanting to rebel, I decided to treat myself to something different, as my life was consumed by the daily drudgery of being a caregiver to my wife. I went to the mall and a young woman pierced both my ears. Back in the day in Vermont, distant relatives in my family history were rum runners and smugglers during the prohibition years. They souped up their cars and made roadsters out of them, so they could outrun the law. From nineteen twenty to nineteen thirty-three, speakeasies and underground bars and clubs sprang up all over the northeast, from Vermont to New York. People were going through such hard times and most folks just wanted to drink to forget their problems and enjoy themselves. This opened many opportunities for making money and my relatives were no exception. Vermont, borders Canada, where liquor was legal, so the men would drive their roadster's and pickups into Canada and buy whisky, then they smuggled it back into Vermont, by way of back roads and secret dirt trails. My father told me a story when I was a teenager about one relation of his, a woman, who was married to a man and they had four kids. Their house was secluded and it was way up towards the top of the state of Vermont. The property was located on a sharp curve in the road, right near a little bridge that went over a small river. When her husband died, she was having a hard time feeding her kids, when a friend of theirs asked if she could leave the back barn door open at night, so he could drive into it and close the doors, if he was being chased by the federal agents. She said yes and many a morning when she went to feed the livestock in the barn, there would be an envelope containing cash that she so desperately needed. There were also stories bandied about by the locals, concerning smugglers in boats, picking up people on the Canadian border, and taking them by boat, to meet other boats, so they could get into the United States illegally. On one such occasion, while being chased by border agents, a man forced his occupants to jump out of the boat near the shore so he wouldn't get caught. Unfortunately, some folks drowned because they couldn't swim, especially with all their heavy clothes on. It's sad to think that desperation forced people to take such drastic risks in life. Those were some of the toughest times in America's history.

SOUL DEEP

Moosie and I shared a love of history and we felt driven to learn all we could about our ancestors. We were so very close, in almost everything, when it came to our beliefs and customs and we shared our thoughts and ideas on every level, throughout our life together. We were true equals with a deep soul connection. I believe that's why we were able to stay happily married for sixty-five years. Going through so many life events and dramas together helps to fuse you both and it gives you strength to last through the toughest of times. We were meant to spend that incarnation with each other. We are very old souls that have incarnated together, throughout many lifetimes and centuries. That's what made it extremely difficult for me to even consider putting my lovely wife in a nursing home. We were both eighty years old and I had been taking care of her for ten years. Our kids thought it was time I let professional nurses take over, so I could get a break from the twenty-four, hour duties that were becoming harder for me to handle. Ten years of that responsibility would wear anyone down, emotionally and physically. Just thinking of taking her from our home and putting her in a foreign place, with strangers, made me sick, deep in my soul. I felt like I was cutting off half of my body, I just couldn't face it. No matter how nice the place might be or how kind the staff was, it felt like I had been gutted. It was like when people can't take care of the family dog or cat because their pet is sick or they don't have money to pay the vet bills, they just drop it off and drive away. The internal suffering of those left behind, abandoned, through no fault of their own, felt so cruel and selfish to me that I couldn't wrap my head around it. Our kids weren't being pushy about it, they were worried about me and my depression and wanted me to enjoy the time I had left on earth and I appreciated them for it. Knowing they wouldn't be mad or upset, helped me make the decision I needed to make, to save us both. Moosie was needing more care medically, which I wasn't qualified to give her and I was so drained by the long days of her care, that I finally knew it was the right thing to do. Not that I felt good about it, I just had no choice. I started searching the internet for good-quality nursing homes near our house. We were both still living in the house on the golf course and it had been paid off and even upgraded years ago, thank God. After a few weeks, I went to visit three, which seemed to have great reviews and were within a two-to-three-mile distance from us. That way, I could be close by so I could visit every day. The first two I saw were nice but I wasn't sold on either one. The last one was a little farther away but still under a fifteen-minute ride each way, which was doable. I liked that it had its own separate wing, designated just for Dementia and Alzheimer's. It was a very big place that had a huge auditorium and an outside gazebo, a structure for those wanting to sit and smell the roses. The staff seemed hardworking and kind, the bedrooms were nice and everything smelled clean. After the tour, I spoke to the director and he filled me in on all the details and gave me brochures to peruse at my leisure. It took me several days to mull over all the pros and cons of each establishment, before deciding on number three. My attorney advised me to take Moosie's name off of the house and to enroll her in Medicare, so the cost of her care, depending on which of us died first, wouldn't eat up our entire savings. With that done by April, of twenty twelve, I now had to set the date she would begin residing there. I took her to our doctor for a full check-up and also bought her some new clothes, making sure she would have nice things to wear. I admit, I dragged the process out an extra two weeks, as it was my way of spending as much quality time with her as I could.

BRIGHT BLUE SKY

The reality of what I was doing was starting to crush my spirit, as the day got closer. I spent every moment looking at her, sitting next to her and just being with her. I wanted to mentally save every second of her being in my mind's memory bank, so I wouldn't add more regrets to the list I already had. It was a beautiful spring morning, on May twelfth, when I drove her and her things to the nursing home. Anxiety in the pit of my stomach was killing me but I tried not to show her because I was feeling so guilty about the whole thing. We walked hand in hand, into the front door and I signed us in, then we made our way to the Alzheimer's wing. The staff greeted us warmly as they showed us to her room. There were two beds divided by a moveable curtain. Her bed was the one next to the window, where I put her clothes in her closet and the dresser drawers, while she was looking around at the other patients wandering around in the hall. I put her dolls and some stuffed animals, on her nightstand by the bed and on the shelf above her bed. I took her hand and we walked around the wing, as I told her about all the details of each space we visited. She probably didn't comprehend what I was telling her but my anxiety was making me chatty. She was quiet and busy taking it all in. Some of the patients were also walking around, watching TV, sitting on the couches or outside, under the shady gazebo. After we completed the tour, a nurse came up to us and we followed her into a room with a chair and some medical equipment. She had Moosie sit down, while she took her blood pressure and temperature. My heart was pounding so hard I could feel the blood rushing in my ears but I was doing my best not to crumble. She let us leave the room and we went to the couch where it was quiet and sat down. When it was her lunchtime, I walked with her to the cafeteria and sat her at a table, while we waited for the lunch trays to be delivered. When her tray came, I set everything up and unwrapped her straw, putting it in her juice cup. I helped feed her lunch, which she ate most of, then we walked back down to the living room with big windows that had a lovely view of a field, across the street while big, fluffy, clouds floated by in the bright, blue sky. I sat next to her, holding her hand and holding back my tears. After forty minutes, she fell asleep, so I placed her hand on her lap, then kissed her forehead. I stood, looking down at her sleeping face, feeling like a sneaky trickster, then I turned and walked out of the wing and out of the building, feeling like I had just killed her. My facade was crumbling fast as I hurried to my car, afraid I'd break down before I could drive away. It was all I could do to drive home, as my palms were sweaty and tears were leaking down my face. There are no words for the emptiness and heart-sick feelings that were ravaging my body and soul. Mel was my wife, my confidante, my rock, my lover, and the mother to our four children. I felt ripped apart with guilt and anger that God didn't spare us, this horrific tragedy and pain. We were good, kind, and generous people. Why had she chosen this disease before birth to be one of her lessons? Didn't she know how painful it would be for the ones she left behind? Even though we believed in life after death, this was like being dead, while alive! Anger and heartache took turns overwhelming me and I was overcome with such grief I hadn't felt since both my parents died, two years apart, when I was in my thirties. I just couldn't see past my pain. I was unable to wrap my head around this travesty and accept that my beautiful wife would never be coming home again. Would never sleep next to me again. The worst of it all, was that she was still alive and physically healthy and I was going to have to see her every day, help her anyway I could, only to return home each afternoon alone, until one of us dies. She was going to slowly starve to death until the day came when her mind would forget how to chew and swallow. I would be helpless, to save her or spare her the long years of daily suffering. My poor love was going to have to somehow adjust to the new and strange surroundings. It was like both of us were living in our own Hell, in that we were both struggling and only death could release us. I had to endure a long two weeks before I could see her again. In the meantime, I had my doctor write me a prescription to calm my nerves, so I could sleep at night and that helped me deal with my anxiety. I called the nurse every day to check on her and they kept me apprised of her progress.

GENTLE BREEZE

After what seemed like an eternity, though it was only fourteen days, it was finally over and I could see her again. I felt like a nervous teenager, fearing she might hate me for leaving her there, even though I knew she couldn't comprehend the reality of her situation, I knew her soul was aware of everything, even if her mind wasn't. She had been through her share of trauma early in life but since we were married, I had bent over backward, to please her and protect her, so at least we had shared many wonderful times during our marriage. When I walked down the hall and found her, she looked up at me with a quizzical look at first, then a spark lit up her eyes as she realized it was me! Even though she didn't know my name, her soul knew me by heart. I hugged her, then we shared looks without speaking, letting our conscious thoughts do the talking. Tears welled up in our eyes, as I took her hand

and we walked down the hall and outside to the gazebo, where we sat together and just let the gentle breeze ruffle our hair. Later, I fed her lunch and then we sat holding hands on the couch, watching the other patients as they kibitzed with each other. Sometimes we both fell asleep, our heads leaning on each other. That same routine went on for a total of eight years. Both of us were healthy but longing for the time when one of us would exit our body and return home, to the celestial realm to be with God. It killed me slowly, more each year, to know she was alone, existing in a warehouse of sorts and not at home with me. Many times she would seem like she was nearing the end and I would call in the Hospice nurses to monitor her health, only to be fooled, when she suddenly bounced back. Before you think I was heartless, I wasn't wishing she would die, but I didn't want to see her wasting away day by day either. Moosie had been there for four years already and I had gone every day through those years to feed her. It crushes your spirit, when someone you love is hurting but you are powerless, to bring them relief. I admit, I took my frustration out on the kitchen staff when they would put food on her tray that wasn't on her dietary list. Since my death, I have watched our life's story hundreds of times and I felt shame and embarrassment over some of my treatment of the kitchen workers. It's too late to apologize now but I would if I could. I turned bitter, angry, and frustrated, beyond any level of emotion I had ever experienced before in my life. Growing up as an only child meant I had all the attention of my parents but their generation wasn't the kind that told their kids they loved them or showed any type of physical affection and I raised my kids that same way, instead of breaking that barrier of negative treatment. When I was eight years old, I remember being with my mother at a school function, when she noticed a lady leaning down and hugging her son. She pointed them out to me and stated; "Look at that woman making a fool out of herself." At the time, I didn't register what she meant by that but as I aged, I realized that she was disgusted by the lady hugging her child. I had grown up with her keeping me at arm's length, so I didn't know any better. It was after our oldest daughter Jem gave birth to her twin daughters, that Moosie and I saw how tender and maternal our daughter was to her tiny babies, it broke down our walls and opened our eyes and our hearts, to how showing love and affection deepens your bonds with others. Holding our first, baby granddaughters, as they crashed into our hearts and melted them, had a profound effect on us. It began our new family tradition, of after every phone call and interaction, we told each other "love you". We both admitted we were way better grandparents than we were parents, something we have to atone for. In the nineteen fifties, folks spanked their kids. It wasn't right, but that's what every parent did back then. The lessons we learned from that lifetime have helped us grow as souls. We realized that the things we thought were reasons to whip our kids with a belt, were not justifiable. Mostly the oldest two kids. We will apologize to Jim when he crosses over, Jem had her apology right after we died and our twins will get their apologies when they cross over. We got to review our lifetime and our kids and grandkids' stories too. It's not a "Film" per se. Things are so far advanced in what we call, The Heavenly realm of God/Jesus/Source. We communicate using telepathy and each Soul can choose to exist in their natural form, as a white light ball of conscious energy, a human shaped crystalline form or they can appear in any human form from their favorite lifetimes on earth. It must also be noted that taking a human-looking appearance in their crystalline shape is what most spirits in heaven choose. All this depends on what each soul wants to be or do. The majority of Spirits project the human form for daily use and only appear in their true energy field state when traveling to other galaxies. When they arrive at their destination, they revert to a human-looking persona. Each being tends to choose the ages of thirty to thirty-five, as that is when they feel they experience many significant experiences in their lives of living in a suit of flesh. It must be noted that at thirty years old, that's when the human's mind-Spirit-body are at their peak performance levels of strength, stamina, agility and mental maturity. The entity known to your world as "Elvis", chooses the thirty-year-old version of himself, because that is his favorite incarnation to date. When you read the story I wrote at the end of this book, you will have a better understanding of reincarnation and life beyond time.

In the fall of twenty fifteen, my neighbor Marge, asked me to go with her to an assisted living complex, so she could check out what they offered. She had been living alone for almost twenty years after her husband died. I picked her up and together, we walked into this massive set up of apartments and amenities. A nice woman gave us a grand tour, as we walked through the place. To say I was stunned, is an understatement, as each room we saw was outmatched by the next. Talk about all the bells and whistles! From the huge dining room to the library and movie room to the separate diner for those who just wanted a quick meal, it was beyond impressive. Moosie and I had lived for twenty years in our own home and I was healthy and fit, so I never even considered this as an option. In the dining room, there was a long salad bar that had soups and side dishes, along with everything one needs to make a gourmet salad. The lunch and dinner menus were packed with healthy choices, such as salmon, roast beef, grilled chicken, and many other options. She showed us the gym, the workshop for people who like woodworking or crafting, the large, indoor pool, and the library, which I loved. On the ride back, to our homes at the golf club, we both were experiencing a twinge of buyer's remorse, as we were dazzled by the tour and seeing all the folks meeting for lunch, walking the halls, and living their best lives. It's like when you buy a car and drive it for ten years, then test drive a new car, with all the new advanced technologies, that you realize all you have been missing out on for the last ten years. The old car did it's job but as styles and new tech emerges that make driving better and easier, a person can't help but feel out of the loop. Marge and I talked a few days later and said she decided she would stay in her house because the cost of her monthly care would exceed her finances. I had been thinking of that complex, nonstop since we went there and I even made a list of the pros and cons of selling, our paid-for, home, and moving there. The pros-It was one mile away from Moosie's nursing home, saving me the ten-mile round trip through traffic every day. Pro-both Walmart and Sam's Club were two miles north of that place. Pro-If I downsized now, instead of waiting till I was older or possibly sick, that duty wouldn't fall on our kids. Please remember, we were antique lovers, so our current nest was decked out in a lot of expensive items. In a two thousand, square foot home, many things would have to be sorted, packed, and moved upon our deaths. The other pros were that I wouldn't have to cook any meals except for my breakfast, something I always ate at home. I whipped up toast or oatmeal with my coffee each morning, so not having to cook lunch and dinner was alluring. I could also use the gym to stay healthy and the library was full of new books to read, a passion of mine. The most compelling pro was that I would be meeting and engaging with a lot of new people and not home alone. In our neighborhood Marge, and I were the only two who lived alone. The other couples were our good friends but most of them were snowbirds, who only stayed during the winters. Pro, I might meet some single men my age to be friends with, which I had been craving for many years. Now the Cons-our house was where our children and the grandkids came and stayed. Moving to a much smaller place meant they would have to stay in hotels. Con-Jem and I had worked very hard to redo our backyard Koi Pond into a Zen Garden, of rocks and boulders and I loved sitting out there among our memories of the project that reflected our labor of love, in the final piece of work done by father and daughter. Con-I could walk to the grocery store across the street and my bank was there too. Con-I was a part of the community for the last twenty years, if I moved, I know I wouldn't see them as often. Another con was the actual amount of labor it would consume to tackle packing it all up and dealing with real estate salespeople and folks coming in and out of the house looking at all our stuff. We had moved so many times over the years but this was the place we enjoyed the most. Not only for the year-round good weather but for the better quality of life for Moosie and me. She and I were fierce and independent and I wasn't used to being told what I could or couldn't do by anyone, let alone an assisted living institution. Con-gardening was my way of connecting to nature and planting new things and caring for them was my main hobby after writing. Maybe my pride was doing the thinking when it came to a move to assisted living, as I walked daily and ate natural food, not greasy, fast food. I felt like assisted living homes were where you went when you had bad health or no other choice. It felt like I was giving up, to sell our house and move in there. One of the biggest cons was that our house held my wife's energy and twenty years of good memories, up till the time Moosie had Dementia and Alzheimer's. Holiday dinners with our family and Christmas spent with the grandkids permeated the very walls inside our home. All of our beloved antiques, that we hand-picked together, wouldn't be able to go with me if I moved, except for a few items that were extra special. Anyway, there was a lot to ponder, between my visits to Moosie and my doctor appointments for my Macular Degener-ation is something that had been with me since a young age and is something I had two surgeries for. A week later, I went back to the complex and met with the lady who gave us the tour. She sat with me and explained how it works, then she took me to one of their vacant, two-bedroom apartments, to let me get a feel of the actual space. That unit was next to the stairs, meaning I would only have one neighbor on the left. Stairs were not an issue, as they gave me a small workout and I could go down the hall to the elevators anytime I chose to. The halls were long, going off on each side of the central elevators. Each floor had a big area in the middle of the long hallways. When you stepped out of the elevator you could take a few steps to the laundry room or walk over to the storage door. Each apartment came with a five-by-seven-foot storage locker to keep their holiday decorations or whatnot in. The apartment was on the second floor and it offered a great view of the lawn, trees, flower beds, and people walking the grounds. So far, I liked what I saw and we went back to her office, where she gave me pamphlets and brochures that explained it all in detail. I left the grounds and drove home, full of thoughts and ideas concerning assisted living, and tried to picture myself in that place. I saw an image of myself at a dining room table, sitting with three other men, eating and enjoying the conversations. I retired from the federal government with a good pension and also my social security added to my monthly income. After selling the house I could purchase the unit I saw and then afford to pay them a monthly fee for my meals, and the cleaning lady, and still have funds left for things I needed like, going out to eat, entertainment, or going to a movie. The pros were adding up and the cons were melting away. No one likes to think about their death, especially when you're healthy. In the fall of two thousand and eight, I had a colonoscopy and they found a mass that needed to have a biopsy. Moosie was still living at home then and I was so worried that if it was cancer or aggressive cancer, I would die, leaving her all alone. It came back as colon cancer and they scheduled an operation to remove it. Thank God, after it was removed it never came back and I had yearly colonoscopies to make sure. Both she and I had life insurance plans and the equity from the house if one of us needed it. I decided that moving there was the right choice, as they even offered to drive residents to doctor appointments and shopping, something that might come in handy if my eyesight got worse.

THE BRILLIANT CAGE

I called up a realtor and listed the house. Because it was a fifty-five, and older community, we could only show it to those that fit the criteria. Within two weeks, a lady whose husband worked at the golf course, showed interest in it, confiding that her husband had the beginnings of Alzheimer's and she knew she wouldn't be able to care for their big house and the large property after he passed away. She paid the asking price because there were other offers also made at the same time, due to the amazing location, the large open floor plan, and the corner lot. There also weren't many properties available, because after twenty years it had become a highly desirable retirement community. I was happy that she was the one buying the place because I felt an affinity with her, in that we were both doing our best to deal with a difficult situation. We had three large oriental rugs that I gave her, as my new place couldn't accommodate such things and she appreciated that gesture. In January twenty-sixteen, I sold our house and I had Jem fly out from California, to help me pack up and downsize. Jem picked out the paint colors and tiles for the bathrooms, then measured each room, so she could make sure I could fit our favorite pieces of furniture in the new place. She made a floor plan on paper and drew each piece of furniture to scale and I was amazed to see that all of my special things would fit! I was able to turn the second bedroom into a den, with a sleeper couch and a large, walk-in closet, into my office. It helped me feel closer to my wife, as she was only a mile away. It was a huge complex with all the amenities a person could need. I ate lunch and dinner in the dining room with my new guy friends. After the first four years, when Moosie was in her new quarters, I didn't need that big house and this new setup was amazing, as I was able to do things I hadn't been able to do for ten years. Gone was the daily stress, except when they would mess up and give her the wrong food when I fed her lunch but other than that, I was free to write, go out to eat with friends, and also visit my cousins who came down from Vermont, every fall till March and have Christmas, Thanksgiving, and Easter with them. Moosie seemed to go through phases of mental clarity and I know she hated the showers but I did my best to make sure she had warm clothes, new stuffed animals, and treats. We both had settled into a daily rhythm of sorts, it wasn't perfect but it wasn't hell either. This new arrangement gave me more vitality since I didn't have cooking or cleaning to do. Gone was the daily stress and anxiety of taking care of her twenty-four hours a day. Moosie and I were both awaiting release, to be reunited in our celestial home with God. Neither of us wanted resuscitation, for we believed that death is a reward since you free your soul from its earthly body and return to your natural state as a powerful, white, light is. Death is just an exchange of a suit of flesh in the third dimension, to a heavenly body of light of a much higher frequency in the Divine dimension. Even if your death itself is painful, as soon as your soul leaves the body behind, all pain and suffering end. Your Spirit, journey's home to the Heavenly realm, to be welcomed by Angels and ancestors, that passed before you. Even knowing all of that, it was still a very long eighteen years for both of us and it was also a tremendous learning opportunity, not only for us but for our children. Moosie and I both chose to partake in everything we went through, the good, the bad, and the ugly. Her sacrifice of choosing Alzheimer's, was a courageous and selfless act, with the hope that none of our children would get either Dementia or Alzheimer's in their lifetime. She didn't want others to suffer what we went through, so she bravely took those diseases out of our bloodline. I am beyond proud of our actions and all our many contributions, to history and our family and friends. Her bravery and determination, let her hang on for all that time, so we could leave together, two months apart, in twenty-twenty. During all those many, long, years of her being affected, by both those memory and mind-stealing diseases, and all that she went through, our family raised thousands of dollars for Alzheimer's research and awareness. One family's fight against those tragic diseases, that took a daughter, a wife, a mother, grandmother, and a friend, away from her loved ones, locking her brilliant mind up in a cage, to never be released. We may have been on the outside while she was on the inside, but we came together as a family and did our part in walks, events, and fundraising, so when she watches her life story from Heaven, she will see that we never abandoned her or forgot about her and her plight. We come from a long line of warrior souls who have fought against injustice and cruelty of every kind, in many lifetimes. We also love helping those in need. Our ancestors fought against the British and a few more, fought against slavery in the South. One of my relatives threw tea at the Boston Tea Party! I was in the Army, and our oldest son Jim, spent thirty-one years in the Air Force. He fought in Desert Storm, two tours of the Gulf War, and two in Afghanistan, as well as a few tours in the Middle East. Both of his sons are Marines and one is married to a woman who is also a Marine. We are proud to call America our home and our kids continue to be devoted to that beautiful land of the free and the home of the brave. We believe in liberty and justice for all.

Moosie and I want to wish everyone who reads this, a healthy, happy, Dementia and Alzheimer-free life...Amen.

God Bless You All! Thanks for reading about one family experience with the mind thieves.

By, Ken Davis

P.S. I hope you enjoy the story, "The Creation Game", I wrote, and that you come away with more knowledge of the supernatural. Wishing you peace and joy on your journey....

Jem's View

CHRISTMAS STUFFIE

Being the oldest daughter in a family of six, often means you have to do the most out of your siblings, when it comes to chores and helping out around the house. My older brother Jim was only fourteen months older than I was, so he and I were more like twins, in that we did a lot of things together. When we moved to new homes, there were new schools and new friends to deal with. The fact that it was the early nineteen sixties, in Virginia, meant that we took a lot of abuse from the local kids in and out of school. Even though Jim and I were both born in Virginia, our parents were from Vermont and Maine, so our friend's parents held that against us. Back in those days, the school principal had wooden paddles hanging on the wall in his office, a daily reminder of what was to come if you stepped out of line, something neither of us had any plans on doing. We both were more afraid of disappointing our parents than we were of getting punished by the principal. It was also customary for folks to spank, and use a switch or a belt to discipline their children. What was a regular custom back then, parents would be jailed for doing so nowadays. I can't speak for all kids, but I can say that I always wanted my parent's approval and love, so I tried my best at school and at home to show respect and follow the rules. But no child is a saint and that's the truth. In the south, everything was "yes mam, no sir, yes please, no thank you." Kids didn't talk back to their elders or disrespect teachers or adults, for fear of getting a beating. It's just the way things were. Every parent was strict and for the most part, they stuck together when it came to parenting. You didn't run and ask your Dad if your Mom said No, at least not in our family. Moving a lot had its good and bad perks. It was sad to say goodbye to kids you liked and schools and teachers that were special but it also held a tingle of excitement because you were stepping into the unknown, a whole new state, new friends, and new places to explore. You gained knowledge from every place you lived and you became more confident, with every new challenge you completed. I remember feeling like a gypsy, setting off for new horizons where anything could happen. My stuffed animals were "Alive" to me. I whispered to them at night in my bed, telling them my thoughts in the dark, hugging them, and feeling like they understood everything I was saying. They became the one thing that was comforting and stable for me during each new move. They soaked up my tears and when I breathed my energy into them each night, I could inhale it back into myself later, when I had a bad day or experience. Their tiny bodies would hold all my "Chi" energy and I treasured each one of them, as they were sacred to me, a bond like no other. They never hurt me or made me feel sad. Even all these many, many, years later, I still have them, this small band of misfit pals that are worn and familiar with their adorable faces and unique silhouettes. No matter where we moved or where we lived, as long as my tribe was on my bed waiting for me, I could get through anything. People who say that stuffed animals are just cloth and don't have feelings, know absolutely nothing. Try taking away a child's baby blanket and see how devastated they are or a dog's favorite stuffed toy and you'll break their hearts. When a person gives their love and compassion to an object, that object holds that energy, and when the child or dog is feeling sick, sad, or lonely, they hold that blanket or stuffie and breathe that Chi energy back into themselves and feel comfort and love. It's a proven fact. One Christmas when I was thirteen years old, I saw this little, light brown, stuffed dog named "Henry" on its tag, in a department store at the mall. My Mother had taken Jim and my Christmas shopping, to get gifts for our dad and our younger brother and sister. I fell in love with that little dog at first sight and I asked my mother if I could please have him for Christmas. She said, "I'm not buying you that rag!" It was two dollars and ninety-seven cents but I didn't have any money of my own that day, even though I babysat for four or five local families, for fifty cents an hour. When we left the store and went home, I couldn't stop thinking about that little dog and how adorable he was. I had already named him "Henny" in my mind. It was still a few weeks before Christmas and he was all I wanted but I was worried that if she didn't buy him soon, they would sell out and I'd never get one, so I snooped around the house to see if she had bought him, something I had never done before. I'm overflowing with curiosity but I've never been a nosy person. We always put our tree up after Thanksgiving and we would decorate it, then put a few early gifts under the tree for the Christmas spirit and as decoration. I saw one that was a small box and the tag had my name on it. The size was just right for Henny to fit in, so I carefully peeled back the tape and opened the box. When I saw a pair of slippers, my heart sank and I wrapped it back up perfectly and placed it back under the tree. Disappointment made me sick to my stomach and I even felt a little angry that my mother might not have bought him after all, so I moped around until Christmas Day. The tiny spark of optimism was dimming fast, as I opened my gifts that Christmas morning, and even the makeup mirror with the lights I had wanted held no joy for me. As we started to clean up the wrapping paper, I was holding back the tears, all hope was lost and I was doing my best to show gratefulness for the things I did receive, when my mom said, "Oh, here's a present that we must have missed, it's got your name on it," as she held it out to me. I looked up at a very small box and knew it was too small for Henny but I took it and unwrapped it. When I removed the wrapping paper, the box top popped off, and out sprang Henny! He had been folded over and stuffed into that small box and I fell to my knees and cried and cried. I never felt so relieved in my young little life. My Love for my mother went up ten notches right then. That's the kind of memory I go back to when I think of my mom. Not only was she incredibly intelligent and clever, but she would also see something, then go home and make it. She could beat the men at their games and she was fearless when it came to making her dreams come true! She was a hard act to follow but she also loved to teach others and was selfless in her kindness to others. A trait both my parents shared! Sometimes, when she pulled off something hard to do, there was a genuine twinkle in her eyes, something that I've only seen on one other person, besides her. She was fiercely independent and a genius, there was no pulling the wool over her eyes. She was strict but once in a while she'd let me stay home from school and she and I would go to the wholesaler or the leather tannery or to the Boston flower mart, to buy supplies for her store. I was a straight-A student, as I loved school, so when she would let me ditch for a mother-daughter day, it was super special. In turn, I babysat the twins, made dinner, and cleaned and did laundry, while she was working at her craft store, Monday through Saturday. When the twins were babies, I was Mommy's little helper, getting her things and doing stuff that she needed from downstairs. When it came to occasions, like birthday parties, Moosie was amazing as she went all out, hand-making games, putting up the decorations, sewing outfits, and baking cakes and cupcakes. One year she made very ornate hats for me and five of my friends, complete with sashes tied under our chins and huge paper flowers that adorned the top of the hats. It was the talk of the block! My older brother Jim, had a pirate party one year when we lived in Virginia, and Mom went all out to create the pirate theme and put up the games. She also had an idea to bake tiny, tool charms and Cracker Jack boy charms, in his pirate cake. Well, all was going swimmingly, until one partygoer bit down on a tiny metal wrench. Luckily, no teeth were cracked and no one choked! Back then we just laughed it off, because Jim was eight years old and he and his friends were used to stepping on jacks and other rough stuff. Looking back over my life, I was grateful we never stayed in the same house all our lives. We were like the "Robinson Crusoe" family, moving to far-off places and our view of people and the world made us appreciate what we had and our love for each other. Dull, was a word never spoken in the Davis house, wherever that may be at the time. I learned to be street-smart at a very young age and I could read people's energies and moods. You learn to turn it on and off as the situation demands. My soul-deep connection to nature and all creatures was so intensely important to me that I felt like a champion of the underdog. My motto was the fair and kind treatment of all of God's creatures, big and small. I remember pounding on two boys who put a firecracker in a frog's mouth and lighting ants on fire with matches! Those poor creatures can't defend themselves and it made me turn into a wild animal. All my life I've saved starfish, snails, worms, birds and turtles, cats and dogs, opossums, skunks, chickens, and horses. No effort to help an animal or a person is too small. Being a strong advocate for animals and their voice. I especially relate to creatures that change their colors to adapt to their surroundings, like Chameleons and the Octopus.

Every new move to a different neighborhood and school, had me making adjustments to my personality traits. I talked fast and sometimes non-stop because my brain was so hyper that if I was having a manic phase, it amplified my anxiety and stress, thus making me talk more and even faster. Everyone made fun of me and I had no idea that I was Bipolar, as no one ever talked about mental health or mental illness in the nineteen sixties and seventies. I tried hard to keep quiet but I felt like I would explode if I didn't speak. My brain would jump all around, lighting on one thought then seconds later I'd be off on a different tangent, zooming like a hummingbird, from thought to thought. My whole body was running at a very high frequency and with it came visions and flashes of information that just popped into my head. The visions helped me solve problems uniquely and quickly like that guy "Mac-

Gyver" did in that nineteen eighty-five show. It's an Aquarian trait, to be able to find unique solutions to any problem swiftly. It's almost uncontrollable when you're young. My brain was capable of deep thinking on a very high level. I understood things about life without ever being told anything about whatever it was. I knew the Egyptians didn't build the pyramids, that the stones were cut, lifted, and quarried by intergalactic beings of divine light, using sound to change the molecular structure of the substance being used and levitating it into place. This was all happening around nineteen seventy-one, while I was in seventh grade. I told my class that aliens were all around us all the time but they vibrated at a very high frequency so we couldn't see them. That brought on laughter and teasing but I didn't care because I knew in my heart it was true! I was gaining access to futuristic information, due to my spiritual openness and my dream of being a psychic channeler like my mom. I was never afraid to try or do a new thing so my curious nature opened up many new doors. Years later, a famous female brain surgeon from Boston, who has bipolar disorder said, "Being Bipolar is like a Christmas tree with lights. When you are in a manic phase, all the lights are going on and off, flashing wildly and when your brain is depressed, only a few lights are on and blinking slowly." Finally, I understood what my brain was going through. It helped me feel I wasn't alone. I was ninety-five, percent manic and only five percent depressive. In nineteen seventy-one, no one had even heard of bipolar disorder. It would be when I was thirty-three years old, that I was diagnosed with Bipolar/Manic Depression. Once you get a diagnosis, then the doctors try different cocktails of medications to balance out your salt deficiency, which causes bipolar disorder. They gave me a mood elevator pill for depression and a mood stabilizer pill for anxiety. Those medications make you feel nothing, numb, and you can't laugh or cry. I decided after being a Guinea pig for seven years, that I didn't want to take a seizure medication that makes you susceptible to seizures if you stop taking the pills! I never had seizures, so it didn't make sense to take a medication that can "give" you seizures. I saw at least a dozen doctors, while I was in my thirties because I moved a lot and had to go where my insurance paid for it. As I got older, I figured out what worked for me and my lifestyle, and my sense of well-being. I was always athletic while I was young. After high school, I worked out at the gym and participated in other sports, as working out burns off my angst and hyper energy. I'm like a racehorse, in that I need to work off all my excess energy or I get fidgety with anxiety. This is essential for hyper people, especially if you're Bipolar. It's okay to live your life according to your loves and desires but to maintain balance in your life, you need to be aware of yourself and your environment. Your surroundings and various situations might affect your mental health or your stability and every part of you is essential, the mind, body, and spirit. If you neglect your body, your mind and spirit will suffer, neglect your mind and your spirit and body suffer. Get in touch with the inner you, that way you can have all three of those things working together to keep you healthy, happy, and safe. It can't be all work and no play or vice versa. Balance is key to a happy life. No matter your age, it's very important to be honest with yourself about how you're feeling spiritually, physically, and mentally. That way you can make proper decisions and choices for a happy and healthy life. If you're experiencing anxiety or depression, please seek help from a qualified doctor or professional in mental health. Don't suffer in silence, your peace of mind depends on you to take action if necessary. After all, you need your body and mind to stay alive and your spirit will guide you in the right direction if you just trust and believe in yourself. As the years sped past, I outgrew my bipolar disorder. I learned what my triggers were, so I could get away from that situation. I've grown into a more powerful, spiritually elevated human being. I no longer take any medications for Bipolar disorder and I treat myself much better. I stopped letting people abuse me, use me or hurt me. I am now at "One" with myself and that's the best medicine ever!

APPLE WARS

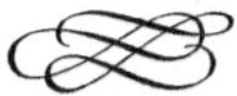

Moving to West Newbury, from Acton Massachusetts, was one of my personal favorites because our house sat on the main street through town. The public library, the apple orchard as well as a huge, cow farm with corn fields, were a stone's throw away. Plus, we ended up living there for six years, an unbeatable record for the Davis family! Currently, it's still the longest I've ever lived anywhere. Having to go to the local middle school, for a year and a half before being bussed to the tri-town junior high and later high school, helped my brother Jim and I, get a footing with our neighborhood gang of kids. It was very country, with more land than people, so three adjoining towns all used the same junior high school and high school. That meant when you entered seventh grade, you were suddenly thrust into a huge school with eight hundred kids, where you only knew about twenty kids from your town. Jim went there first and it was a local tradition that seventh graders told their younger brothers and sisters scary tales about the new school, hoping you'll freak out. We were really lucky because there were about twelve to fifteen kids that lived up the street behind our house, so there was always tackle football, ice hockey, sledding, dodgeball, bike riding, and apple wars. Lucky for us, our neighborhood had a library, a huge apple orchard, and a large dairy cow farm. On the weekends a gang of us would go pick apples and Robin's mother would make us candy apples. One time we were at the edge of the orchard picking apples when all of a sudden, the seasonal migrant workers saw us and the men started chasing us! I was eleven then and wearing real army boots that a neighbor gave me that were five sizes too big. I had a paper grocery bag filled with fresh apples from climbing the tree and reaching the best apples. Everyone else was running fast but the clumpy boots weighed me down and a Hispanic man was almost on me. I threw the bag of apples over my head and adrenaline kicked in and I sped away! Phew! That was close! We didn't know what the men would do to us if they caught us, but we weren't waiting to find out! If you've never played in a cornfield that has stalks over six feet tall, you don't know how scary and thrilling it is to play tag in one. There were at least ten acres of mature, cow corn and when you were in a row, you couldn't hear or see anything but the mosquitoes. After we got to the end of the corn, we were in a clearing that was backed by trees and the woods. Some boys were chasing the dairy cows in a pasture, which I never did, as it's mean and they get blood in their milk if they run. I was busy picking some wildflowers when all the kids started yelling and running towards a tractor road in the dirt. By the time I saw the huge bull chasing them, he saw me standing there and careened my way at full bore. Reacting quickly, as he was almost to me, I turned and ran towards a huge oak tree. I ran around the tree with a pissed-off bull thundering right behind me, so I did a second lap around the tree then took off towards the tractor path that my friends had gone down. As I sprinted down the path, I mentally reviewed my options, to the right were towering pricker bushes that were impenetrable, and to my left, was a barbed wire fence with a field on the other side, where all my friends were safe behind the fence. The bull was so close behind me that his hot, snorting breath warmed my back as his hooves shook the ground like an earthquake! Mike Melanson, yelled my name, as he stood and pulled the barbed wire up with his hands, then he used his foot to press the bottom wire into the earth. I dove through the two barbed wires at a sprinting speed while friends pulled me away from the fence. I lay flat on the ground to catch my breath, while the fuming bull trotted back and forth past the fence. We went into some woods and came out near where we left our bikes. That was my first brush with death. I never told my folks what happened, as I knew they would be upset or worried. Even the Apple orchard wasn't safe when they flew small planes over it and if they saw you in their orchard, they shot rock salt at you. My first crush Chucky and I got separated from the gang when a plane flew overhead and we had to stay hidden for hours till it got dark before we could get back home. The last time we went to the farm, the local sheriff was waiting for us by where we left our bikes. He read us the riot act and most of us were getting too old for those silly things so we stopped going. In those years, Jim was shy and quiet, and I was energetic and hyperactive, so I bounced through school loving it, not only for the academics but for the new friends and the sports. When kids would tease Jim in fifth and sixth grade, I'd beat the boys up, even though I weighed only sixty pounds and my nickname was skinny. I also played right wing on a boy's ice hockey league for seven years, until the mothers got together and tried to have the town council remove me because I was a girl. I went to the town meeting and spoke up for myself, saying that my parents paid taxes in West Newbury, so why should I have to go to the next town over to play hockey? The boys liked me because I was fast and furious on the ice and I scored a lot of goals and I wasn't afraid to play rough either. From the very first time I put skates on when I was ten years old, I skated like I had done it in a past life. That's how easy it came to me, so I just kept playing hockey until I graduated from high school. My parents were very good about getting us lessons in things we wanted to learn. Since my father had a master's degree in education and my brilliant Mother possessed a degree in teaching as well, they took pride in granting our wishes. Jim started with piano when he was seven, by taking lessons in Virginia, from a lady who lived down the street. He was going because he wanted to please our mom and he had an ear for music, plus the lady's son was Jim's age and a friend of his. One day when we got home from school, our mom sat us down and told us that Jim wouldn't be able to go to lessons anymore. She said that the lady brought her son home from school and when they entered their home, they found her husband, the boy's father, had shot himself in the head with a shotgun, right in their living room rocking chair. We were shocked. I still remember that day like it was yesterday. I recall thinking how tragic that was, but why hadn't the man gone into the woods and shot himself, instead of having his wife and son walk in and see that, then have to keep living there with his bloodstains in the floorboards? Jim was seven, and I was six at the time. It was so tragic for the mother and son, that eventually they moved away. Jim took up flute years later in Jr. High and he was very good at playing it.

BUSY BUMBLEBEE

I'm a very competitive person, but only with myself, that's why I chose sports that make you push yourself harder to be the very best you can be. I was a good sport when it came to teams but I preferred individual sports. My Mom found me a teacher for floor tumbling, and acrobatic/gymnastics classes in Haverhill, Massachusetts, a large city twenty minutes away. I was eleven at the time and had been throwing myself around the yard trying to do flips and handsprings and she thought I was going to break something unless I had a teacher. She was probably right! Doris Casey's dance school was a small storefront studio on the main drag in Haverhill, complete with mirrored walls and smooth hardwood floors. Doris was old school and didn't believe in using any floor mats or cushions, so when you did a headstand, it was on a hard floor. Let's just say that her students learned fast because we knew how much it hurt if we messed up. Talk about a learning incentive! Doris looked like a woman that had been through it, with her dyed, jet-black, hair tossed up in a messy, beehive hairdo. She wore garish red lipstick that showed she had trouble staying in the lines and her thin body was always encased in a baby pink leotard with matching stockings, complete with a droopy, tutu and worn, black ballet slippers. Did I mention she was a chain smoker? She puffed up a storm as she put us through the paces, standing by with the long stick that she used to "Tap" her students with when they broke form. We the students were probably high off the nicotine vapors that swarmed around her in the breathless room. Being older than most of the students at eleven, I took private lessons until I was caught up with my other classmates. After my third year, I performed a solo, gymnastic, floor tumbling/acrobatic routine, to the song, "The Dawning of the Age of Aquarius", in front of three thousand people at Methuen High School. Unfortunately for me, I came on after a beyond adorable group of six-year-olds, who danced "The Busy Bumblebee", which was cuter than a bug and a hard act to follow. Show biz had a slogan back then, never come on after animals or babies! I could relate!

In the summers I went for two weeks to a local day camp on a Morgan horse farm. They gave me a horse to take care of and ride each day. When working around horses who can sense your energy and understand everything you thinking and feeling, one must stay on their toes. Horses can spook easily and one day as I was riding my horse, outside in the open ring, with rock walls surrounding it, a kid rode up on his bike, and the chain on his bike made a big racket when he stopped. Trispers, the horse I was on, was advanced in her pregnancy and extra skittish. She reared up, like "Roy Rogers", horse used to, and took off running at a frenzied pace, while shaking her head wildly, bucking and kicking! Perched on a tiny English saddle, wearing slick riding pants, I clung to the reigns, as she flew around the track until I was thrown off, landing head-first into the stone wall. My Mom had pulled up a minute before the boy rode up on his bike, so she saw the whole thing through the car windshield. I got up shakily on my feet, with the breath knocked out of me and everyone ran over to see if I was all right, which I was, thanks to my English riding helmet. When I got in our car, I could tell my Mom was shaken up and worried about me having a concussion or a head injury but I kept telling her I was okay. She drove to Amesbury, fifteen minutes away, and took me into a store and told me to pick out something I wanted, (which was super rare, as back then you only got gifts on holidays), so I picked out a bottle of suntan lotion, then we went home. My poor Guardian Angels spent many years working in shifts because of my wildling behavior and risky spontaneity. I've been told they even make bets behind the scenes about the outcome of my impulsive ideas and daredevil charades.

NEW AGE

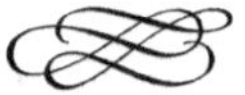

These are just a few of the best reasons why I loved living in West Newbury, during my teen years. Our gang of friends was a tight-knit bunch that watched out for each other and played hard but fair. Going through my teenage years in that old house, with my best friend Robin five houses behind me, helped me grow into a strong, fair, compassionate, team player. All of us kids were supportive of each other and that made it an amazing time. At home, we were the kind of family that joked around, laughed a lot, and played pranks on each other, as it made life more carefree and lighter. It helped balance out, the energy of the old house. Positivity drives back dark, menacing, forces, so it might be the reason we all made it through living in that old, haunted house unscathed. Many people that live in haunted houses, don't have that knowledge of ghosts and supernatural entities but since both of my folks read spiritual books like, "Seth Speaks" and "Over Soul Seven" by, Jane Roberts also books by, Carlos Castaneda, as well as Uri Geller, who were all sharing their psychic experiences and their knowledge of the supernatural. My parents were hip to things that went bump in the night and it helped us, kids, by them being knowledgeable and aware of spirits, good and bad. The seventies, had a "New Age" movement that coincided with the hippy-dippy theme, as it encouraged people to be open and expand their minds with freedom of expression and harnessing the intuitive powers that you are born with. I chose that era of time to be a teenager in, before I was born, that way I could piggy-back off my mother's and father's psychic skills of Channeling Spirits and communicating with higher, frequency entities at an early age. I needed to be old enough to want to learn about my psychic powers and to appreciate how amazing it is when you start to develop your abilities. Much of that understanding about what I was and what I could become, came from trial and era and proper training. I am forever grateful that my parents were open-minded and caring with Jim and me. They trusted us and we had an open and honest relationship with them. One particular day, Jim and I were roughhousing around and running downstairs as he tried to catch me. Between peals of laughter, we burst into the kitchen and I scooted around behind my mother and squealed, "Help me, help me, Mom-moo-ser!" The three of us cracked up over that and the name got shortened to "Moosie", which started as something we kids called her but the name stuck and was used by everyone who knew her, right up until she died. It was just one of those nicknames that stick with you your entire life. While shopping for clothes with her one day at the mall, I shouted out loud, "Moosie, what about this dress?" Other ladies in the store near us, gasped in shock. They thought I was calling my mother a Moose! We found it hilarious!

MANY FIRSTS

Living in West Newbury while I was in junior high and high school, held so many memories for me because those six years shaped who you are and the person you're going to be. There were a lot of "Firsts" while living in that haunted house. My first kiss, first boyfriend, first lead in a play, first prom, first time driving, and other important milestones in a teenager's life. Those memories are stored, not just in our minds, hearts, and souls but also in every house or dwelling, even man-made furniture, antiques, and other objects can also hold either negative or positive energy. The interior of your home also holds the residual energies of those that have spent time or resided there before you. From love to hate, happiness to depression, those emotions soak into the walls and ceilings, like smoke from a cigar. That's why sometimes when you walk into a house for the first time, you can feel comfort, love, and happiness, while other times, you feel a sense of foreboding or negativity. Every time you think a thought in your mind, it goes off into the universe, where others can pick it up and sense your thoughts. It's a proven fact that thoughts are very powerful. Even unspoken, your thoughts are projected out into the entire atmosphere, where they travel unrestricted, becoming part of the Matrix that surrounds planet earth. It's called, "The Collective Energy " and it blankets the Terra Firm-a of mother earth. It's mind-blowing how interconnected we all are as Light Beings here on earth. The more we try and think positive thoughts, the better it is, not only for us and our well-being but for the collective energy of our precious Mother Earth. Whenever you are in a situation where you don't know what to do, it's far better to send out a message in your mind, asking for advice from God/Jesus/Source, to please help you with your problem, than to just let it go around and around in your head. That way you aren't making things worse by worrying and fretting over it. Those negative vibrations that come from fear, anxiety, doubt, worry, insecurities, and hopelessness, are what feed the dark energies that keep us all in a cyclone of repeating negative things, instead of moving forward and away from our problems. Just to give you an example of the power of thoughts, every time I think of someone, they call me within one to twenty-four hours. I was at a friend's house I hadn't seen in six years. I asked him if he had heard anything from his friend Billy, who had helped me install his sink when I remodeled his kitchen six years ago. He told me that he hadn't heard from Billy since that day but he had heard through a friend that Billy had moved away. Less than thirty minutes later, while we were still sitting at his kitchen table, his phone rang. He looks down at his cell phone and it's that guy we were just talking about, calling! It shook my friend up, guess I'm used to it. Another time, while at a house with five people, I asked out loud if they were going to answer the phone. It wasn't until I said it out loud, that I realized the phone wasn't even ringing. Just as everyone started to laugh, the phone rang for real, not even twenty seconds later. Now that even freaked me out!

HAIR THAT WIGGLES

I always had so much positivity and I was very bubbly until we moved into that house in West Newbury. Even though things looked good on the outside, honor roll, student council Vice President, art committee, student advisory committee, and an athlete, inside I was on a roller coaster of teen angst and anxiety. I didn't let that stop me from acting in plays, horseback riding, doing gymnastics, or playing ice hockey, however, living with an undiagnosed mental disorder, takes a toll on one's daily life. I hardly ate and I was in constant motion from bell to bell. My hands shook if I held them out in front of me. I slept four hours at night and never napped. My natural energy was through the roof but it wasn't a "good" kind of energy. It was a potent mix of hyperactivity and anxiety at the same time, so when I got nervous, my body and mind went to a very uncontrollable and scary place. My face would turn beet red and my scalp would tingle and itch. I had to push past all that and do my best to control my shaky hands and nerves. I wasn't afraid to do things, but my energy was always like I was on speed or a lot of caffeine. If I drink caffeine I have to lie down, as it puts me to sleep! Crazy, I know. It was the spirits in that house, the ghosts, that would use me to write poems (automatic writing) that were nothing like me at all. I could feel their dark and heavy, negative energy, it was so frightening! Here's the start of one poem, I still remember to this day...

Hair that wiggles chair legs that stand

Meaning one motive to come to take my hand

Entering the passage to Hell's burning flame

Twisting and turning and calling your name

The flames get higher as you draw near....

I forget how it ends but a happy twelve-year-old girl just doesn't write that stuff. Especially because I loved everyone and I was an upbeat person, that protected my family, friends, and animals. I started getting depressed and I fantasized about suicide. Back in nineteen seventy, you didn't even know the word "Depression", except for The Great Depression and I didn't know how to deal with such overwhelming emotions of sadness, hopelessness, and wanting to die. The spooks in the house were trying to dwell inside me and sometimes I'd just explore ways of killing myself, in my mind. It was such a juxtaposition to my reality. This twelve-year-old "TomBoy" started dreading going home. Pressure to compete in school, pressure in sports, peer pressure, and the fact that I was a people pleaser, meant that I just had to keep going and I had no one to confide in about what was going on with me. This was all way before "Oprah" and folks never spoke about that stuff or anything private. Being good at school, no one suspected that I was being tormented by demons dwelling in the same cubic space as I was. Jim and I had started using our parents' Ouija board a few times after school and one day the spirit controlling the planchette flew from letter to letter so fast that Jim's and my pinkies were barely hanging on. It said scary things and swore at us, so we put it away and never touched it again. The few times we used it may have opened up a portal that let more negative and evil entities into our home and neither he nor I knew how to do things, such as protect ourselves by putting white light energy around us or using Sage around the house. We couldn't tell our folks, for fear of being punished for even touching the game in the first place. He was thirteen and I was twelve, so we were too young at that time to fully grasp what we had done. All through junior high and high school, I spent all but my senior year living with demons and ghosts that were using me like a puppet because I was already psychic but didn't know how to control it or how to protect myself. Night time was the worst because that house was so big, that when I came home and everyone had gone to bed, it was beyond frightening to walk up those stairs with the floorboards announcing my approach, creek, creek, as I turned off the lights behind me. It also didn't help that I have always had amazing dreams that are so detailed, they are like being in a color movie. I have complete conversations within them and some were even time-traveling or Astral Traveling dreams. For me, sleep was filled with hours of wildly realistic movies, with people and places from the past, present, and future. I had a recurring dream that there was a ghost living under the floor in my closet. In one dream, my closet door, which was at the left of my bed's headboard, was open and I could see flames like in Hell, shooting up from below. Also, my floors would creak if you walked on them. One night, I had just gotten into bed, I was twelve at the time. I lay awake in the dark, with my little alarm radio playing softly, on my nightstand to my right, when the door to the closet on my left, opened and the floors started to creak, once, twice, then I felt someone sit on my bed and the sheets got tight over my feet! I was so terrified, I might have passed out because I didn't remember anything after the ghost sat down, when I woke up the next morning. By now I was fighting a nervous breakdown from all the stress and fear but I had to keep it all inside, packed down tight because I didn't know how to strike up a conversation back then and I didn't want to have my folks mad at me or be a bother. Looking back now, I can't believe how much stuff I went through in those eighteen years.

My Parents still had their "Trine" mediation group at our house one Wednesday a month. I would sneak downstairs, just out of sight, and sit in the dark and listen to my mother, as she spoke in different voices and accents, as spirits imparted wisdom to those listening. If you've seen the movie, "Ghost" with Whoopi Goldberg, you get the idea. I was very titillated by the whole psychic thing, especially because I wanted to know a lot more. I needed to learn how to not see ghosts and how to fend off evil. I was so startled on one such Wednesday night, though hidden just a few feet away on the stairs, the Spirit speaking through my mom, said my name! None of the group knew I was sitting there but the jig was up, so I went down two steps to the landing and sat there in sight, as I didn't want to be rude. The guest Spirit speaking that night, went on to tell me about some of my many past lives and as I listened, I made a mental note of a common thread that seemed to be in every life they spoke of. I was a girl in one life that lived in Athens Greece and I used to run foot races with the boys. In another life, I was a Native American girl that raced ponies with the boys. I would later go on to hold the nineteen seventy-five, Massachusetts, state record for the fastest time in the ladies' 50-yard dash. My ancestry DNA report came to me a few years ago and how shocked I was when they included my "Traits." Seems I have the sprinter gene in this life too and I also started horseback riding in third grade and went on to own two Egyptian Arabian horses and a tan and white Quarter Horse called a "Paint," as you see out west. I flew out to the Arabian Nationals in Scottsdale, Arizona, in nineteen eighty-eight, and wound up buying that Paint horse from the University of Tucson, as a souvenir, tee hee. That same night when that spirit spoke to me, he asked if I had any questions after he told me things about my past lives and I said "Yes". I told him that I was afraid of ghosts and I asked if there was any way I could Not see them. He told me that it could be arranged. I felt such relief that I had been able to tell someone of my fears and now my dad had heard what was said but often when a Psychic is in a "Trance State", the person doing the channeling, steps aside in their mind and allows a Spirit to use their voice, so they may not be aware of what's being said through them because they aren't the one speaking. It depends on how deep the speaker is while in a trance. That night changed a lot of things psychically for me. Hearing someone else's voice coming out of my mom didn't scare me, it empowered me, to not let the evil in our house rule me. I felt like I had opened a channel, a dialogue if you will, between my parents and me in a higher form of communication. It bonded the three of us on a whole new level because now I felt like I could tell them what was going on with me, instead of keeping it bottled up. I felt like I had superpowers of sorts, in that I could find lost objects, and do automatic writing and drawings. I had a firmer grasp of what was going on around me. I felt grounded and more sure of myself. Now I was ready to take on anything!

HIGH SPIRITED

It's true that in the incarnations we make on earth, we plan it all out before birth and decide what traits and skills we must download, so that we can complete our missions successfully. It appears that in most of my life when I'm a female, I come down here to challenge the boys at their games. I have very strong feelings about equality. It goes against my beliefs when all beings aren't being treated equally. I detest anyone who bullies others or those that pick on people for their enjoyment. Women are always looked over for jobs and promotions and we never get paid the same as men do, even when we perform the same duties. I must admit, nothing makes me happier than proving I've got what it takes to do whatever a guy can do. There's a saying I find sadly, to be true, "You have to be twice as good as a woman to be thought of as half as good as a man." Obviously, my mother and her mother Vivian, have the same traits! We are high-spirited rule breakers, risk takers, and smarter than the average bear, kind of ladies! We can cook, clean and sew but watch out boys or we just might steal your seat at the table, or at least your heart! I thank my most wonderful dad and mom that let me explore life at my own pace and didn't cut me off at the knees when it came to letting me be a wild child. God bless them for their guidance and their patience because they helped me get past a tough time and make it through all those trying years that were filled with fearlessness and foolishness. Their love and support truly brought me to where I am now.

BARRACUDA

As I mentioned earlier, in nineteen seventy-five, we moved from West Newbury to the smallest city in the state of Massachusetts, called Newburyport. It was such a quaint little place, full of old-time New England charm and loads of history. The very first United States Coast Guard station was established on the waterfront, a stone's throw away from our building and I used to ride my skateboard on their freshly paved parking lot. A store owner my mom knew, talked me into entering the Miss Coast Guard pageant. My nerves got the best of me and I came in second but it was a fun experience. My folks bought an old sail loft building, which they hired a contractor to renovate. The wooden building was located right at the mouth of the Merrimack River. We could see the ocean from our second-floor deck. Our living quarters were on the second floor and the Craft Center store was below us on the first level. All six of us loved that place because instead of a yard we had the waterfront, stores, bars, and restaurants and it was only two miles to the beach. By then I was seventeen and I commuted to high school in West Newbury, driving my dad's nineteen seventy-one, Ford Mustang. I wanted to finish out my senior year in West Newbury, so I would have a yearbook full of good friends and memories. Jim was eighteen and owned a nineteen sixty-nine, Plymouth, Barracuda, that he bought in seventy-three. He was great about letting me drive it after I got my license at sixteen. I custom pinstriped the hood of his Barracuda with flames. When I was fifteen, my father bought another car and he let me buy his Mustang for seven hundred dollars. I was earning money that summer, working fifty-five hours a week at a bakery for two dollars and fifty cents an hour. That sure beat fifty cents an hour babysitting! I learned amazing skills working all summer in "The Lovin Oven". The owner was a man in his thirties, who was there every morning at four am to bake donuts, pastries, and bread. He even made a huge pot of fresh, baked beans every Saturday, that you could smell coming down the street. My Mom's craft store used to be just around the corner back then and I'd go see her on my lunch break. A young woman in her mid-twenties taught me how to decorate cakes, even wedding cakes, so I have fond memories of my first real job. One large wall inside the bakery had a hand-painted mural on it that had ladies with very large breasts, barely covered in a tight, white blouse as they wore in Sweden, in days of yore. Sometimes I'd catch a husband gazing a little too intently at the scene and it would make me stifle a giggle when his wife would catch him and slap his arm!

Now that I had graduated high school, I was attending jewelry school in Boston, at the North Bennet St, Industrial School, located in Little Italy, in Boston's North End. It was September of seventy-six, and I was up at four am, every morning except weekends. It's a forty-five-minute commute to Boston each way, depending on traffic, so sometimes I'd drive twenty minutes to the train station in Beverly and ride the train without worrying about the traffic and parking, especially in the winter. Being a petite girl, going in and out of a huge city alone was thrilling. Once I got off the train in Boston Gardens, I'd walk a quarter mile through old historic streets and buildings that held such character and were also steeped in rich traditions. The Italian North End was home to pizzerias, bakeries, butchers, restaurants, and churches. The very first few times I went, it felt like I was transported back to Italy, in the nineteen thirties, between the people and the wonderful smells, emanating from everywhere. It was as if I had gone abroad to study jewelry making in Italy itself. I was captivated by it all. I had heard it said that Italian men love Irish women, or blondes and as a young woman, I was attracted to those men with dark hair and eyes. After a while, it felt like home and I was never afraid or scared, it was as if I had a large Italian family watching out for me. Regina's pizza was on my route and I'd often stop to grab a slice. You haven't tasted real pizza, unless you've eaten in Little Italy, in Boston. The school itself sat on the corner of North Street and Cross street. The "Old North Church", where Paul Revere rode his horse yelling, "The British Are Coming", was right behind our school, in the same block. Talk about history! Across the street, to the side of our school, was a small coffee shop called, "Frankie's", where I would go every morning for a small carton of orange juice and honey-dipped donuts, drool. Frankie was in his early forties and always greeted me with a big smile and Dante, the "Bookie", was dressed to the nines while taking bets from the pay phone. Frankie told me to be very wary and stay focused, as I went around Boston alone in the seventies. It was relatively safe but when you are eighteen years old and alone, you attract attention. My blonde locks made me stick out like a snowman in Florida. I had lived in a lot of places but had mostly grown up around black and white people, so to become immersed in Italian culture was an amazing experience for me. As the weeks went by,

Franky and his crew took me under their wing and told me where it was safe and where it wasn't, in the Boston area. Back in those days, each neighborhood had its own culture and tolerance level of what was acceptable behavior. The crime wasn't that bad in the late seventies and early eighties. When the original families immigrated from Europe, people from each country grouped and formed mini versions of their places of birth, which divided the city into sections. The North End of Boston was Italian, the South End was Irish, the blacks lived in Roxbury and the Asians reside in China-Town. There were other smaller warrens and dens throughout the city, where the Polish, Portuguese, Jewish, and wealthy folks lived. With all its diversity "The Hub ", Boston's nickname back then, was a vibrant city, sprinkled with a multitude of historic places, as well as some skyscrapers and modern architecture, that somehow just seemed to flow. The Boston Gardens is where the train station is and it's also a huge sports and event stadium, where I watched many Bruins, and hockey players, duke it out with other teams, and way too many rock concerts to name them all. Sandwiched in between Boston Gardens and ChinaTown, was a section of blocks that housed what the locals called, "The Combat Zone". A red-light district, with several streets full of strip clubs, peep shows, street hawkers, and men with suitcases, full of all sorts of items, (most were stolen)! Hookers paraded around all day and night, in scantily clad micro, miniskirts, and thigh-high boots. Only men went there unless you were a woman of the streets. Let's just say that every city has its charms and also some seedy areas that you wouldn't want to be in at night. By the end of my first year, making gold and silver jewelry, I was doing custom work for the Italian "Wise Guys", who wanted gold, pinky rings, and crosses. Gold prices hovered around eight hundred dollars an ounce and when I made jewelry for clients, I never hallowed out the undersides of my pieces, which from a business perspective, didn't leave much in the way of a profit but I was also learning and making great contacts with the Italians. I have always been a perfectionist, that demands high-quality work from myself, above and beyond what is called for. Go big or go home. The two other girls in my class had become best friends to me and sometimes after school, I'd go to one of their houses, meet their families and enjoy dinner and conversation. When we were at school, we would get a bunch of us and walk together uptown to the jeweler's buildings and purchase supplies, like silver and gold solder, wire, precious stones, and tools. If it was late, we would go to the Museum of Science and check out their displays or go to a Boston Red Socks game at Fenway Park. We went to school all year long, except for a week at Christmas and the month of August because there was no air conditioning back then for that old fourth, floor building. At lunch, we would walk out onto the roof since we were on the top floor with the cabinet-making and inlaid furniture class. One day at lunchtime, just Sally, Jeanie, and I were eating up there, when we heard a screech of tires and a commotion on the street below, in front of Frankie's Coffee shop. We went to the edge of the roof and peered over. Four floors below on the street, a dark brown Lincoln had slid to a stop and a passenger in the front seat opened his door and stood up. He yelled something to someone in Frankie's Coffee shop and then a bunch of wise guys ran out and guns were drawn. After a heated exchange of words, the guy got back in the car and they peeled off down the street. Jeanie, Sally and I were stunned but we also thought it was the coolest thing we'd ever seen! Never a dull moment in the North End. The next day I was dying to know what it was all about but I didn't dare ask Frankie when I got my donut and juice. Those guys were sweet to me but I wouldn't want to be on their bad side. Sometimes they'd talk about some guy named, "Blackie Pete" and from what I gathered, he was a very bad dude because they all seemed to have a healthy respect for him.

NO BONJOUR NO

One of the benefits of being Psychic is that I can read people and their intentions in seconds, which comes in handy. I also walked fast with a confident stride, that gave off a "don't mess with me vibe". That's crucial when you're a woman, no matter where you're from or how old you are. One Morning, as I walked from the train station through the North End to school, an old man was outside of a bakery sweeping the sidewalk and putting out little tables and chairs. It was six forty-five, in the morning and as I got closer, he looked up at me and waved me over to him. Seemed innocent enough and most of the locals knew I went to the school and were used to new, young, kids coming in and out every year. I walked up and stood five feet away and said, "Bonjour no" to him. He stepped closer and pointed to his cheek, indicating he wanted me to kiss his cheek. Well, good-ol-me the people pleaser, didn't want to be rude, so I leaned over and went to kiss his cheek but as I did so, he turned his head and kissed me full on the lips and put his hand behind my head to hold me! I pushed back, then stepped around him and started walking fast to school. My face was red hot with embarrassment and anger at myself for even stopping to speak with the old guy. I just hated to be rude to my elders and I didn't want to stop trusting people out of fear. Why do men always put me in these predicaments? Maybe, I put myself in those situations because I'm too nice and too trusting. Frankie could tell I looked startled or upset by something and asked if something had just happened but I said no, I was just running late and having one of those crazy mornings. He wouldn't let me pay for my juice and donut, so I hugged him and went over to my school. It's tricky when you're in another neighborhood because you don't want to upset or anger anyone when they know your routine and that you're alone. Even being Psychic, you can still be surprised by an event you thought was going to be fine, only to have it be a negative experience. I refuse to become nasty or rude and I also think it has a lot to do with growing up. I was raised to be respectful and obey my elders so it was hard for me to be suspicious or untrusting of folks older than me. It's also very important for young people to learn to be aware of their surroundings and to listen to their intuition or gut feelings. Never be afraid of doing what "You Feel" is right for you. If you get a hinky feeling about something, exit quickly. Trusting your "Gut" feelings is also the first step, in opening a dialogue with your Angels and Spirit Guides. Once you acknowledge that Angels and Guides exist, you are sending out a signal that you're ready to welcome them into your life. That small attempt on your part, shows those beautiful benevolent beings, that you believe in them and that you know they always want the very best for you. Each time you receive something you prayed or wished for, give a verbal, "Thank You" to the Spirit Realm and God/Jesus/Source and soon, you will notice more and more things happening that you used to think were just a coincidence, happening much more frequently. When you show gratefulness and appreciation, the Universe will respond in kind! Be brave, and trust yourself to know what's right for you!

I loved my Trade school, especially my teachers. The headMaster was a very smart and kind, Afro American man in his sixties named Paul Revaleon. The younger, six-foot, five-inch teacher, was a gentle, bearded giant who went by the name of "Joe". In nineteen seventy-six, black people never went to the North End, as the Italians and the blacks didn't get along. For a black man to be the teacher, at the North Bennet Street school, located in the Italian section of Boston, was unheard of. For Paul Revaleon, it was a very brave and radical thing for him to do. Both of those teachers were so patient and loving to everyone and what they taught me is worth more than platinum and diamonds combined. Everyone at the school, felt like one big family because of its unique curriculum and small classes, such as piano tuning and technology, camera repair, locksmithing, watch making and repair, custom cabinetry and lastly, jewelry making and repair. They had a cafeteria on the first floor, that served great Italian food at low prices for the students. One day in the cafeteria, I asked for some gravy on my mashed potatoes and she scooped marinara over them, and "that's" how I learned the Italians call their spaghetti loop sauce, gravy! During my two years at school, I had gotten the reputation of finding lost stones for my classmates. Someone would be over at the torch station ready to solder when they would drop a tiny diamond melee or a ruby on the linoleum floor. They would come to get me and I'd go over and stand still, closing my eyes and looking at the scene in my mind's eye, and a little red light, in my vision would light up, showing me where the stone was. I'd open my eyes and bend down, lick my fingertip, and touch the stone, picking it up and placing it on their soldering pad. They all got a kick out of it but since age seven, I had done this while playing with kids when they'd lose something in the grass or a pool. Early one spring morning, in my second year of school, as we students were all standing in the hall, waiting for the teachers to come let us in, a classmate came up to me with a worried look in his eyes. I could feel his desperate energy, so I asked him what was wrong. He said, "I lost a bag of jewelry and there's a three-carat diamond ring and some other pieces I brought with me from the jewelry store I do repair work for. If I don't find it, I'm in big trouble!" "The diamond ring alone is worth over ten thousand dollars!" He asked, "Can you do that thing you do and please help me find it?" I took a step back and answered, "I've never tried to do it on an object that isn't nearby." He grabbed my arms with tears in his eyes and said, "Please try, my boss is freaking out on me and I can lose my job!" I felt so bad that I took his hands in mine and said, "Okay, don't panic, let me think about it tonight and I'll tell you tomorrow where it is". He looked so relieved, while inside, I was freaking out. I got on the train that afternoon, frantic with worry. What if I couldn't find it? Would he lose his job? I was so tired from being up since four am, that I closed my eyes and laid my head back on the seat. You know when you're tired but not asleep and you're in kind of a twilight lull, between sleep and awake? All of a sudden, I had a vision of a white refrigerator, with both doors open with the bottom drawer on the right pulled out. My eyes flew open and I knew where the bag was! There were no cell phones back then and I forgot to ask for his number, now I would have to go all night, so excited that I could barely sleep before I could tell him. I sprang out of bed the next morning and raced through my morning regime, then I drove like a bat outta hell for school, instead of taking the train. I was the first one upstairs, waiting outside of our class door, then a few other students arrived and asked me if I found it but I said they had to wait until Mark came to hear it. Minutes felt like hours and when he came walking up, dragging his feet, I put my hands on his shoulders and said; "I know where it is!" He sprang to life when I said, "Look in the bottom drawer on the right side of your refrigerator". The other students started laughing saying, "That's ridiculous, no one puts expensive jewelry in a fridge!" Mark didn't have anyone at home to call and have them check, so we had to wait another full day to find out if he found it. The next morning, he walked up the stairs, straight to me, with a serious look in his eyes, which made me nervous but as he got in front of me, he reached down, picked me up like a bride, and twirled me around while everyone laughed! His grandmother saw the bag on the kitchen table two days before and thought it was his lunch, so she put it in the bottom drawer of the fridge, then she went to visit her sister in Jersey and she didn't know he had lost a brown lunch sack! There were cheers all around and at noon we all walked to Regina's, where he bought everyone pizza for lunch. I was so elated because now I knew that my talents had layers that I hadn't even discovered yet, which meant that the possibilities were limitless!

TWO STEVE'S

From nineteen seventy-six to seventy-nine, while attending jewelry school and working in Boston, I was still living at home over at the Craft Center, in Newburyport and I worked there to help out after school. While going to jewelry school in Boston, I got wild hair and decided to go to night school in Boston, to be a professional bartender. This was a predominantly male-driven field, making me the first woman at nineteen years old, to enroll in the Boston Bartender School. I went at night for two weeks and I learned so many things about not only pouring drinks but what your duties are behind a bar. I also learned how to layer liquor in a small glass, from the densest liquid first to the lightest at the top. I never imagined there was so much responsibility when you're a bartender. I graduated with a mixology certificate and was looking forward to putting those skills to the test. After graduating from North Bennet Street school in the fall of nineteen seventy-eight, with a degree in jewelry making and repair, I worked in downtown Boston, in the Jewelers building, at three thirty-three, Washington street. Only men worked there, in nineteen seventy-nine, unless you were a sales girl in a jewelry store but no women were jewelers in a trade made up mostly of Armenian, Israeli, and Jewish men. The place I worked sold wholesale supplies to jewelers like, gold and silver wire, flat stock, and chains, they also sold tools, gold and silver mountings, ring shanks, and cut gems like sapphires, rubies, emeralds, and diamonds. Think of it as a "Home Depot" for jewelers. It's what's known in the trade as a Stone Jobber or Findings wholesaler. When you got buzzed into the room, there were three big glass, display cases and a wall behind the counters, full of tiny drawers, and a back room that held the bigger tools and equipment. Each small drawer held tiny wax paper envelopes full of gems, findings, and other items that jewelers need. The first week I worked there, no men would let me wait on them. The two owners, Steve and Steve, really needed my help but the men thought I was just window dressing and that I didn't know my butt from my elbow. I tried to help them but they would just ignore me, until one day, red-haired Steve said, "Either she waits on you or you can leave", as he walked out back, leaving eight startled men just standing there. "Come on, give me a chance", I said. Well, they had no choice but to let me and I filled their orders fast and knew what I was talking about because

I was a jeweler, whereas my two bosses had bought out the old owner, after they got back from VietNam and they weren't jewelers. Word quickly spread like honey in the Beehive, that is the Jewelers building, that a young girl was working at C.W. Somers, who knew her stuff and before long my line was out the door. I loved that job because I learned even more about how the jewelry business works, from how it's made to how it's sold. I'm forever grateful to both "Steve's" for giving me a chance. I left after eighteen months, to open up my own custom jewelry and repair business back home in Newburyport. I started doing repair work for a few local jewelry stores and I rented a small office space on the second floor of a building on busy Pleasant Street, in downtown Newburyport. I made custom wedding bands that I carved from wax and then cast into gold. I also made a lot of custom pieces for the store owners in town.

HEY GIRLY

Back in nineteen seventy, nine, I was earning five hundred dollars a week making and repairing jewelry but I was bored. I landed my first bartending job at a local seasonal event bar, that was on a road heading from Newburyport to Salisbury beach. I worked weekend days and most nights at this popular club that had bands and dancing at night. It catered to locals, beach goers and events like weddings, during the spring and summer. It was a large venue. What an exciting time to be a bartender! The Bee Gees came out with a killer Disco album, right at the same time Rock and Roll was in its prime. Everyone got along and people were kind and friendly. In the winter that place closed, due to the snowstorms and bad weather, so I found a new place the next spring. I heard through a friend of mine that "The Boat Club," a big two-story building on the river that rented out dock space and moorings to club members, was hiring a new bartender. It was kind of like the American Legion, but for boaters. I aced my interview and got hired on the spot. The old men took a while to adjust to me being a female bartender but I won them over with my fast service and my repartee of funny jokes and retorts. I don't think being a chesty blonde hurts either. I thought it was funny when the older men called me "Girly". "Hey girly, get me a beer!", was a daily remark along with, "Are your boobs real?" It was within those walls that I learned a "boatload" about people, especially men, and their thinking process and traits. An indisputable fact is that when people are drunk, they have absolutely no filter when they speak. It's also very hard to "lie" after three to five drinks and since the bar itself started serving at eight in the morning, I was dealing with professional drinkers! In fact, men were waiting outside at seven-thirty every morning for me to open up! Alcohol is like a truth serum, in that it loosens a person's inhibitions and their tongue. The boat club was a working man's bar during the day and at night a younger, mixed crowd of guys and girls would come by for cheap drinks. You couldn't get served unless you were a member or if you were sponsored by a member, which made my job a little easier, and less riff-raff. Bartenders have a front-row seat for all sorts of crazy behavior and they never know when a fight will break out. You have to be two parts mixologist, three parts entertainer, four parts psychologist, and one part bouncer. Every bartender has the right to shut you off if you've had too much and to throw you out if you are causing trouble. It's a delicate balance because you have to stay on your toes, making sure the whole place runs smoothly during your shift and you also have a list of chores to do to leave the bar set up for the next shift. Being a small female, you are more cautious while working behind the bar. You're constantly dancing between making drinks, breaking up fights, and fending off male advancements. It can be challenging until you prove yourself to be a person who means what they say and isn't afraid to back it up. I've had to literally vault over the bar and get between two big men to stop a fight. When my adrenaline gets pumping, I go from my usual hyperactive self to a flying monkey that is surprisingly strong!! All those sports and gymnastics really helped me during some of those strenuous times. One thing is for sure, you get Bartender Ears, meaning that while you are busy making drinks and washing glasses, your ears pick up conversational tidbits without looking like you ever heard a thing. Information is currency while you're behind the bar. You can find out who's sick, who's broke, who has it in for someone, and who is cheating on their wives, etcetera. Those tips can help you anticipate trouble way before it happens, making it invaluable. Now I was making jewelry by night, so I could work days at the bar. My income had risen to a grand a week. Not bad for a female in nineteen seventy-nine! I had moved into my own apartment in the nearby historic district of lovely Newburyport, right before my parents moved back to Virginia with the twins. Now I was living alone in my own place, paying my own bills and decorating with all my antiques and the two custom couches I had made. Life was sweet!

TWO FIRE ROOSTERS

I felt on top of the world…until the day a tall man walked into the B.C., while I was pouring drinks behind the bar. Before that day, I had heard some of the younger guys my age talking about a guy that was six foot, two inches tall, had long, curly black hair, and was a "Wild Man". I never spied on my customers nor do I have a nosy personality but I was intrigued by the stories bandied about at the bar. Old men seemed afraid of this guy, young men had a healthy fear of this guy and well, the women all wanted this guy, even though he was married with three kids! I had just turned around to face the bar and hand a customer his drink when the door opened and the silhouette of a tall man was backlit by the bright sunlight, as he stepped through the door. Instantly I felt like I had stuck my finger in a light socket that shocked me! The hair on my neck and arms stood up as he moved closer to the bar until I could make out his features. Tall-check, dark black curly hair-check, dark eyes-check, powerful male energy checkmate! So, this was the "Wild Man" that was on the wagging tongues of the Boat Club members! Now I had a body and a face to put with his name and if the sparks going off between us were any indication of what was to come, I was in deep trouble! Our energy met in the space between us and then we both got shocked by how strong our attraction was. He came up to me at the bar and being short, I had to look way up and when our eyes met it was epic! Even to this day, some forty-five years later, I still remember that day as if it was an hour ago. Here was the guy that everyone had been talking about and he looked very surprised to see me behind the bar and not a guy with a mustache named "Ian". He ordered a White Russian, (Kahlua, vodka, and milk), which I poured with shaky hands and set it down in front of him. Right away he started hitting on me and I threw him some great one-liners while we verbally sparred until my shift was over four hours later. Dennis was his name and it became a daily ritual to see him in the bar almost the entire day when I was working. After six weeks went by, I asked his best friend, Danny, if he was happily married. Danny told me they were separated but he still lived at home with his wife and kids, while they were both seeing other people. I didn't want to be a homewrecker, so I stuck to just flirting, until one day his wife came into the bar with her new boyfriend, then after seeing those two together, I knew they were seeing other people. I decided to surprise him a week later when I answered, "Yes, I'll meet you tonight for drinks". He lit up like a Christmas tree when I agreed to go out with him that night. We decided to meet at eight pm at the "Frolics", on Salisbury beach. I had my girlfriend Cindy go with me because the Frolics is a huge complex, right on Salisbury Beach, that holds several hundred people and they have big concerts and bands on the weekends. I wanted to get there early to have a drink to soothe my nerves, as I was hyped up with anticipation and regret. What was I doing meeting a married man?!? She and I had a drink when the band started up and thirty minutes later, he hadn't shown up, so we had another round. Now he was over an hour late and it was incredulous that after all his flirting and asking me out over the last two months that he was standing me up! I told Cindy, "If he's not here when I finish the second drink we are leaving". Just as my straw slurped up the last of my drink, I looked up and saw Dennis, hobbling towards me on crutches! Crutches!! We both stood up and rearranged the chairs so that Dennis and Danny could sit down at our table. As soon as we ordered a round for all of us, Dennis started explaining that he broke his foot in a fight a few hours after I got out of work. He had been at the hospital getting X-rays and a cast. Cindy and Danny were laughing about it and after their drinks were gone, so were they! Danny stood up and offered Cindy a ride and they took off. I gave Cindy a scathing look for abandoning me, as Dennis pulled my chair, with me in it right next to him. He leaned in to kiss me but he bit my cheek instead! I had never been bitten before and I sat back aghast, while he just chuckled. My mind was at war, with one side wanting to jump up and run out the door, while the other side was intrigued as hell and wanted to see where this was going! My curious side won the battle and I asked Dennis if he was a caveman and we both laughed hard at that. We listened to the rock music blast, as we kissed like two people that hadn't seen each other for many years. We both sat staring into each other's souls, speaking without words and drinking each other's drinks. When we left, he was feeling no pain from his broken foot as he hobbled on crutches, while I strutted on four-inch heels next to him to my car. It was quite the trick when I had to fit his six-foot, two inch frame, in the front seat of my tiny Toyota Celica GT with the crutches! On our trip back to the Boat Club where I was going to drop him off, I turned down a back road near the river and drove towards some seven-foot-tall marsh grass I parked right in the middle of the grass, as it swallowed us up. He grew up in Newburyport, but I had only lived there three years and spent those first two and a half years in and out of Boston, so he asked how I knew of this spot. I replied; "A Lady Never Tells" and we made out like teenagers and messed around doing the wild thing before I drove him down the street and back to the Boat Club. I felt like I was the dude that picked up a chick then made it with her and dropped her off back at the bar where we met! In my mind I figured a man like him was only looking for one thing, then he'd "bee" off to the next flower but the next morning my phone rang and it was him asking to see me again. Rats…my plan backfired. Let's just say that my life was forever altered the day we met. It's very hard to date again once you've had that kind of "Soul Deep" connection as we had. It would be over thirty years later, while doing some research on Chinese Astrology, that I found out that Dennis, who was born in early March of nineteen fifty-seven, making him a "Fire Rooster," the most auspicious of the Rooster signs and also, that I was wrong about my own Chinese Astrology Sign. I was born in the first week of February, nineteen fifty-eight, a year later, so I thought I was "The Dog" but I didn't realize that in February, nineteen fifty-eight, the Chinese New Year wasn't until February seventh, making me a "Fire Rooster" too! No wonder sparks flew the day we met! Two Fire Rosters facing off in an intense encounter of epic proportions! We both felt such electric feelings for each other right away, it was Kismet.

MILITARY POLICE

Before I go on, I believe this is where I should tell you more about Dennis and his shady background. That day in late June of nineteen eighty, when he walked into the Boat Club while I was bartending, was a week after he was released from the "Lawrence House Of Corrections" jail, in Lawrence Massachusetts, after serving one month, out of a twelve-month sentence, for being caught with two pounds of marijuana, when police raided his apartment in nineteen seventy-nine. Since it was his first arrest, he was to serve one month in jail, with eleven months suspended and three years probation. That means if you are caught doing anything bad in three years, you must do the eleven months-plus whatever new charges are added, as a result of your second arrest. From gossip around the bar, I learned that Dennis had been in the Military Police while serving in the Army in Germany.

It's not easy to get into the police division in the Army but Dennis was an intelligent guy, even if he didn't excel in school. He had a natural talent with math and strategy. His father owned a machine shop that repaired small motors and appliances during the sixties, seventies, and early eighties. Dennis could fix small motors or repair cars with ease. He had a natural talent for fixing automobiles, boats, and motorcycles. To put it simply, he could fix anything. I've always been drawn to men that can do more physical things, rather than men in business suits. It's not fun as a woman, being the butch in a relationship. Even though my dad was a white-collar worker, I've always preferred men with trades. Living in New England, it's almost a matter of life and death to know how to change a tire, jump start a car, build a shed, plow a driveway, or make emergency plumbing and electrical repairs because the temperature drops below zero in the frigid winters and if you live in the country, help may not come. Pipes freeze, and the ground freezes, so the knowledge of how to operate a generator or other equipment proves extremely important.

"BONNIE AND CLYDE"

Dennis was a male version of me, in that he was very independent and held lots of skills and trades under his belt. Together we became inseparable, like Bonnie and Clyde. Not in the killing cops and robbing banks way, but rather in the way that we were constantly together the first three years of our relationship. It felt like it was always "us" against the world. I had never felt that deep sense of commitment and understanding with another human being in my life before. It transcended any human connection I had ever experienced in my life. We communicated with just our eyes, it was surreal in nature. We told each other everything and had each other's backs. That's what women want, a man that can handle what life throws at them and stands up for his woman. Money never did it for me. I was used to being independent and earning my own money. I wanted my man to be tough when needed. Through Dennis, I learned how he made his living. Some days we spent at the machine shop, with him fixing motors and some days we spent picking up weed from a dealer that was moving five hundred pounds at a time, bringing it up from Mexico into Boston. I felt like I was back in the North End, hanging with the Italians. Dennis was second generation Sicilian, on his Mother's side and his father was part German and a mix of other European peoples. In nineteen eighty, while everyone was getting along and the vibes were "love, peace, and chicken grease", the local Newburyport police had other ideas. The war on drugs was ramping up since the Vietnam war was over and our men had returned home. Drug task forces were springing up everywhere, especially in cities near the water, where boats could bring loads to the shore at night. It wasn't unusual for locals to find bales of marijuana washed up on the beaches in our area. I didn't care as much for drinking alcohol but I liked pills and weed that mellowed out my hyper nature. Back then Dennis had some clients that were nurses and doctors who were smoking pot, snorting cocaine, or taking pills. He had a crew of guys he could trust, who picked up the weed from him and only sold it to other friends of theirs, not to strangers on the street. It was a suspenseful and also a thrilling adventure when he and I worked together and we made the most of our time as a couple. He and I would pick up fifty pounds of Thai stick, (high-quality Marijuana from Thailand tied onto a 4" thin stick) that was selling for big money and

Dennis's dealer always had the primo weed. We brought it to the stash house we rented and divided it all up and bagged it to sell. Sitting on the floor, surrounded by piles of marijuana and stacks of cash was an exhilarating feeling. Everything is new and exciting when you are twenty. You don't worry about the consequences or about getting caught because you are young and you feel invincible. Things were going well and by the end of the first year, a new product came to town, one that would change history, Cocaine. I had heard of it but had never used any. I'm naturally hyper, so much so that people were forever asking me if I was on "speed", which was ludicrous since I was an athlete and was born with a heart murmur. If I had a dollar for every person that wanted to buy some of my energy, I'd be stinking rich! One night, Dennis came to my apartment and when we sat down to watch TV, he had a saucer from the kitchen, then he took out a small, one-inch glassine bag from his pocket and opened it, dumping out the white powder. He then took a razor blade and divided the piles into several long white lines. I'm next to him, mesmerized by what he was doing. I looked on in wonder and amazement, as he took a three-inch, cut plastic straw and snorted a line up his nose! I had never seen anyone snort anything up their nose before, so when he handed me the straw, I leaned back on the couch and said, "no thanks". He did another rail and told me I shouldn't judge unless I've tried it. I just felt out of my wheelhouse and wasn't comfortable trying it. I wasn't a prude, as I smoked weed and I tried

LSD and many other hallucinogens while in high school. I just couldn't get past the "snorting" part. We watched the movie and near the end of it, Dennis got up to use the bathroom and while he was in there, I slid the plate in front of me, picked up the straw, then bent down and held my left nostril closed with my finger and gently snorted a tiny amount of the coke up my nose. It only took three seconds to feel the rush of speed engulf my whole body. I felt like I could run a marathon without even stopping like I was super ener-gized. Colors were intensified, as were sounds and my lips felt numb. When he returned from the bathroom, he noticed one of the lines was shorter and he sat down giving me a big smile. "How was it?" he asked, "Not too shabby", I answered. After a few weeks went by, I was a pro when it came to sniffing up lines but since my heart already beat fast, I only used coke after I had a few drinks, to feel perky or more awake. Cocaine tends to "snap" a person out of a drunk or lethargic state, making it an essential party favor among adults and heavy drinkers. Soon, friends were asking us to get them some, and then, their friends asked them to get some, so before we knew it, we were dealing with larger amounts every week. I can recall sitting on the floor in the living room and counting out fifty to eighty grand and putting rubber bands on it, while George Michael belted out the "Careless Whispers" song in the background. We were raking in a lot of cash, so we bought a small, three-bedroom house from his older brother and we remodeled it inside and out, complete with a security fence and alarms. All of this was happening in the early eighties. The local police heard rumors of what Dennis was up to, right from the start and when I joined him, they knew who I was from my mom's store and her being the Vice President of the Chamber of Commerce. The cops would try to catch me alone while I was in a store or at the gym and ask me what I was doing with that bad guy. In my defense, I was in love with Dennis and he loved me. We had something rare and wild. We were both strong-willed, tough souls who had each other's six. The people that we dealt with were over twenty and friends and families we had known for a long time, we weren't selling to kids or strangers. The whole country was loving weed and cocaine, like folks love liquor and cigarettes. The Bayer Aspirin company put cocaine, opium, alcohol, and marijuana in their cough syrup, back in the eighteen hundreds. No wonder folks worked so hard! Another fact in history, is that in the eighteen hundreds, they made a liquid medicine that contained opium called "Laudanum", which parents gave to teething babies and they also used it in snake oil that lots of people became addicted to. Folks didn't like prohibition and opened Speakeasy's and secret bars, just to bring alcohol to adults that wanted to relax and have a good time. Life's hard enough sober, people want choices. Now marijuana is legal in almost every state, as it should have been, back fifty years ago. Considering smoking cigarettes gives you lung cancer, at least marijuana can help calm anxiety and stop seizures, so it has medicinal properties and benefits. Taxing its sales has brought obscene sums of money into cities and towns to fix roads, and build better schools, hospitals, fire stations, and other programs that benefit the people, towns, and cities. It's a win-win. My life with Dennis was so insane for those eleven years, that you wouldn't believe the things we went through. The feds wanted to put him in jail so badly that they decided to arrest him for "Continued Criminal Behavior", an unprecedented charge that took our savvy lawyers five months to get him out! The cops violated him for suspicion of continued criminal behavior, without any proof. It was a bogus charge but the cops took a gamble because his three-year probation was almost up and since he was smart as a fox, they felt they had nothing to lose. It happened right after I found out I was pregnant. He was in jail from the time I was three months along until I was just a few weeks away from delivering the twins. I had to live alone for five months, while I was pregnant and no one would hire me but I still had bills to pay. I drove three times a week, forty minutes each way, to the Lawrence House of Corrections Jail. One time in February it was a blizzard and the snow was getting deep as I was driving our big seventy-two Lincoln, down route, four ninety-five at sixty miles an hour and I couldn't see a thing in front of the car because it was a total white out. It was like driving blind! God and the Angels brought me there and back each time! People who owed us money blew me off, knowing Den was locked up and I was in no shape to kick their butts. While in jail Dennis got hepatitis from having to use a metal can for a toilet. He incited a whole prison riot by setting sheets on fire and having the men throw their dirty poop buckets at the prison guards. The prison was very old and didn't have proper sanitation, so many inmates also got tetanus and hepatitis while in there, and a few years later the prison was shut down and the inmates all sued the prison for mistreatment. Danny, Den's partner, would throw me some cash from time to time and parents sent me fifty dollars a month to help out. On one visit to see Dennis, Danny had rolled up half a pound of weed into joints, putting them into a men's black sock, which I smuggled into the jail with a pint of whisky. Usually, there was a cardboard trash box, inside the door of the visitor's entrance, where I'd put the contraband but that day there was no box. I was doing my best not to freak out because I didn't want to get caught with the weed or the alcohol on me. When it was my turn to see Dennis, I let on that I still had the goods on me, and what should I do. It was decided that I should just try another time. When my thirty minutes was up, I turned to leave, walking outside towards the giant gate entrance, when an inmate yelled to me from behind a four-foot wall, on my right, to throw the stuff to him. I was so scared the guards inside would see me throwing the sock filled with weed or the pint of liquor but I tossed it fast anyway. Walking towards that gate entrance seemed like forever, like I was in slow motion, as I waited for alarm bells and guards to run out and stop me. My

Angels were watching out for the pregnant me, and I made it out of the jail yard, then safely home. Dennis traded the weed for better food so that's why I did it. I was crazy in love in the first three years and all your emotions run high when you're an expectant mother. I also delivered fifty pounds of weed to a guy in the Kmart parking lot one night, as I needed money to eat and pay the rent. On one visit to see Dennis at the jail, I had gotten there early as always and I was sitting on a chair in the waiting room when I watched a really tough character walk through the front door. He was a poster boy for a tough Irish gangster. His body was lean but all muscle like a boxer's. My ears perked up when the man told the guard at the desk, he was there to see Dennis Brown. The guard pointed to me when he told the man that I was here first, so he had to ask me if I'd split the hour's visit. When the tuff guy approached me, he asked if I'd split the visit and I said, "Sure, you can go first". I wanted to go after him so I could find out what he wanted. This guy was a serious thug. When it was my turn to see Dennis, I sat down and asked who that guy was. Den said the man told him his name was Red Shea. He also told Dennis that Whitey Bulger from the Winter Hill gang in Boston's Irish section, sent him to deliver a message. Red went on to say that Whitey didn't want Dennis doing business with the Angiulo brothers in the North End. Dennis told Red to tell his boss, "It's too late, I'm already doing business with the Angiulos. I'm half Siciliano, and Raymond Patriarca Jr. and I are tight." Since Dennis ran the north shore areas of Boston Massachusetts, and the southern New Hampshire areas, the Winter Hill gang stayed in Southie and they had their own territories. There were so many insane events and crazy wild things that happened during the eleven years Dennis and I were together but that's for a ten-book series I'm writing about my life with Dennis. Here are just a few of the highlights....

DOUBLE TROUBLE

In November of eighty-one, I found out I was pregnant. I was on birth control for years, so I was shocked! I was freaking out over this news. I was too young to have kids, Dennis wasn't divorced yet and I craved freedom! I knew I would be tied down with raising a child and I wanted a few years of freedom before that commitment. I detested doctors but I had to go see one and he sent me to the hospital for an Ultrasound. The technology of Ultrasound was just invented, making me one of the first in that hospital to get it done. I went to my appointment alone because I'm a very private person that doesn't like to ask for help unless it's unavoidable. Hospitals are scary, especially if you only go to one after you break something or get stitches, something I'd done three times by the time I was ten. My older brother broke my left pinky finger, while we were roughhousing in the car, while our parents were inside a store. A girl in Virginia fell on top of me on the street when she tripped, while walking behind me, which was followed by six stitches for the gash in my left knee. My older brother pushed me down a flight of stairs when I was ten and when I stood up, blood was pouring from a deep and huge gash under my chin that required seven stitches. Now you get an idea of why I'm not a fan of doctors. A nurse had me lay flat, on a hospital gurney covered by a sheet, when another young nurse came in and set up the ultrasound machine. It was chilly and my hands were shaking. She put the gel on my stomach and started moving the handpiece around my belly on a treasure hunt for a fetus. I was so nervous already but when she said; "Oh my, it seems you have extra parts". I started shaking uncontrollably. I asked her what she meant by that and she said; "I'll be right back, I'm going to get a Doctor!" Then she ran out of the room like her skirt was on fire, and I started to panic. Extra parts?! Now tears were sliding down my face, all alone in that room for what felt like forever. She finally returned hauling a harried doctor behind her who sat down in the seat and said, "Let's take a look here". Holding my breath while he probed around my midsection, mentally kicking myself for taking LSD in high school and in suspense until he sat back and asked; "Do you have any twins in your family?" I said; "Yes, my younger brother and sister." I didn't like where this was going...He said; "Well congratulations you're going to have twins too!" I almost fell off the table. Twins?!? I wasn't ready for even one baby, let alone two! My mom was fifty-seven inches around when she was pregnant with the twins and she's five feet seven inches, what will I do? Dennis already had three kids, how was I going to tell him about this new development? The nurse and doctor left the room while I changed clothes and I sat there and balled my eyeballs out. I was twenty-three years old, it was too soon to even think about kids and all the heavy responsibilities that come with them. I had spent eleven years as a babysitter for my brother and sister and the neighbors' kids, I didn't want this at a young age. I was earning great money but I wouldn't be able to bartend in that condition, as you run on your feet eight to ten hours a shift. So many things were going great, that this news wiped all my dreams off the board, like words written in the sand when the tide came in. Women always have it the hardest when it comes to kids, that's why I was on birth control, to begin with. Now I understood how my Mother must have felt when she just had my older brother and then found out I would be coming fourteen months later. So many racing thoughts going nowhere. I had to decide what to do before I told anyone. I drove my seventy-two, Plymouth Scamp back home and later that night when Dennis arrived, I told him, "I'm not having a baby". He looked so confused since he wasn't aware that I was even pregnant. Then I said, "I'm having two babies!" Dennis took it far better than I did. To his credit he was elated, especially when I threw down the "Twin" card with the picture of the ultrasound that showed two tiny panda bears, floating in a kidney bean-shaped pool. Before I could decide how and when to tell my folks, Dennis called them behind my back, telling them about the pregnancy. I knew they would be disappointed, as they weren't a fan of Dennis and his lifestyle, to begin with. My parents asked him how come I didn't call to tell them, which made me even more upset, as I was super close to my parents. I know he did it so I wouldn't consider having an abortion if my dad and mom knew about my condition. I have to admit, it had crossed my mind for a moment. I called my folks and told them the details and the three of us just accepted it, since it was already done. I want you to know that I don't dislike kids, it was just the timing and our young ages. I had just gotten a taste of pure freedom and I didn't want to be tied down, at least not at twenty-three years old, or to a guy that was making a living the illegal way. We were wild then and I feared losing what we had between us. Things change after you have kids and I knew that for sure. My doctor told me that my due date was August eleventh but I told him, "Don't go away the last two weeks of July"! I went into labor on July twenty-fifth, on a Sunday but the hospital sent me home saying twin labor could last for days. On Tuesday I had a spurt of energy and cleaned the whole house. Then at seven am on Wednesday morning, July twenty-eighth, there was a knock on the door and I got out of bed to answer it. I was surprised to see my dad and mom there. I let them in and we sat in the kitchen. They had driven up from Virginia, on their way to see my moms, mom, Vivian, in Maine and they wanted to check on me. I told them I wasn't feeling too well, so they said they would go to a diner and have breakfast, then stop by again before they left for Maine. I saw them at the door and went into the bedroom where Dennis was sleeping and laid back down. No sooner did I lay down, when I felt water gushing out, so I got up fast and put on a dress. I wrote a note for my parents that said, "Water broke, gone to hospital" and taped it to the door. Off we went in the rain to the nearby hospital. After seventeen hours of hard, painful labor, I gave birth to twin daughters, totally naturally and without pain medication. Justine came first then eighteen minutes later out popped Jade, guess she wanted to make a grand entrance, show off! They had their Dad's dark Italian hair and olive skin, making them look like mini Hitmen for the Mob. Their eyes were big and blue/green which later turned to amber gold. In their teeny, tiny hospital gowns and caps they looked so cute. The doctor said they were premature but I told him they would be born in the last two weeks of July and I knew they would be girls, because they came to me in my dreams, looking like twin brunette Barbie dolls. Justine was only four pounds, eight ounces, and Jade was four pounds, eleven ounces. Together they were kept in the preemie ward in incubators until they weighed five pounds. I was going to need all the energy I could get to take care of twins! Once my daughters were three years old things got much easier. They loved going out on the ocean on our sport fishing boat. In the summers we would all sleep on the boat while it was docked behind the Boat Club, where I used to bartend. We also bought a forty-two-foot, lobster boat, and two hundred wire traps and buoys. He and I went lobster fishing at four am and later we had cookouts with lobsters, steaks, farm fresh, sweet corn, and other summer foodie delights. Our parties were legendary and Life was sweet.

TRACY'S SHOES

A long with my psychic powers starting at an early age, my sense of fashion developed when I was five years old. I wanted to be a model when I grew up, like Twiggy, she was my first Idol! I posed in our front yard, while my dad took my pic with a Polaroid camera but I wasn't photogenic at all. After seeing myself in photos, I was upset that I looked different from how I thought I looked. When it came to clothes, I wore what my mom laid out for me, until I turned six years old. I remember one day while living in the blue house in Virginia, It was a steamy, hot, summer morning when my mom chose what I call a "Bubble" suit. It was a one-piece, lightweight, sear-sucker cloth, that had elastic around the top of your thighs and more elastic around your bust. It had thin straps on the shoulders, making me look like a bubble! Well, I thought I was too old to wear something so babyish and told her I didn't want to wear it. She replied that I could stay in my room until I put it on. Aquarians are a fixed sign, so we are born stubborn. I lasted almost three hours until I finally put it on because I was hungry. I wasn't rude or fresh, it's just that I already had ideas of what kind of clothes I wanted to wear. Later when we moved to West Newbury, my multi-talented mother made me a long, purple suede vest that was open in the front, with a twelve-inch-long fringe that had colored beads. I wore a pretty tie-dyed headband over my long hair. I still have the picture of me wearing that outfit during the late sixties. When I reached junior high school, I learned to sew in school and I would make miniskirts and stuffed animals from hand-drawn patterns. When my folks opened the Craft Center, in nineteen seventy, I was in seventh grade and I was babysitting for my brother and sister, as well as for some school teachers and neighbors. I was making money to buy my clothes and makeup, plus my best friend lived at the top of the street behind our house, so Robin and I would share outfits, making it look like we had more clothes than we did. By the time I graduated high school, I had a reputation for being a trendsetter and a clothes horse. I wore tasteful makeup and was known to suddenly cut my hair short then a few months later I'd get a perm. That's how I was named, "Best Dressed" in my high school yearbook. This area of my life shaped me from a Tom Boy, into a person that could also rock heels and dresses, which came in handy later on in my life. In nineteen eighty-four, I woke up one day at six am, sat upright, and said out loud, "I'm going to open a shoe store! "Wait! Who said that?!" I sat there a moment and I did some noodling about the idea, just long enough for it to ferment, then I thought; "Hey that's a great idea!" My twins were two years old and since I wasn't doing jewelry or bartending, I needed something to be an outlet for my creative passions. My parent's store used to be in Newburyport and the whole area only had two small shoe stores back in nineteen eighty-four. You could drive thirty to forty miles either north, south, or west to get to a big mall with more current stores. This was, way before department stores started to sell more shoes. The only two shoe stores that were local, sold Florsheim and other sturdy, heavy leather shoes, so stiff that it took months to break them in. Not to mention the blisters! They had what you'd call, "sensible shoes". I jumped up, got dressed, and headed into Boston to get my DBA (Doing Business As). I registered the name, "Tracy's Shoes", so I could get my tax ID number. Then I drove back to downtown Newburyport and slowly cruised up State Street, then took a right onto Pleasant Street, looking for an empty store to rent. Those were the two main roads that housed all the shops, stores and boutiques, and restaurants. I wanted to be on one of those, and low and behold Bingo! I found an empty store on the right. It was the third store in, from the corner of State St, on Pleasant Street, right across from the locally famous restaurant, "Angie's", a very busy Greek diner. Next to Angie's, was a vintage "Wool-worth" store, with its lunch counter, probably from the late forties, and early fifties. I called the number on the "For Rent" sign and a man came over and showed me the twenty by sixty-foot store that came with a full basement the same size. I could feel the Spirits and the Divine energy working its magic, as each important task was getting crossed off my list and it wasn't even dinner time. I poured my heart and soul into that space. I painted the walls and went to Danvers, Massachusetts to a big warehouse that sold store fixtures, new and used. I had slat wall panels installed on both sides of the walls, so I could hang moveable, clear acrylic, shoe-sized shelves to display the boots and shoes. Then I had a company make hexagon pedestals that came in three heights and could fit together in groupings or be laid on their sides. I had one set of three in medium purple and another set of three in off-white. I bought wooden benches to sit on while you try on shoes and I had a sales desk made by a friend. We put up a partial partition three-quarters of the way down the store, to make a small back room for stock, as well as shelving units in the cellar for more storage. The nice thing about selling shoes in retail is, that you only display one shoe from every style and you keep the other half in their boxes in the back, so it's very rare for a pair of shoes to get stolen while you are in the back or if you have to run downstairs to get shoes for a customer. The cash register was locked with a key I kept on my wrist. Back then, stores didn't have cameras but we did buy a new computer, which was a behemoth, so we could track inventory and sales, without running downstairs, only to find out of those shoes in that size. I worked the store alone from nine to five for the first six months, then I hired a girlfriend to work some days, giving me more time with my twins. Before the store opened, I had just missed the big wholesale shoe show by a month and since I didn't know what I was going to do, I opened a "Glamor" magazine and when I saw a shoe ad that appealed to me, I called their one, eight hundred, number and they sent a salesman out. All shoe stores in general back in the early eighties were owned by men. "Tracy's shoes" had a radio jingle and we took out quarter-page ads in the Boston Globe, for five hundred dollars each ad. Those ads brought the airline stewardesses, who were on layovers in Boston, out to my store, forty minutes away. It also stirred up some controversy, as I paid a very good artist that draws people extremely well (she did the art for Grolier encyclopedias), to draw my ideas that were considered by some, to be suggestive or kind of risqué at that time. There wasn't any nudity but one ad showed a woman with her arms around a man's shoulders and a pair of sandals hanging from her fingers. It was only drawn from the bust-up, but we received phone calls from strangers, who thought the ad was naughty and provocative. One lady bluntly called it "Smut"! What can you expect from New Englanders anyway? The ads were the talk of the town because they ranged from funny, to sexy, to whimsical. One of my favorites was a cartoon-looking raccoon, with a Santa-like sack over his shoulder and a few shoes he dropped on the ground on his getaway. The caption was, "Shoes Are A Steal" at "Tracy's" store-wide shoe sale. Another favorite, was of a checkered picnic blanket, on the ground with food laid out and no one there but the ants, that were carrying the shoes away. "Get carried away at Tracy's store-wide summer shoe sale". Anyway, the store was such a success and the net was two hundred thousand the first year and just shy of three hundred thousand the second year. I never even thought about the fact that at twenty-five years old, I had earned two hundred thousand dollars. I let Dennis handle all that and I designed the window displays and did the ordering and shoe designing. It wasn't until I was writing this book, that I suddenly realized, in two years in business, I had netted almost half a million dollars! The store had a Dun and Bradstreet Rating of B plus in the second year and I was delighted with the progress. We were the first store to sell "Reeboks", the sneaker that kicked off all the other sneaker companies like, Adidas and Nike. Reebok started the sports athletic shoes you could wear all day. It was all about comfort, ease, and style! It was Iconic and awesome to be a part of the footwear culture during the mid-eighties. We carried Men and Women's shoes but mostly sold ladies' high-fashion shoes like Mia, ChopStix, Jasmin, Ital, Chinese Laundry, and Peter Fox. I had grown up going to the crafting wholesalers with my folks, to buy for the Craft Center but it doesn't work that way with shoes. Shoes, ahhhhh wonderful shoes, where to begin? They soothe my "Sole". Tee hee. When you sell anything seasonal, it's very important to stay on trend. You have to read ladies' fashion magazines and twice a year, in spring and fall, they have huge shoe conventions. You need to order your footwear six months before the season starts, so you buy in early Spring for the coming Fall and you buy in the early Fall for your Spring collections. That means you order shoes for each season, six months ahead and you pray you chose the season's top hits, as you have to pay for them whether they sell or not. The "Justin Boot" company just happened to be in Manchester, New Hampshire, an hour away from my store, so I drove up there and introduced myself. They were great and they let me choose from all kinds of colors and prints of leather and suede. That meant when I ordered twelve or eighteen pairs of boots or shoes I had designed, they were the only shoes like that in the world, which brought me even more business. Now I was catching on, shifting gears, and giving it the gas! I found out they were having a big shoe convention in a hotel in Manhattan, NY, and Dennis made our reservations to stay in a corner suite, on the fortieth floor, in the Helmsley Palace. The convention was at a hotel a few blocks away and I was very excited to walk to each booth and check out the coming season's designs. On the fourth and fifth floors, all the hotel rooms had their doors open to show their shoes on display inside. I'm blessed with size five to six in ladies, so I could try on the sample shoes myself and make sure they were comfortable. It was at that show that one shoe company offered to hire me to model their shoes. Funny, my dream of being a model finally came true, for my feet! Ha ha…I thanked the man and let him down gently. Word among the ladies was spreading like wildfire in a fifty-mile radius of the store and life was sweet. I never bought designer clothes, not because I couldn't afford them, it was because I had an eclectic style and bought what I liked. I loved wearing wild outfits and creating a look that was my signature. Mixing a vintage motorcycle jacket, cowgirl boots, and neon-colored, tight dress with Native American antique sterling and turquoise jewelry. The jewelry I made was also futuristic and bold, just like me!

VROOM VROOM

What I desired now was a fast car. I had grown up drag racing cars on the backroads in the country. My older brother and I had been going to the drag strip since we were fifteen and sixteen years old. Going to New England Drag way, watching the "Snake" and the "Mongoose" drag race each other, was a passion of mine and I loved Chi Chi Muldowney. When she raced against the men, she was my idol. Since I worked hard, I bought myself a nineteen eighty, eight Porsche Targa 911, Signature Series, Anniversary Edition. The front seats were embroidered with the Ferry Porsche signature and they only made twenty Carreras and eighty Targas for nineteen eighty-eight. I had one of only eighty Targa 911 Porsches that year. It came with a bronze medallion, heated front seats, and a built-in radar detector. I loved that car so much, as it was the nicest thing I had ever owned. She drove like a dream and handled like a boss. The twins fit perfectly in the back seat and giggled when we drove with the Targa top off. Driving her gave me confidence and pride that I had done so well, when in fact, I was just pursuing my passion. Making money was a perk but not my driving force, it never has been. When my parents decided to move to Vermont on the lake and leave Virginia, I was so happy they would only be four hours away. It was an eleven-hour drive for me to visit them in Virginia and now I could see them more, now that they would be closer. One Wednesday night, I drove my Porsche up to Epping, New Hampshire, to New England Dragway. It was "grudge Night" at the drag strip and I paid twenty dollars to race the quarter mile against whoever pulled up beside me. What a thrill to rev her up in front of the Christmas tree lights, then punch it and fly down the track, shifting as fast as you can! I also raced a Ninja bike on the highway at one hundred and forty-five miles an hour. The car felt like it was floating. I loved the thrill of speeding fast, whether in a car or on a motorcycle and I had no fear when driving fast. I still ride my custom Harley Sportster, bobber, twelve hundred but I enjoy cruising these days more than speeding. It's funny, as you get older life seems to speed up while you start to slow down! If I had lived in California when I was a teenager, I would have loved being a stunt woman in Hollywood! Having a background in acrobatics, trick riding, horse jumping and motorcycle riding, and swimming, I'm sure I would have had a blast! I think of myself as a mix between Evil Knievel and Mae West. I'm fifty percent wild woman and fifty percent dareDevil, a perfect mix for this life! It's important to know yourself. We all have many sides to our character. Each of us has half male and half female energy. Like the Chinese sign for Yin and Yang. Some women tend to lean into the Tom Boy side and others stay way over on the Fem Fetal side. The trick is to be like Flux, to go where the heat of your desires draws and pulls you. Some situations call for a woman to be meeker if it will help them out of a jam. Others will require a woman to "Man Up", as the saying goes, and kick some butt. The same goes for men. If they are at home, playing with their kids or grandkids, they will be tender and kind, making sure the child's needs are met. That same guy on Sunday is watching football with the guys and he will act differently in that scenario. We are all here figuring things out as we go. Be kind to yourselves! No matter how well you prepare, it's always possible for an unexpected event or a situation to pop up. So, expect the unexpected. I guess what I'm trying to say is, that it's okay to be yourself, no matter what the situation calls for. If you follow your heart and your desires, good things will come your way, as long as your intentions are positive and good. When you are honest with yourself, the door to "Self-Discovery" opens, letting you get closer to your divine goal of total enlightenment of Self and Soul.

COMING UNRAVELED

Dennis found a house about thirty minutes northwest in Kensington, New Hampshire. It was a two-story, new build with a garage, on five acres of land. The area was so rural that you couldn't even see the neighbors, except for their mailbox and driveway entrance. Dennis wanted to relocate, so we had more land and also so the detectives from Newburyport couldn't spy on us as easily. They were still trying to catch him doing something illegal, as they wanted to seize all of our things but the shoe store was making a quarter of a million in profit each year, so my accountant could prove where all the funds came from legally. It was nineteen eighty-six when we moved in and it took a lot of getting used to. The house was set back over a hundred feet from the road and had a stand of trees that lined the entire five-acre property. It was a huge lawn to maintain. Dennis was gone almost every night and because we had moved so far away, we had very few visitors. I became immersed in the local elementary school's PTA when I enrolled the twins in first grade. We designed a parade float to compete in the local Christmas parade contest between schools. We decided on a Disney Prince and Princess theme. Hard work and our creativity won our school first prize but the real joy was being a part of a group of parents that wanted to help their kids have fun. Kensington had a small population with lots of farmland and the local gossip mill ran wild when I painted our new home in a boysenberry color with gray trim. The display at the store showed the house painted gray with dusty purple trim but I reversed it, just to give folks something to talk about! The eight-foot, black rubber-coated chain link fence with a foot of black razor wire, fueled the tales with speculation about who we were and what we were up to. That's why I made a point of being a part of my daughter's lives and their schools. Once the parents met me and saw how genuine and kind I was, it went a long way toward helping the twins make friends in their class. Living in that secluded area turned out to be harder than I thought it would be. Everything was thirty or more minutes each way, which meant a lot of driving just to get groceries or go to the gym. Dennis was very seldom home and that created lots of arguments because I felt lonely, ostracized, and trapped. I was in my late twenties and I didn't like feeling so far away from everyone and everything. I also knew that Dennis was cheating on me and that hurt me deeply. Everyone in Newburyport knew he was taking out other women, it was humiliating. He got more ass than the toilet seats in Logan airport! After I dropped the twins off at school, I was driving down our street when I saw him driving towards me. I whipped my Porsche around and he had pulled over and gotten out of our Caddy, walking towards my car as I parked behind his car. I looked through the rear window of the car and I saw a dark-haired girl in the front seat, trying to sink down and hide. He hadn't come home last night and now he's got a chic in our car. I looked him dead in the eye and floored my Targa, almost knocking him down because he was standing by my car door. He jumped back in the nick of time and I was going ninety miles an hour as I hit the on-ramp for the highway. I was crying so hard and also seething with anger and I drove a buck twenty till I came to my gym exit. When you can't get up and leave a terrible relationship of extreme abuse, physically mentally, and spiritually, it makes you feel helpless, weak, and sick inside. To have to play the role of a mate to somebody evil inside and out, while you fantasize about poisoning his drinks but know that you'll end up in jail and your kids need their mother. Fear, anger, and frustration were my constant companions, so alcohol and drugs became my only escape. I still kept the house beautifully maintained, dinners were always gourmet, and the kids were clean and well cared for while inside I felt dead, like a robot going through the motions. It's the loneliest feeling of all. To not be able to tell anyone what's going on for fear it will get back to Dennis. Even the girlfriends closest to me were having sex with him behind my back. They all wanted to replace me, they wanted to live in our house and drive my car. They had no idea what kind of a hellish situation I was in. I had no friends because when you live with a career criminal, you can't ever tell anyone anything personal. After all, they could be feds or trying to set you up. It felt like he put me away, like a princess in a tower, so I wouldn't catch him with all the women he was sleeping with. I decided to close my shoe store after three years because it was too much to handle, living so far away. I put the twins in a private school, ensuring they would get the best education, and drove them both ways every day. Things were unraveling fast once we moved to Kensington. It was so sad but Dennis did what he wanted to do, no matter how I felt about it, we were barely speaking. I wanted to leave him but he threatened to kill me and take the twins. At six foot two inches, he was a foot taller than me and a really tough guy. My nickname for him was the "King of Crude", due to his rude and colorful vernacular. I knew being with him was going to be challenging right from the start, that's why I didn't want kids with him, as I knew he would use them against me. I was very lonely and secluded living out in the country while he was out living it up every night with women in bars. At night it was so pitch black and scary in the country and when I'd hear a noise outside, I would take his Beretta, sixteen-shot automatic pistol, and stand just inside the twin's bedroom at the end of the hall on the second floor. Because of what he was doing, I had to be paranoid of the police, DEA, the Feds, and other drug dealers, who would try to rob us because they knew you had cash and couldn't call the cops to report the crime. Some nights I stood in their room, till sweat rolled down my face and my arm shook from holding the gun. By now I was suffering from PTSD and severe anxiety from being beaten, abused, and in fear for my life and my twins' lives. Paranoia, fear and rage coursed through my veins for more than ten years. I felt helpless and trapped between Dennis and the cops. I was caught up in a major crime syndicate, with local, state, and federal agents tapping our phones and tailing us everywhere we went. My younger sister Doreen had rented a small cottage in Hampton beach so I brought my twins over one day to hang out with her. I got up to get a glass of water and my eyes caught sight of a scruffy man in a green army coat and long hair with a beard. He was standing on the edge of Doreen's driveway, taking pictures with a big camera. I opened the door, and yelled "Hey", and the man bolted away towards his beat-up car, so I grabbed my car keys and ran to my Porsche and chased him down small roads with both of us driving almost sixty in a twenty-five mile and hour zone. I was right on his tail and I memorized his license plate. I let off the gas as we got into some traffic and went back and got my kids. I called Dennis and told him to meet me at the house. When we got home, I told him that I had been followed the day before while driving my kids to school and that the guy taking pictures looked like a bum but that I believed him to be an undercover cop. I'd been in the game for nine years and I could vibe a gangster, Fed, cop, or a DEA agent just by looking at them. My Spirit Guides would tell me in one sentence who they were and whom they worked for. They were never wrong. As Snoop Dog says, "Gangster knows Gangster". By now I knew that they were getting close to catching him because of how many times they were following us and the Feds were trying to use Colombian guys to pose as dealers but were actually federal agents. After I spoke to Dennis at the house, I left with my girls to go visit my younger brother Dean who lived in the next town over in Amesbury. When I took a right onto the road to Amesbury about a mile from our house, I looked to the left at a group of cars and men all talking together on the side of the road. Standing right there was the guy I had just chased with my car near my sister's cottage!! Now I knew they were cops and federal agents, so I slowed as I rolled my window down, and smiled as I waved! "Gotcha"! Letting them know I knew who they were. They stood there with their mouths hanging open because I just caught them less than a mile from our house, which let me know they were also the ones who followed me home after I got my girls from school. When they followed me that day, I went down a country road and lost them as I maneuvered my Porsche around those sharp curves at high speed. The detectives were so blatant, that Dennis would be out at night eating at an expensive Italian restaurant and he'd send our limo driver outside to deliver take-out meals for the detectives sitting in their cars. He loved playing games with them without regard to what that meant for me and our twins. If he had just kept a low profile while dealing, instead of wearing flashy suits and tons of gold that was worth more than a cop's yearly salary, they wouldn't have made him priority number one. He put not just me and our daughters in danger, he also put his Ex and their three kids in peril. I prayed for the cops to catch him so I could be free of him, his lifestyle, and all that stress.

OPERATION BLIZZARD

One afternoon in September, I had just gotten home, after getting the twins from school in Exeter, the next town over. Dennis was upstairs still sleeping when I walked by the glass atrium and saw a SWAT team careening into our driveway on two wheels, with men hanging off the side of their armored vehicle. I grabbed my twins and called upstairs to Dennis, telling him, "It's the cop's!!" SWAT, DEA, and other officers pounded on our front door while I stood still with a twin under each arm, my hands up. Dennis came down in his bathrobe and opened the door while a dozen men poured inside with M16 machine guns and dressed in full SWAT uniforms. Our dogs were shaking and they made us all sit down on the couch, while they went through our home, throwing stuff on the floor and being rough with everything we owned. One of the DEA agents took me outside to sit in his car.

He asked me where the drugs were and I said; "You may have a search warrant but Den never keeps anything on the property." The officer then threatened to get a backhoe and dig up our yard and I said, "Please do, I want him out of my life, so do whatever you have to!" He said if I cooperated, they would put me in witness protection but Dennis had warned me if I ever hid myself and the twins from him, he'd kill my younger brother. Since he had killed Vinny Lupo, Boston's most notorious Mafia hit man in nineteen eighty-four, who had murdered thirteen people that the State Police knew about, and was on America's most wanted list, I had no doubt Dennis wouldn't hesitate to take me out. He told me they'd find my body floating in a river. Unbelievable how all the cops and Feds wanted me to rat Dennis out, when they were all terrified of him! What did they think would happen to me if I snitched on Dennis. They searched through everything in our home and found nothing for the second time. They raided our apartment in Newburyport, two months after my twins were born in eighty-two and they didn't find anything then either. I was so weary of the whole situation and wanted to leave but I knew he would find me wherever I went. Dennis had a lady on his payroll that worked in the police station in Newburyport, so he used her to look up license plates and addresses. He also had a huge network of people running his bookie operation and his prostitution ring. I never liked, supported, or wanted any part of that. What started as just some small amounts of weed or coke, had morphed into a huge drug and crime syndicate, something I had no part in. Once he branched off into all those other criminal activities, our relationship became one of abuser and victim. It was his way or the highway. He did what he wanted but if I did something he didn't like, I got a beating. I was forced to stay or risk being killed and have my daughters raised by a psychopath. Better to live with a snake under glass, than a snake under your bed. Easy for people to tell women they should just leave a guy that's abusive because it isn't as easy as that. What kind of life would you have, always looking over your shoulder in fear, alone, cut off from your family and friends? Dennis had me choose fine suits and ties so he could class up his act, especially after I opened the shoe store. I believe he was jealous of my success, so he came home drunk and beat me up. I started going up to Vermont more, now that my folks lived there and I did all I could to protect my children. I wanted to sell my Porsche and stash the cash but Dennis told me if I did, he would beat me, so I didn't dare. I knew he was being sloppy and not taking proper care of business, now that he didn't have my shoe store to siphon funds from. Folks weren't buying as much cocaine, now that "Crack" had moved into town. Den had gotten spoiled having all that extra money from my store and he was treating me horribly since I took away his cash flow. We had heard rumors of the local cops wanting to raid my store, calling it a money laundering, drug front. The cop's wives shopped at my store and I was furious they would even think of raiding my successful and legitimate business. We knew the cops were just doing anything they could to ruin our lives so they could take all our stuff. I said screw that and shut it down. Everything Dennis touched was tainted by his evil, negative energy, he ruined everything and everyone he was associated with. He started talking about these three Colombian drug dealers that wanted to sell him ten kilos of cocaine at ten thousand per key but they wanted my Porsche title as collateral, which I flat-out refused to do, as I had paid cash for that car with my earnings from my store. A psychic friend of my parents gave me readings during those years because it's harder to read for yourself and I was afraid that since everything was in my name, they would arrest me too, so they could take it all. I never wanted that house or anything in my name but he didn't have the platinum credit as I did. He bought that house without even asking me or letting me see it and with my earnings from the shoe store. Dennis knew I was on to him and all the shady stuff he was doing, so he threatened me not to see my psychic friend but I went anyway. I desperately needed some information that came by way of Spiritual advice. I knew in my heart the end was coming very soon and I wanted to get away from all of it if possible. In nineteen ninety, on the Thursday before Labor Day weekend, Dennis had gone out as usual that evening and he didn't come home that night, which wasn't unusual for him. The next morning, I got a call from a friend that told me Dennis had been arrested last night in a parking lot in Danvers,

Mass, and was being held without bail, as he had two ounces of cocaine in his possession, at the time of his arrest. As bad as it sounds, I was so relieved that my prayers were answered, that I broke down and cried like a baby, letting some of that stress pour out of me. I don't wish bad on anyone but when they pistol whip you and hold a gun to your head on Christmas Eve, then try to throw you outside in twenty-degree weather when you are in a tank top and shorts and bare feet, you lose all connection to them. Every time he hit or kicked me, I withdrew from him more and more. After the first three good years, I had lived through eight years of hell and I just wanted my life back. No amount of money or possessions can make up for being beaten and cheated on by someone you love. I was a prisoner of a psycho, my life and my twin's future all hung on my actions. I didn't even have enough money to run away with. He had been spending and hoarding everything I earned so he had taken away all my options. But the worst was yet to come. That next morning on Friday, I packed my car with the girl's clothes and stuffed animals and drove over to my sister in law's house in Newburyport. On the way there, I passed a small hamburger stand and saw all the local detectives standing and talking by their cars. When they saw me, they waved me over. I thought they wanted the keys to search the house so I pulled in. When I got out of the car, they told me I was under arrest, which sent my stomach plummeting to my feet, in shock. I asked what the charge was and they said, Co-conspiracy. They explained that after fourteen hundred hours of wiretap on our phone, I answered when a guy called and asked if Dennis was home, I told the guy Dennis wasn't home, and he asked me to tell him he called. I said, okay and we hung up. No mention of drugs or anything else, it was such a bogus charge but I knew they wanted the property, cars, motorcycles, and our boats. Damn him for putting all that in my name! The only way they could grab all our goodies was by convicting me of a crime, since it was all in my name. I was freaking out because I had my twins with me and they were scared and crying. The detective I knew let me use his police phone to call my sister-in-law to come to get the girls. I'll never forget that day, as I stood next to our car, with my twins looking at me through the back window with tears streaming down their little faces as my sister-in-law drove them away. While I was riding in the back of the police car on the way to some jail in Boston, the detective I knew said that on Thursday night, after they had arrested Dennis that afternoon, he had the best night's sleep he's had in ten years. That's how afraid of him the police were! Dennis firebombed the federal judge's house, who had first put him in jail, right after he was released from jail and right before I met him. Now you know why I was helpless when it came to just leaving him. I was a mere trophy and he wasn't going to let anyone else have me. He was never going to let that happen. That Friday morning on Labor Day weekend, I spent five days in a holding cell without a blanket, pillow, or anything warm. Sleeping on a hard wooden bench. The DEA took me out of the cell once each day and brought me to a room, to grill me for hours about Dennis and his operation. The ten-year file on him was so thick, I knew they had enough to keep him in jail for a long time. My parents drove down from Vermont and were staying with the Random's in Newbury, after they got the call, I was arrested. My anxiety was so severe I couldn't eat, sleep or calm down. They shoved some McDonald's food under my door three times a day but I wouldn't eat it, so they put me on suicide watch. I didn't know how my babies were doing, they had never been taken away from me before and I wasn't allowed any phone calls so I didn't know where they were or if they were Al rightfully . I was a total wreck. I lost fourteen pounds in five days and when they brought me into the courtroom, I saw my parents in the back of the room and I almost collapsed on the floor with weakness and relief. I was in the same clothes I had on for six days, not even a brush for my hair. Thank God I was bailed out, using our house as collateral. It was only then that I realized, not only had Dennis and I been arrested, but his whole crew was also arrested and many of them didn't get bailed out. Turns out those three Colombian drug dealers, that I had warned Dennis about them being Fed's, really were DEA agents that wanted my car title from Dennis! They wanted to set him up and arrest him, but ironically, he had gone to Danvers, Massachusetts, to meet a guy to pick up half of a kilo of coke. His regular guy was out of town, so he told Dennis to meet his guy instead. He met the guy and got into his car. The dealer only had two ounces, but Dennis took it anyway and was walking back across the parking lot to his car, when a team of DEA agents, doing surveillance from inside a parked RV in the back of the parking lot, noticed him because they were watching the guy he had just met. When they saw that it was Dennis that had met their guy, they almost peed their pants because they had been after him for ten years but they never had enough evidence to arrest him! They jumped out of the RV, swarming Dennis's car, yanking him out, and searching him, finding the two-ounce baggie of cocaine in his pants. That single event changed my life in a very profound way. I had been Dennis's partner for the first three years until the twins were born, then I had stayed out of anything illegal because I was a mother and I wanted to make a living the legitimate way, to be a good example for my daughters. I stayed home with my girls and I put all my time and energy into raising them with good manners, values, and compassion for all things. I taught them how to be loving to animals and wildlife. How not to kick rocks because everything has feelings. I instilled in them the fundamental laws of doing the right thing, being respectful of others, and sharing their things with their friends. My wildly, successful shoe store was proof that I had made it the legal way. The cops knew I didn't participate. After Dennis beat and kicked me very badly one night when he came home drunk, I spoke to a local cop outside my gym the next day and told him I needed help getting away from Dennis. The cop said I would have to be an informant, tell them everything I knew, and that I might have to go into witness protection. Once you do that, you can never see your parents, siblings, or anyone you care about ever again, as you start your life completely over somewhere far away, praying he won't ever find you. I was so traumatized by then, as I was facing ten years in jail for just answering the phone and I was working two jobs to support my girls without any child support. I obtained a great Boston attorney and plead "Not Guilty". My lawyer and I were building a solid case for my defense and I had a clean record, so I knew I could win. There were numerous counties, across three states, local detectives, DEA, ATF, and other federal agents, all in what was deemed, "Operation Blizzard". An intensive operation that spanned over ten years. Dennis was the biggest drug kingpin north of Boston. Whitey Bulger and his Irish, Winter Hill gang, ran Boston's, South End, aka Southie. The two Angiulo brothers ran the Italian, North End Mafia, where I had gone to jewelry school. Dennis bought coke through Sonny Angiulo, who owned an Italian restaurant located on the first floor of the Prudential Center in Boston. He also bought it from a woman that got it from Raymond Patriarca Jr, who ran the Rhode Island Mob. Because Dennis dealt in New Hampshire, Maine, Rhode Island, and the North Shore of Massachusetts, many state agencies and officers were involved. Dennis was working with Raymond Patriarca Jr, from the Rhode Island Mafia and who had ties with the Gambino crime family in New York, NY. Two years before, we had been to a Mob rehearsal dinner, the wedding, and then the reception. I was sitting right next to guys who were the real deal. While I sipped my drink at a table during the reception, a well-dressed man sitting next to me, asked if I would watch his silver metal case for him. I said, "Sure". After he left the table, I mentally went over a list of what could be inside his weird silver suitcase. Money? Drugs? Guns? Body parts? Meatball sandwich? Meanwhile, outside, the FBI, DEA, and other law enforcement officers took down everyone's license plate numbers, while we ate, drank, and danced. For the eleven years Dennis and I were together, the high points were amazing but the low points were so extremely bad. I had a very high chance of winning my case, until one night, as I climbed into bed at eleven pm, the phone rang and the voice on the other end belonged to Steven Story, the head agent of the DEA office in Boston. He was the one that grilled me every day I was in jail about Dennis's operation. I will never forget that voice. He told me that if I fought my case, he would personally plant a bag of cocaine in my car and that I'd go to jail for forty years! I was thunderstruck!! I didn't have a way to record that call or I would have owned the DEA. My lawyer charged them with intimidation, which only pissed them off more, so finally, I called my attorney and told him to strike a deal where they could keep the stuff and I would get probation. It went against my belief in being innocent until proven guilty, but after that phone call, I knew they would just keep coming for me and my nerves were shot from all the stress and anxiety. I was alone and supporting eight-year-old twins without a car or money. I started my life over, at thirty-one years old and moved with my twins to a nice condo complex, closer to the beach. They took everything but our clothes and furniture and that was fine by me. Just having peace of mind helped me and my daughters acclimate to a normal life. Years ago, when I was a jeweler, I had given my parents seventeen ounces of pure industrial grade, twenty-four karat gold bullion, to hold in their safe deposit box at their bank. I sold all my diamonds, jewelry, and gold, just to get another car and set us up for a few months till I landed a job. I didn't have any friends while I was with Dennis because he slept with all of them. Every chic wanted to be me because they thought I had it so good, but I worked hard at my shoe store, and it wasn't given to me. No one knew how bad my life was, the beatings, him cheating on me with skanks. I had stopped letting him touch me because I didn't want an STD from the cheap trash he was sleeping with, so he raped me when I wouldn't cooperate. It was a living hell, being trapped by a vicious demon. Starting over, allowed me to let people in my life again, and to trust people again. I met wonderful ladies that became like sisters to me. For the first time in eleven years, I could do whatever I wanted to, without fear of what Dennis would do to me. He wasn't going to get bailed out. He ended up getting two consecutive life terms, plus one hundred and forty years. There were so many times I begged him to quit and to use the shoe store money to buy some land and flip it, the legal way, so we wouldn't have to deal with the cops, but he wouldn't listen. He lived for that cat-and-mouse game with the detectives. He was a stagnant man, losing his grip on everything and everyone around him. The world was evolving around him but he was still stuck in the past. I was growing as a person, mentally and spiritually, while he was still doing the same vile and negative things over and over. It was very sad because what we once had was so powerful but in the end, greed, crime, and retaliation became his rituals. Mix copious amounts of alcohol with that and you're living with a bomb. Negativity breeds negativity. It was only through the strength of my convictions, and my belief in a higher power, that I could rise like a Phoenix from the flames. He did his best to break my Spirit and to crush my faith but he didn't know just how strong I am and that just made him madder. His biggest mistake was to underestimate me. Other men in my life would make that same mistake! They all tried their best to break me, wanting to control me, to use me, to keep me under their thumb but in the end, they were the ones that suffered by losing a good, kind, and loyal woman. Thanks to God, Jesus, my Archangels, and my "God Squad", I was finally able to break free of his evil and wicked grip on me. Some people chase power, and some chase fame. Better to live a life full of good intentions, followed by good deeds. If you think life on earth is hard, what would an eternity in Hell feel like? It doesn't cost anything to feel positive or to put out positive energy and thoughts, that way you are part of the solution, not part of the problem.

OOPS!

I worked one summer at a tattoo shop near the beach. I met a guy at the gym, who asked me if I wanted to make one hundred dollars a day plus tips, to be his tattoo assistant. Brad was from the Bronx, in New York, and was six feet, seven inches tall, with blonde hair that made him resemble Hulk Hogan the wrestler. I grew up with everyone around me, being over six feet tall, it didn't bother me. I had a small tattoo that I got when I was twenty-eight, of a sea serpent. Never did I imagine I would become a tattoo artist! I waited on customers, helped them choose their designs, drew up each stencil, then photocopied their license, (you had to be eighteen) and I set up Brad's station for the next client and cleaned up after his last client. I watched over his shoulder, thinking, I can do that! No way would a man teach you because they wanted all the money for themselves and no competition. So, I knew better than to ask him to apprentice me. At the end of the season, I found a guy in a city, an hour away in New Hampshire, that offered to teach me for twelve hundred dollars. My parents watched the twins while I stayed for three days of intensive training. I slept on the floor of his attic in forty-degree weather and ended up with strep throat! Tattooing is the hardest art form, as you can't erase your mistakes, you have to do it right the first time. No client ever wants to hear a tattoo artist say, "Oops!". Luckily, I picked it up pretty fast and then I had to open my studio, as no shop run by men would hire me. "Sacred Skin" opened in nineteen ninety-two, in Portsmouth, New Hampshire. Because I was one of only three female tattoo artists in the whole state of New Hampshire, word traveled fast, and within a few months, I was booked up six weeks in advance. Tattoo artists earn over a hundred dollars an hour, plus tips, and it's a cash business. I tattooed from ten each morning till ten at night, six days a week, earning over a thousand dollars a day. I loved creating beautiful wearable art and I met so many cool people that shared similar values and philosophies. It's like being part of an artistic tribe. I went to tattoo conventions and tattooed people, as well as being featured in a few tattoo magazines. Tattooing as a whole was hitting its stride, in the early nineties, so my timing was impeccable for jumping in. The twins and I lived in an apartment over the shop which helped a lot and they could walk a few blocks to school. Everything was going great, but the winters were starting to get to me. Everyone wanted to get tattoos in the summer but it's bad for the fresh tattoo to be in a pool or the ocean or in the sun for that matter. I hired other artists and a girl who did body piercing, to make the most of the five months of warm weather. I also hired a young girl to sit at the front desk, schedule appointments and take the customer's payments. Then things would slow down in winter and I was still working a lot of hours but I was burning out. It's hard on your back and wrists, so you make the most that you can while your body can handle the pain. I woke up one day in late February of ninety-five and decided I wanted to move to Florida, where it's warm and sunny. My folks drove down and stayed with the twins while I took a flight down to Miami and I went into tattoo shops with my portfolio, on South Beach, to see if I could get a job. I finally made contact with a young guy, who had a tattoo shop in Sarasota, Florida who was opening another shop and asked me if I'd run it. We agreed on the money split and the terms. Back home, I sold my current tattoo business to a young guy, then we packed up and moved to Sarasota in July. Sunny and warm Florida here we come! Once we settled in Sarasota, on the gulf coast of Florida, I went to the shop to meet my new employer. When I got there, he told me there had been a change in plans, that he had decided not to open the other shop, so I would be tattooing with him in that shop. I was pissed off. Not only because that wasn't our deal, but as I was bringing my equipment into his shop, he was being a jerk about how I was setting my stuff up, criticizing every little thing I did and I knew he and I would not work well together. As I listened to his rants, I psychically got the feeling that some bad Ju-Ju was going on. I felt very negative energy around him so I didn't argue with him, I said I had to get back to my kids, and left, saying I would see him tomorrow. When I drove back to our new apartment, I kept going over things in my head. I was trying to figure out my next move. I was thirty-five years old and I didn't want to work with a guy who had a big ego and who would boss me around and who could be another "Dennis". I had already lived through enough miserable years of that. Never again! That night I took the twins with me to the mall next to our building and we went into a steakhouse. While we ate, I saw a couple of big guys at the bar, so I went up to them and offered to pay them one hundred dollars to go with me to that tattoo shop the next day, so I could get my stuff. I was thinking if I went alone, that weirdo might try and stop me from getting my equipment but if I had a big guy or two, he wouldn't dare. The three of us walked right into his shop the next day and the men stood near me while I grabbed all my stuff. The shop owner didn't even make a peep when I told him this wasn't going to work out. A week later, there was a knock on our apartment door. I open the door and the lady standing there says, she's responding to a report of someone tattooing in the apartment and throwing dirty needles in the trash. She flashed her badge from the Board of Health. That lie was not even worth getting upset over. I told her I know who called in the fake complaint because I just moved in and only he knew where I lived. I went on to tell her that she was welcome to look around, as I had nothing to hide. She was nice and could tell by how great our place looked that it was a false tip. After she left, I did something I hadn't done since I was a kid, I put a hex on that guy. I had uprooted my children, and moved us over fifteen hundred miles away, only to have him change the deal and not call and let me know! I know it's not kind to put the whammy on someone, especially if you are a psychic but after he sicked the board of health on me, I was livid. I got lucky with a job in a local tattoo shop and met a lady my age, also from Massachusetts, that is now, like a sister to me. We loved working together and when I told her my story about that guy, she asked our boss if he knew who he was. It's a tight-knit community among tattoo artists and he did know of him. About a month went by and one night, our boss told me that the guy I was supposed to work for, had gotten into a fight and broke his hand and couldn't tattoo, then when he was driving back from Miami to Sarasota, he got pulled over and busted with five hundred, Ecstasy pills and was sentenced to ten years in jail. Then we heard his beautiful, young wife and their new baby left him! And "That's" why, I don't put hexes on anyone anymore, because they work! It's also not good Karma. I was so glad that I never worked with him because my feelings were spot on and he was totally up to no good. A few months later I opened a tattoo shop in Sarasota called, "Galaxy Girl" and because of its location, I started to get a lot of clients. My shop was situated in a small strip mall, off a busy road. I was wedged in between a lady's nail salon and a very busy men's barbershop. Eighty percent of my clients were either tanned or dark-skinned. Seems some local tattoo artists were telling people with darker skin tones, they can't put color in their tattoos because it won't show up, which upset me. They were just being lazy and after a few months, I was packing color in so many tattoos for happy customers that things were going great. After two years, the guy I was dating said his company was moving him to Ft. Lauderdale and he asked if I would go with him, Heck yea, I took the twins and we headed southeast. Sarasota is a very nice area, but I was looking forward to being back on the east coast and new surroundings.

THE TOY RUN

Ft. Lauderdale, is exciting and enticing. Not only are the beaches beautiful, but the huge city also has a lot of cultural events and art shows. It's also only forty minutes from Miami and a few hours from Key West. The city had a much younger vibe and everywhere you went, people were partying and on vacation, so it was never boring. I worked at a tattoo studio for a while, then I got a job bartending in a sports bar. I made good money and I enjoyed it. The twins graduated from high school in two thousand and I had a girlfriend get them a job at the brand new "Harley Davidson" store, in the motor clothes division. My daughters are beautiful and when they both sat at the front counter answering the phones and doing sales, people would say, "Are you, the Harley Twins?" The name stuck and the owner hired them to be the Brand Ambassadors for his four motorcycle dealerships. They emceed all the

Harley events at all the big bike shows. Every December they rode on the first vintage fire truck with Santa, dressed as Santa's elves with the kids with disabilities, in the annual "Toy Run". A yearly, one-day event to raise money for the Miami Children's Hospital and Toys for Tots, which had Marines collect all the new toys that the bikers donated, that filled the whole eighteen-wheeler big rig! More than half a million motorcycles rode two by two for seven miles on Interstate ninety-five, which the police had closed down for seven miles to Markham Park. It was a huge outdoor event space with bands, contests, vendors, food, and entertainment. My twins would help sell the raffle tickets for the charity and Mcee the bands and the events. Each year it grew bigger and bigger and in one day they raised more than half a million dollars for the hospital. Last I checked, the bikers raised enough to build a new wing of the children's hospital! Bikers are good, loyal, hardworking folks like me, who want to help make a difference in the world. They support so many charities and always help those less fortunate. When you're on your bike and you break down, another biker will help make sure you get yourself and your bike to where you need to go, proving their loyalty and their motto of never leaving anyone behind. It was a thrilling time for the three of us! There was so much to do and see in Ft Lauderdale and we became well-known in the motorcycle industry. I started bartending in a large bar that was run by the motorcycle club, the Outlaws. I also tattooed in a camper in the back by the bands. They were like the Hell's Angels, a group of riders called the, "one percenters". They felt they represented one percent of the American men who were tired of the government sending them off to war, then treating them like trash when they returned home. Riding motorcycles was their way to rebel against the broken establishment. After the soldiers came home from Viet-Nam, the young men rode motorcycles and lived the biker lifestyle. They formed clubs and operated them as the Armed Services did. They had a ranking system and a set of rules and codes to be followed. They also punished any member who broke the rules. On the back of their leather vests and jackets, they have patches that are machine embroidered with their club's name on top and their location on the bottom rocker. (Rocker-slang for the big curved patches with the lettering) They call their vests, their "Cuts". Those vests and jackets are treated with the utmost respect because it's proof, they earned their rank in the club. Dennis and I always rode as "Independents", not wanting any affiliation with any club. Those wanting to join a club had to hang around the club for up to a year or more, doing all the grunt work and passing any initiations the club rules stated. They were slaves who had to prove their loyalty in any number of ways, often by illegal acts. They are called probates or hang-a-rounds. Girlfriends were made to wear shirts or vests that had printing saying, "Property Of The Outlaws." When I bought my first motorcycle in nineteen eighty, I wanted to drive a bike, not ride on the back of one. When I walked into a motorcycle dealership, I told the man I wanted a bike, he showed me a four hundred, I told him if I wanted a Moped, I'd have bought one. I got a Yamaha six, fifty. It had a teardrop gas tank and looked kind of like a Harley. Dennis had a Harley Davidson, Wide Glide, and a nineteen sixty-three, Harley Pan Head, which was a Coke can red and had been featured in Easy Rider magazine because of its custom paint and chrome accessories and the fact it was owned by a Hell's Angel from New Hampshire. My younger brother taught me how to ride on an abandoned strip of highway. One day Dennis was in his open rail, four-seater dune buggy, I was on my motorcycle and we were going for a ride to the beach. He pulled out of our driveway first and as I started to pull out behind him, a car came flying around the sharp corner near our house. I couldn't stop my bike because the front tire was up on the road pavement, the back tire was lower on the driveway and there was a deep ditch between the tires. If I stopped, my feet wouldn't be able to touch the ground and my bike would have fallen on me, so I hit the throttle, shooting me like a rocket straight across the street! Because I was a new rider, I didn't realize I was giving it too much gas and when my foot hit the back brake, nothing was slowing me down. I drove through the field across from our house, at forty miles an hour and when I squeezed the front brake, I was instantly launched up and over the handlebars as the bike came to a sudden stop! In the meantime, Dennis saw me in his rear-view mirror, flying into the field and he thought I was trying to race him, he didn't realize I was trying not to crash. I landed hard, flat on my back, knocking the wind out of me. After a beat, I jumped up and ran to my new bike, freaking out that I had dropped her. I was more worried about my bike than the fact I had just flown eighteen feet through the air! When I found out I was pregnant two years later, I sold my bike. I wanted to make sure my twins had a mother, but I never stopped loving motorcycle riding!

TRUMP SNOW

Back in two thousand and two, I was bartending at Rudy's Clover Bar in Ft. Liquordale, when a regular customer named Mark, came in and asked me if I knew how to gold leaf. I said, "No, why?" He said, "Well you better learn, I got you a job gold leafing Donald Trump's, front entrance walls of his, "Trump International Golf Club" in West Palm Beach. I thought he was joking, so I made his drink and put it in front of him laughing. He finally convinced me he was serious about it and I went home that night thinking about how to do gold leafing. The next day I drove to Pearl's art store (I had worked there for a while in the custom frame department before I got another bartending gig.) I asked the counter girl, "What do I need to gold leaf and do you have any tips or advice on how to do it?" She explained the process and then asked what I was gold leafing. You should have seen her face when I replied, "Donald Trump's walls!" Let me give you a little backstory on why I was given this opportunity. Every good bartender gets a following, especially if you are fast, friendly, and funny, flirting helps too. The guy who offered me the job was a very smart man who ran his own business and knew a lot of people. He had a friend that ran a crew of guys that detailed and maintained rich people's statues, art, and signs. One of his guys was buffing the dark granite on one of Trump's front entrance walls and had accidentally buffed off some of the gold leafing of the carved inset lettering, in several spots and the man wanted to fix it. He didn't want to risk losing the Trump account. My friend knew that I was not only an artist but a multi-medium artist, so he figured hiring me would help his friend out of a tight spot, and get my art talents some exposure. It was a win-win. I drove up to view the walls in person on a Tuesday and took a notebook, measuring tape, and went about examining each of the two forty-foot walls. Each letter was carved in, almost three-quarters of an inch deep and they were more than a foot tall. I had no idea how many sheets of twenty-three-karat, Italian gold it was going to take because I was a newbie at gold leafing. When a well-dressed man came out and introduced himself as "Lyman" and asked what I was doing, I introduced myself and said I would be redoing the gold letters. He was very kind and helpful. He told me that there was the Women's Open Golf Tournament, coming in nine days, so it had to be finished before the next Friday. Talk about pressure! I drove home to my apartment and I tried to figure out, approximately how many sheets of gold, how much sizing, and how many gallons of primer and sealer I needed and called the man who was hiring me. I told him that both signs needed to be done completely over. Whomever gold leafed the walls first, had used German Gold, which is a reddish, muted color, and Donald Trump, had everything else out front done in Italian Gold, which is yellowish and bright. There was no way I could just patch new, shiny, leaf over dull, faded, red gold, it would never blend or match. I am committed to being a perfectionist, good enough is not, good enough. If I'm going to do something, it's going to be done right. I told him I'm super busy and that this is a rush job because of the time constraints, so it would cost five grand. He was silent, then I said, "Please let me know asap", and I hung up. My boyfriend looked at me and asked, "Who are you?!?" It hit me so funny, that we both rolled around laughing so hard that snot bubbles started popping! The fact that I had zero ideas of what I was doing, or even how long gold leafing takes to do, especially to do it right, was hilarious. I had been bluffing during that entire phone conversation! I was a lunatic, what if I couldn't finish it in time?! Twenty minutes later, my cell phone rang and the man said, "Okay, do it. I'll give Mark half of the cash up front for the supplies, so please write me a receipt. "No problem," I said. Well, well, things just got more interesting…hmmm. I'll never forget the first day on the job. My friend Barbie and I were busy setting up on the front lawn, in front of the left side of the entrance, at six in the morning on Thursday. It was still dark out and she and I were getting supplies in place on the wet grass when an older man walked up to us and asked, how we were doing and when we thought we'd be done with the whole job. I was sitting on the grass and I had to crane my neck up, to speak to him. I told him if the weather held out, we would be done by next Thursday afternoon, right before the LPGA tournament on Friday. He was delighted and said, "I know you'll do a great job, I can tell a good artist when I see one." I stood up and thanked him, then as he walked out of earshot, I asked Barbie, "Was that Donald Trump?!?" She nodded her head yes and we both freaked out! He didn't look at all in person like he did on TV, he seemed like a regular guy and I felt embarrassed that I didn't jump right up when he came over to us. Even though I had never gold leafed, I had painted many houses, apartments, murals, paintings, and boats, so I was no stranger to remodeling things and refinishing furniture and metal with tools and paint. First, we had to use wire brushes, to clean every letter and then wipe the whole thing down with alcohol. Next, we painted each letter with a white, marine primer they use on boats. No one told me any of that, but I remembered when we had two wooden boats, we had to dry dock them and clean and paint the hulls. Using a marine primer ensures its last ability. I found out that most gold leaf artists prime their project with the same color gold or silver paint, as the gold or silver leaf they use, so if they miss a spot of leafing, it won't show but I thought that was being cheap and lazy. Anyway, not a single store in Florida had any "Sign Painters One Shot" paint, in Italian gold color. We didn't have time to order it either and that's when I remembered about the Marine paint standing up to water and sun better than anything else. After the primer dried, we used razor blades to clean any paint off the granite slabs. Painting the clear, sticky "sizing", was the next step. After forty-five minutes, we took popsicle sticks, covered in felt, as fingers, to push the gold leaf into the lettering, saving our fingertips from being raw and sore. While we were doing this, people were starting to enter through the front gate, walking by us as they headed into the golf club. Barbie and I were both in our early forties, she had long brunette hair and I had long blonde hair. We were both in shorts and tank tops, due to it being hot in the Florida sun. She and I were going home at three thirty in the afternoon, showering, and then going to our bartending jobs, from five at night, till two thirty in the morning, then sleeping for two hours and up at five thirty, to go work outside all day on the gold leafing. Barbie was doing the final detailing of the first wall, while I was finishing the last of all the gold leafing on the second wall. She and I had done many faux painting jobs inside wealthy homes and we worked well together, plus we both worked for the same bar. Barbie acts tough but she's really sweet and a hard worker. When I first worked with her, she told me that when she and her boyfriend were at home, she was on the couch in the living room and he was in the bedroom cleaning his gun, when it went off and the bullet went through the wall and into her stomach. She almost died from that shooting. We bonded over our love for art and our misfortune with men. The locals told us they call the gold flakes that come off and blow in the wind, "Trump Snow" and we were handing out the wax paper squares with some twenty-three karat gold flakes still on them, to the people taking our pictures, as they entered the gates and they loved it! Every day while we were there, Donald Trump came over to speak to us or he pulled over in his Lamborghini sports car and waved me over to chat. One day he introduced me to Melania, and he asked me how they found me since I wasn't his regular art guy. I told him who the man's company was that hired me and that they wanted to make sure his lettering looked amazing. He told me to make sure I gave them my number, so he could hire me again. I can't tell you how many times I've kicked my rump, for not pursuing his offer. I was making good money bartending and tattooing and I didn't want to be a corporate artist, as I had spent many years tattooing and I loved being free to ride my motorcycle and do my own thing. But I have often wondered, what kind of life would I have had, if I had just left my phone number, with his right-hand man, Lyman. We had two days left on the job when Lyman gave us a heads up that the man who does all of Trump's gold leafing, might stop by and give me a hard time and he was right. I was almost done leafing the second wall and Barbie had painted a clear, marine, acrylic over every letter on the first sign, sealing it so it would last a very long time. Out of the corner of my eye, I caught sight of an older, heavy-set man with dark hair, speaking to somebody at the guard shack in an elevated voice while waving his hands around. My antenna was quivering, as the man went over to Barbie and asked her a question. Gotta luv Barbie, she didn't say a word, she just pointed to me, oh great, now he was marching towards me, foaming at the mouth! I calmly kept pressing the gold into the lettering as he stopped three feet behind me. "I do all of Donald Trump's gold leafing", he sputtered. "Not today!" I retorted. "Who hired you?", he asked. I bowed my head like a frustrated mother does, and turned to face him. I said, "Look, I'm really busy here. I had to drop everything I was working on and jump on this job. Why don't you give me your card and maybe I can throw you some work since I've got tons of jobs lined up." That shut him up. He wasn't expecting that. I could see the gears smoking in his head. He pulled out his wallet and handed me his card. I took it and tucked it in my bikini top and said, "Thanks", and I turned back to my work, leaving him standing there with sweat rolling down his face. After he left, Lyman strolled over to me, curious as to what the man had said and when I told him, he laughed. He said, "Good for you", then we both laughed! I'm willing to bet that the gold leaf looks just as good today, twenty-one years later!

COMPLETE MY MISSION

I wanted to share some of the events of my sixty-five years on planet earth. Like most people, I've hit some home runs, and I've also suffered many defeats. Ever since I was five years old, I've been studying people and observing their behaviors. I felt like an observer of humanity and I was extremely curious about why folks did the things they did. Since I could feel their moods and emotions, I went around thinking people were mad at me or disappointed, not understanding that they were feeling that way about themselves or another person. It made me even more eager to please people because when they were happy, I picked up their happy energy and I was happy. At seven years old I didn't know about Karma or Auroras or anything like that. That's why I loved animals so much, as I could feel their loving nature and their pure innocence. They only reacted to their environments and didn't have thoughts of revenge, greed, jealousy, or malice. They simply wanted to survive. Being a Voice for the meek, the tiny, and the innocent became a way of life for me as I was forever saving and helping all of God's creatures. I've spent ninety percent of my life pleasing other people, it's my main mission and why I chose to incarnate on earth at this time. I've lived in fifty-eight places so far and I like to think I left people happier, that I helped people, and that I left a good impression on folks, by putting my unique spin on everything and everyone I meet. My compassion and kindness to others are what I give freely from my heart and soul. I love sharing my energy, my ideas, and my nonjudgmental, loving light, with all I meet. Many times, men mistook my kindness for weakness, only to be surprised by my stubborn refusal to bend to their will. Those that acted nice at first, then dropped their act when we moved in together, using cruelty to cage me, to break me, to put out my loving light. Yes, I've had some success, but I've also suffered mentally, physically, and spiritually at the hands of those narcissistic men who wanted to snuff out my faith in myself by any means necessary. I've experienced just about every human situation there is. I've been raped many times, I had an abortion and a miscarriage, I've had a DUI, been homeless. I attempted to commit suicide several times, I committed myself to a mental ward for fear of killing myself, I started taking pills from eighth grade through high school, I tried mescaline, THC, blotter acid, four-way, window pane, purple microdot, orange sunshine, peyote, and psilocybin mushrooms. All the while doing this, I was on the honor roll and no one even noticed I was on anything. I was bullied at school for being the "Weird" kid because I wasn't afraid of going after guys' sports. Because I was a gymnast I could do the iron cross on the boy's rings, I could push up from a head-stand into a handstand and I beat the boys in four squares. I didn't hang with the jocks or the smart kids, I hung out with the "Stoners" or I kept to myself. People are afraid of those that march to their own drum or are eccentric, so they make fun of you and pick on you but I never let them know it bothered me. Things always get better after you get out of high school, way less drama. After I met Dennis, I snorted cocaine and tried crystal meth and angel dust, (PCP), then in my thirties, I took Xanax and muscle relaxers, that was prescribed, I snorted heroin, smoked weed, took hydrocodone, ecstasy, soma, and valium. I was trying to mentally escape all the anxiety and daily abuse, while still going to the gym, taking my kids to school, and having dinner on the table. In my forties and fifties, I only smoked weed and took my prescription pain pills and Xanax. I'd also been self-medicating with alcohol off and on, as an escape from all those horrific past traumas, the anger and frustration of having to keep all those terrible things done to me, buried deep down inside of myself. I was suffering inside for so long that it began to feel like I had a separate part of me that took that pain and locked it up, so the rest of me could get up every day and push through another day, another week, another month, another year. I've been beaten by men, thrown out of a car in downtown NY city, and left there with no money or way to get back to where I was staying thirty minutes away, to get my little dog, so I hitchhiked on a major freeway. I went on a dinner date and came to the ER, coming out of a cat scan, with a concussion, a broken jaw, eight stitches in a gash under my chin, my face beat in and two broken teeth, after I was drugged at a restaurant and taken to someone's house and sexually assaulted. I've broken over thirty-three bones, been thrown off horses, flipped over my motorcycle, had skin cancer surgery that cut the whole end of my nose off, and a Beverly Hills plastic surgeon botched my close-up surgery, leaving me with a hideous nose. I multi-rolled over my Ford Expedition and was ejected through the windshield, landing twenty feet from the car. That accident killed my beloved little fourteen-year-old, long-haired Chihuahua, named "Chewy", my soulmate and my road dog. We were airlifted to a hospital, Chewy to a vet. Chewy had head injuries and I told the vet not to let him suffer but she wanted to keep him another night against my wishes. On Monday night at two in the morning, I heard him bark in my left ear, as he was saying goodbye and going to Heaven. I couldn't even cry because I had such chest trauma, I had to keep it in, until seven weeks later when I broke down and cried my heart out. I had a concussion, eleven broken ribs, front and back, broken left shoulder, a punctured lung, a sprained back, banged up both knees, broke my left foot in three places, four toes, and lots of stitches from going through the windshield. I could barely move, as I had shaken all my organs loose in my chest and ribs. It happened on a Sunday at seven thirty am, as I swerved to miss a coyote. A tow truck driver was on his way to a call when he just happened upon my car wreck. Being an EMT he immediately called for a Medivac. That was my third brush with death. If that tow truck driver hadn't driven by, I would have died due to my lung being punctured and Chewy would have died there with me, as we were in a remote country area. He told my daughter Jade it was the worst accident he's ever seen. On Thursday, I told the doctor to take me off the morphine and give me pain pills. I told him I was checking out Saturday, and his reply was that I had to show them I could walk first. So, on Saturday morning when a chipper physical therapist came into my room with a walker, I told him to move it out of the way and I rolled to the right, grabbed onto the bed's handrail and pushed myself up, took a deep breath, then I stood up, walked out of the room, past the nurse's station and back to the room. My twins drove me home to Los Angeles, where after a four-hour bumpy car ride, I climbed up three big flights of stairs! It took me weeks to even walk again and the pain was unbearable but I pushed myself every day to try harder and harder. I've learned in life that it's your own will and determination that can get you through anything.

PEELING BACK THE LAYERS

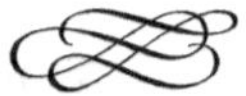

When you can speak telepathically to Angels, Spirit Guides, and Intergalactic and Interstellar beings from the seventh dimension and higher, it's like you are never alone. I stopped channeling in two thousand ten and I opened up my telepathy powers, so I don't need to meditate or enter a trance state. My God squad and I speak all day long and I know each one of their vibrations, Archangel Michael has his tone, and Robert the Angel has his. The intergalactic beings of light are my family members so I've been their voice on many missions on other planets. It took me over fifty years to piece together all the clues to finally know who and what I am and why I'm here on planet earth. Everything makes sense now. I peeled back the layers and found the keys that opened the most precious thing of all, My Inner Self and My True-Life Path. I am a Renegade Member of the Family of Light- Systems Buster. Using intuition, dreams, Psychic powers, my Family of Light's coaching, my Angels Saving me, and Spirit Guides guiding me, I've become "One With Myself". I'm tasked with relaying messages from God, Jesus, Angels, Ascended Master's and Intergalactic and Interstellar beings who are trying to save humanity. I am sworn to help save as many humans from the demonic forces that wish to crush out all Spiritually and faith in a higher power. I pledge to help anyone who feels lost, alone, afraid, scared or overwhelmed. Uniting those who need help, so that together we can raise our vibrational frequency and move up to the higher fourth and fifth dimensions, while the warring Angels take out all the evil and demonic trash here on earth. It is something that we cannot put off any longer! You must make a choice now, either your life is a wonderful life with those that love you or you stay behind in the third dimension to be slaves and suffer at the hands of those that don't want you to be free or happy. I know it's a lot to take in, but we are out of time and God has given his Intergalactic benevolent beings of light the green light to start showing humanity their starships in our skies. God wants you to know you can thrust him and Jesus, that these ships are here to help us, to support us in our time of need. Please know that they need our help to raise our vibration by all of us praying, staying positive and keep watching the skies. Don't be afraid, trust in the process. It's the only way God can get us safely in his barn while his troops round up every evil entity and kill them. We will all be okay if you trust in yourself to be brave, we can do this!!!

I Love You All and I'm Here to Help You! We Can Do This! Be Strong!

FAITH IN MYSELF

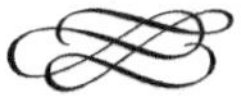

No matter what gets thrown at me, there's one thing, just one thing, that always gets me through it, My Faith In Myself! I won't let the negativity of others move, bend or alter my total belief in myself, my faith in my being, and my abilities to do whatever I set my mind to. I'm resourceful, savvy, and driven in my quest of perfecting my Spiritual connections and my powers. All with the selfless purpose of helping others, reach their own life path goals and dreams and help them discover the clues and the keys that unlock their abilities and skills. I have faced off with bullies in school, protecting a student with physical disabilities. I've spoken up about things that weren't right, at my own peril, I've gone over and above to help the homeless in my area and wherever I travel. In one of my past lives, I was incarnated as Joan Of Arc, in France. I wore men's clothes and I was ridiculed for it. I fought alongside men in battles to free the French people. Wearing armor that didn't save me when they burned me at the stake. I will always volunteer for the toughest missions, whether it's on earth or in another galaxy or dimension. My Faith is stronger than my Fear! Only you can save yourself. Only you can protect yourself and keep yourself safe. Once you tune your vibration to match the "Christ Consciousness" you will gain all the knowledge, skills, abilities, and traits needed to fight for what's right and for what benefits you and the whole. You will "Know" how loved and needed you are, how loved and cherished you are, how grateful and blessed you'll feel to be a part of this spectacular group of pure, loving, and compassionately Divine Soul's! No more living in fear and anxiety after you align yourself with God, Jesus, and "All That Is". Existing in a higher frequency not only elevates your vibrations but also envelopes your total being in a quilt of loving light and energy. You are now operating on multiple levels of conscious frequencies at the same time. Zero negativity can exist and neither do the evil, low-level entities or beings. It's like being in heaven but you're not dead, you're simply blending and hooking into the magical matrix of Christ's Consciousness. It can heal your earthly traumas, heal your aura and past pains and allow you to plug into the mainframe, letting your calcified skull melt away, to be replaced with a complete, indestructible, crystalline body form, shaped like you were at thirty years old. I've seen myself wearing my crystalline form in July of twenty, seventeen. I got up at five am and went out and laid down on the couch. I closed my eyes and I was instantly standing in a dimension of complete whiteness. Archangel Michael was standing beside me and I lifted my arm to stare at it, amazed that the outside was clear like acrylic, and the colors were iridescent like a rainbow. I held my arm closer to my face and saw millions of teeny, tiny clear bubbles, each one holding a natural being or species. One had a seal, one had a palm tree, an elephant, a flamingo, and on and on. Then Archangel Michael told me that humans are an Angelic race, who incarnate in the "Creation Game", to work towards total enlightenment of their souls. Then he went on to say that everything in the cosmos is made from the "Divine Electromagnetic Energies" of "All That Is", and that "We" too, are children of God. We each contain all we need to create any reality we wish to be in or live in. We can choose between staying in this outdated, heavy frequency of the third dimension or, we can elect to reach a much higher frequency of positive energy and loving consciousness, in the fifth dimension. I have personally been through three very challenging Ascension processes over the past ten years. Your whole body feels like it's being squeezed through a straw as you are releasing fourteen generations of traumas, all during three to five days and without sleep. Thank God I had Xanax because, after two days with no sleep, I thought I was dying, or losing my mind. Your whole body is being infused with a much faster frequency and if you didn't know what was happening to you, you'd swear you were going insane. None of you will experience any of that, I had to because I need to get through it fast to help others when the time comes. Make no mistake, we are in a Spiritual war between good and evil. Whether you want to or not you must make your choice, so I pray you chose to have an amazing life as part of the rebirth of Mother Earth. We can all see that the government doesn't have our best interests at heart and that things are going down fast. Once everyone gives up without trying or fighting then the demonic side wins. Right now, you must start thinking positive thoughts and do positive acts, to help yourself align with the good side, as you don't want to be on the side of negativity and evil, it won't bode well for you. Be Thankful that we have an escape route at our disposal, otherwise, we would have to remain here on earth as prisoners in our own homes. It's never too late to help others, to do good deeds, and to think positively. Angels, Jesus, and God have your back, choose love and light and you too will be saved!

MY SPIRITUAL PATH

Throughout my life in this incarnation, I've been blessed with discovering my psychic abilities. As a kid, I thought everyone could find lost objects using their mind. My mom's ability to channel those intelligent beings helped me to learn how to do it at sixteen years old. I went through a Tarot card phase but quickly decided it was faster to channel a being of the Source. I give psychic readings and I analyzed clients' dreams. While living in New Hampshire after Dennis was in jail, it was like I was reborn! I hadn't had freedom since I was nineteen. I could be myself without fear of being beaten. I felt lighter and I increased my psychic routines and methods of communicating with my Spirit Families. I didn't have to live in fear or anxiety anymore so I could meditate and practice my channeling any time I wanted to. Soon things began happening faster than I had hoped. I even let the spirits move my body. It started as moving my right hand up if the answer was yes and my left hand up if the answer was no, to a question I asked in my mind. Soon I had Mastered martial arts, using my body to do complete workouts of fast Tai Chi, and other forms of Asian martial arts like Qigong! My complete trust in the Spirits, advanced my levels of knowledge so much, that at times I couldn't tell if I was moving me or if they were moving me. We seemed to be operating as one, in simpatico. I could do this with my eyes closed or open. One time while doing it in a parking lot, a lady commented on how good my Reiki forms were. I didn't even know how to do Reiki but the Spirit moving me did. A few times while living in Ft Lauderdale, being a bartender, I told a man who was hitting on me, to please stop. After the third time, I don't remember how, but I came to, straddling him while he was flat on the floor. It was my night off and I was wearing a nice dress and talking to two of my regular customers when he kept interrupting us to drunkenly ask me out. I'm not a violent person but I believe my Spirit guides took over and put the man on the ground because I don't remember doing it. My customers were in shock at my fast maneuvers and said they would have taken care of the guy if I asked them to. That same thing happened when I was with my tattoo girlfriend from Sarasota. She and I were out one night when a girl got in my face saying I was dancing with her man, which was a lie because I love to dance by myself all night long when I go out. I don't like dancing with anyone as I love to just let myself do my own thing. She started to reach for my long hair and the next thing I know, a bouncer was lifting me off of her and I didn't hit her but I surprised her by getting control over her so fast. I don't remember doing it but Cindy said even the bouncers were caught off guard because I'm always so sweet. Nice to know that my Spirit Guides are there for me when I need them. My dreams have always been full-color movies and now I can tell if it's a past life dream, a future dream, or an Astral Travel dream. In one past life dream, I was a middle-aged man living in France during the Second World War. My pretty wife was a French can-can dancer and I was a jeweler. I watched myself sitting at my jeweler's bench making jewelry and I was a beefy man in my forties. We were smuggling Jews out of Europe and it was a very scary time for everyone. Another life, I lived in a little village near a Fjord, when the snow melt water started rising so fast we were all running up some stairs, trying to get as high up as possible but sadly we all drowned. In one of my Native American lives, I was a nine-year-old girl holding a little weasel that was my pet, when we were attacked by another tribe. I put my weasel down under a bush so it wouldn't get killed but my whole tribe was wiped out. Astral traveling is my favorite thing to do! One night in nineteen ninety-two, I fell asleep, and in my dream, I was in a room that had no windows or doors, and in the upper right-hand corner near the ceiling was a large black mass of evil energy. It started throwing me around the room like a rag doll, saying,

"Where's your savior now? You think you're so tough no one's going to save you!" I knew if I didn't get away from this evil mass, it would annihilate my very soul. I screamed out, "Jesus Save Me", "God Save Me!" Next thing I know I'm inside a clear tube that's above ground. On each side of the tube, there was a bench to sit on and a place to stand on each side too. They were made of those flat escalators they have in airports but the bench on one side is going away from something and the other side I was on was going to something. I looked outside and it looked white and sparkly but it wasn't snow, somehow, I knew that it wasn't safe to be outside as there were dead black, skinny tree trunks here and there and a few small hills in the distance. When we got to the end, it emptied into a humongous domed mall of sorts. There were beautiful people with light brown skin and other beings that weren't human but they seemed intelligent and kind. I could tell I wasn't on earth, I was in the future. I wanted to know what shoes looked like, so I went into a small store. I saw cool stuff and they had a tall cylinder that opened up and you hung your clothes in there and they sterilized them clean in three minutes. The clothes were like lightweight onesies. As I was looking at more stuff a man approached the sales counter and when he went to pay, he held his hand out flat and the coin he had showed a 3D rainbow-colored hologram with a picture on it, letting the sales lady know how much the coin was worth. I wanted to buy something to bring back to prove I was there and I picked out a cheap hand-sized calendar. When I went to pay, she saw my American money and her eyes got wide, as she stepped back reaching for a phone on the wall behind her saying, "You're a traveler!" Right then a young girl grabbed my arm and said, "Come on!" And we ran down another hall then she stopped by her friends. I asked, "How do you dance?" And she and her friends taught me some quick moves then I asked, "What about earth?" She replied, "The Wasteland?" Then I said goodbye and I jumped into a tube and my hair flew straight up as I fell fast back into my bed. I woke up laughing out loud. The last thing she told me before I jumped, was that the year was two thousand one hundred and ninety-six. Since then, in two thousand and nine, I've been to three more planets with three different timelines. Each time I'm me, but I'm doing different things in each astral travel. I'm in high school in the year two thousand two hundred and fifty-one. I'm fighting against the evil takeover of a planet whose water has had something put in it that turns people into flesh eaters, so my team and I are shooting darts into the citizens before they change into zombies. Until we can clean their water and give them an antidote. That is in the year three thousand and forty-one. I now understand what they mean when they say everything is happening at the same time. We are such advanced Beings of Light, that we can put a cotton ball size chunk to animate our bodies, during physical life on many different planets and dimensions all at the same time! We are truly capable of doing anything we set our minds to! The only thing holding us back is our fears and insecurities! I've seen myself doing incredible things on other planets. My friends and I rode on a Segway that flies through the air. It has a small windshield and the controls are on the handlebars and you stand on a small platform with a post that connects to the handlebars. They can fly straight or you can adjust the amount of lift and height while you're flying. I was told we will have those on planet earth in a few years. We took capsules that contain oxygen for when you're floating in an anti-gravity tank. They also let me ride in a cigar-shaped tube that has a nose cone and you lay almost flat inside it, except your shoulders are sitting up as you close the clear bubble over your head. It's got small wings and it's a personal aircraft that is just big enough to fit in. As a missile looked, it lifted up silently as we flew over the treetops then we came to a big open field with a domed mall. Outside there were four, twenty-foot round plates on giant springs, where you land your little craft, the springs absorb the landing, then we climbed out and we went inside the giant dome. That planet has a lot of trees and also some canyons as we have out west. The domes protect the buildings and they keep the air clean. That's the planet where I'm in high school, Sigourney Weaver is my mom and the planet is called Minotaur. I also know what inventions they have in the future. I dreamt of indoor wave pools ten years before they were invented. I've seen new-age tattoo machine technologies that I want to develop myself. I knew the Covid pandemic was coming on

April nineteenth of two thousand nineteen, nine months before it hit. I've predicted many things for my customers as well as found their jewelry on the east coast while I was on the west coast. We all have amazing powers just waiting to be discovered, so please believe in yourself as that's the first big step. Your skills are only dormant because you haven't given them a thought. Once you are honestly open to trying new things, your Spirit Guides will help you connect to them and then the veil will be lifted and your gifts will come to you like magic! Once you trust in yourself and your Angels and Guides, the rest will come so easily. I'm praying for you all and I know you can do it, you've got this! Go You Go!! Don't give up!

The Following Poem and Story are by, Ken With
A Pen

THE SOUL TEAM OF THE TRINE

A team of souls was gathered 'round, for yet another inning,

In the game, each one hoped

they had a chance of winning

All the gifts and talents gained

In many lifetimes shared,

They planned the time allotted

And how they would be paired

Mixed among the challenges

And lessons to be learned,

There had to be a place to meet

Not easily discerned

Using bits of pottery,

A yard sale and a store

They found a way to meditate

And let their spirits soar

This team of souls will gather 'round for yet another inning

And brightly glow because they know together, they are winning

Ken with a pen

1991

Dedicated to Mel, who gives Ken the form and substance of his life and who speaks for the Trine, all those, seen and unseen, who sit in the circle of the Trine, and to Lynn, who keeps asking the good questions...

GENESIS OF THE GAME

In the beginning, "All That Is" existed in a void. Complete nothingness is incredibly boring and unproductive so "All That Is" decided to make up a game to relieve the monotony. "All That Is", wanted an action game: something challenging with movement, color, sound, excitement, and most importantly, a useful purpose. The first version of "The Game" filled the void with an incredible number of glowing objects that moved in a pattern of cycles and layers all inter- woven in a complicated design containing nearly everything that could be imagined. This beginning of the universe was fascinating, but "All That Is" felt it lacked an essential element. Then "All That Is" had an inspiration. In an effort beyond imagining, "It" took from the very essence of "It's" being, that which is "Life" and sent that essence out into the universe in an explo- sion of perfect light that contained all of the souls that are or will ever be. And thus began the "Creation Game". The souls, like glowing sparks from a cosmic bonfire, flew into the universe, bumping and careening off each other in a joyous flight of freedom, until at least each one came to its farthest point from "All That Is" and some were at a great distance.

THE KNOWING

E very soul near and far became still and quiet so that it could experience what "All That Is" called, "The Knowing" and thereby understood the purpose of its existence. "The Knowing " is different for each level of players depending on their distance from "All That Is" and their special place in the universe. This explanation is for those souls assigned to planet earth, which is a place where first-level players can exist in and manipulate a physical world. It is not possible to explain all of the rules because The Game is complex and has many intricate and ever-changing aspects. Figuring out how to play The Game is a major element of The Game and players are free to do anything they want to do because nothing is right or wrong in itself. As drops of water may join to form a flood, one player or group of players may do something that has a profound effect on many other players. First-level players that get better at playing The Game, move to higher levels of Spiritual Attainment until at last, they no longer need to play The Game on a physical level. These souls may choose to return as teachers, guides, and Spiritual leaders often acting as a catalyst for positive change. "All That Is" conveyed the myriad elements of The Game in an instant and each soul understood its complexities and purpose. However, since a written explanation has to be sequential, the basic aspects of The Game presented here should be thought of as a counterpane made up of connected pieces that together form a warm and lovely quilt that covers the body awake and dreaming. First of all, everything in The Game that appears physical is an illusion shared by all the souls to provide a playing field of wonderful complexity. A secondary, but equally important, playing field is the dream world which allows the soul to go in with The Game while the physical self rests and renews itself. The Game is played in a place of opposition which requires physical beings to constantly make choices and decisions that affect themselves and others. Alone and collectively, souls in physical form exist somewhere on the continuum between the extremes of agony and ecstasy in a world of light and dark, noise and silence, war and peace, and during the time between birth and death. There is a logic and order to the universe that physical beings experience as repetitive cycles of time. This illusion of measurable time provides a framework in which to place a past, present, and future with its history, evolution, and potential for the advancement of life. Present existence is nothing more than the instant that the physical being is experiencing. That instant when gone becomes the past and that instant yet to come is the future. To most players of The Game, the near past and the immediate future are thought of as the present time. The illusion of time is essential to physical beings so they can assess what they have created and can focus on what they will create. Measurable time also provides for the growth and aging process which is an integral part of each physical life. Thus, the ageless soul has a framework for emotional and mental existence in a variety of physical conditions during each lifetime.

In experiencing physical birth, the soul moves into the sunlight of the earth, and in physical death, the soul moves into the light of the spirit. Thus, the soul always moves into the source light of "All That Is". The opposites of positive and negative are a major factor in The Game, beginning with the flight of souls from "All That Is". As the souls flew through space touching each other in flight positive and negative reactions took place that ordained the interaction of souls in the physical world. Positive reactions became kindred Spirits that players are drawn to for no obvious reason, while negative reactions became those with whom players experience conflict and discord. The Game requires that players turn all negative reactions into positive feelings of acceptance and love through physical action. Souls that touch are destined to be forming teams that play out various relationships in many physical lives together.

Souls that are touched with great positive force become highly charged and those are called soulmates. The most powerful physical and emotional aspects of The Game are experienced through the sexual force of male and female existence constantly interacting to perpetuate The Game through reproduction and the nurturing of life. The first decision made by a soul selecting a physical life is the sexual choice because every experience in that life will flow from the sexual orientation. The physical and emotional characteristics of male and female are blended by choice and environment in each being to make possible the amazing diversity of those souls playing The Game. This blending of feminine and masculine traits is one of the most creative parts of The Game because it assures an infinite variety of players interacting and reacting on many conscious and subconscious levels. Physical beings use the senses of hearing, sight, taste, touch, and smell to experience their physical environment. These senses form the creative basis used to communicate and express emotional and physical sensations. Civilizations, cultures, and religions used these sensual elements of The Game to express their thoughts, ideas, and beliefs through art, music, literature, and dance. By denying themselves one or more of the physical senses, souls may experience lives that challenge and inspire themselves and others. The soul's that play "The Creation Game" on earth work together both in and out of their physical bodies to keep "The Game" in constant motion. There is a "Society Of Souls" that serve as advisers, helpers, and coaches when not playing the physical part of The Game. They never act as critics or judges. Those who develop their extrasensory abilities can tap into the resources of Society which are always available to those who want or need them.

THE FORGETTING

To play "The Creation Game" it is necessary to suppress The Knowing and the knowledge of the soul during its physical life and this requires what "All That Is" calls, "The Forgetting". "The Forgetting" allows souls to be born into a physical life without conscious knowledge of why and how they are playing the game. The soul to be born into a physical life, in cooperation with the other souls to be involved, selects the environment and circumstances needed to learn the lessons of that life. With the physical birth, the soul knowledge begins to fade as the player becomes absorbed in the new experience. The Game is played through what is considered to be a lifetime and may be short or long in what is thought of as the earth cycles known as years. The soul has selected the length of time that it will play The Game and how it will end The Game, though it is possible to alter any aspect of The Game and how it will end The Game at any time, as circumstances change. Souls constantly review and select probable futures in a subconscious level of awareness not usually accessible to the players. What players may think of as luck, fate or God's will are actually what the players have chosen to include in The Game? The quest for the meaning and purpose of life is an underlying drive of most physical beings. This search has created a variety of religions that have both advanced and retarded the progress of souls in their playing of The Game.

THE REMEMBERING

When the soul leaves the body and passes into the light of the Spirit, its experience's what "All That Is" calls, "The Remembering". The returning player is met by a Being Of Light who guides them through a review of the life that just passed. This allows the soul to judge itself in terms of what was gained or lost in that lifetime.

From that review, the soul once again remembers all that it has experienced from the beginning, and can continue its progress toward the final goal of being reunited with "All That Is".

Be creative in living and dreaming.

Be loving and kind to everyone and everything.

Be patient with yourself and others.

Be joyful whenever possible.

Be concerned for those less fortunate.

Be positive that goodness and love will prevail.

Be glad for those more fortunate.

Be protective of all that surrounds you.

Be aware that you are a part of,

"All That Is"

Every player should be making an effort to create the world of perfect love and beauty desired by "All That Is". No matter how simple or complex they make it, everyone is playing The Game.

The Game ends when the last soul returns home to be reunited with "All That Is"!

Wishing You All an Exciting Life!

See you on the other side....

By, "All That Is" and Ken Davis

TREASURE MAP

Life on earth is like a treasure hunt. The ultimate prize is "Self"' You already have it, but you must discover it anew. Uncover your hidden talents and powers that your "True Self" is capable of. To do that, you must forage through the waste and desolation of human life and appreciate everything, whether you understand it or not. You are an observer of life and also a participant. Only through learning from mistakes and hard times, can you realize that what you have been searching for has been inside you the whole time. Suffering is your teacher, your reason for self-discovery and reconnecting with who and what you truly are. It's the reason you reincarnate on earth, to begin with. Once you realize that you have untapped potential and powers, you step closer to your inner self and subconscious mind. If everything was easy on the earth, you would just stay in your celestial home, relaxing in your state of constant creativity and bliss. You came to earth for several reasons.

GLOW FACTOR

Life is an introspection of "Self", helping you to get closer to the grand prize, to obtain the rank of "Adept". When you have completed many lifetimes, you are wiser and your connection to nature and compassion are instinctual and blessed. You will see through the stains and smudges of life's looking glass and hone in on what is truly important and impressive, the gift of life itself! Do not look upon these hard times as being forever, for deep in your subconscious, you know that this is just a warped reality, created by evil men's need, to chain the weaker souls to debt, poverty, and disease, all for their material gains. Your true self knows of such trickery and will separate you from those links of misery, through your hard work and "Self" discovery. You will then find Heaven on earth in the simplicity of life itself. What is "Self", you ask? "Self", is the true nature and form you were born from and your state of well-being, in life beyond time. When the galaxy dispels chunks of stars from its cosmic energies, these chunks will float off into the galaxy. The truly large ones will become stars. The smaller pieces, the Stardust and Star seeds, will become what we call, "Souls". These souls will be gathered and taken to the seventh dimension, where they will attend a school of sorts, an orientation if you will. Each new Star seed will have to learn to control its powers and also how to conduct its behavior appropriately, so it can obtain the most out of its unique talents. Many planets across the galaxies and universes will not allow entry to a soul unless it has graduated from all the classes of the Spirit realm. Skills and behaviors like common decency, compassion for all beings, and unconditional love are necessary for every white light being. Star seeds must be well-versed in all knowledge and experiences of what each Soul needs to have, to function as a high-frequency entity of light. In your true form, you look like a bright, pulsating ball of holy, white light but you can choose a human form that appears crystalline in color. You will still have a "Glow Factor", however, you won't be so blindingly intense. In the seventh dimension, the frequency is very high, allowing you to use your innate power of constant creation. You have only to think of creation and it will instantly materialize before you, completely as you perceived it in your mind. Art, architecture, and inventions are possible, simply by using your creative talents of conciseness to make them happen. Because the space in the seventh dimension is endless and your soul is eternal, your possibilities are infinite, when it comes to the instant manifestation of whatever your heart desires. Creating a gorgeous mansion on an island or a mountain retreat is just a few thoughts away when your desires and creativity run wild and free. Since happiness, compassion, and love are the only rules you have to govern you, your Spirit thrives in the beauty and boundless environment of the Celestial Realm. Some souls will attend school but decide not to incarnate on earth, choosing instead to stay in the Holy realm and devote their energies to working behind the scenes and dedicating themselves in service to the Spirit realm, much like a nun or pastor does on the planet earth. It requires a tremendous effort and a huge force of beings, to see to the managing of every Souls daily affairs and their safety, while they incarnate on earth. Since there are now over seven billion souls on earth, those in charge of the Divine Realm are kept extremely busy nonstop.

RECYCLED SOULS

Each new lifetime takes meticulous planning and attention, right down to the most minute details. Even then, with Free Will on behalf of each soul participating, it can alter, slow, or advance each participant's completion of whatever lessons were prearranged before their birth on earth. Let's say you tended to let people use you or control you in previous lives, so you enter a new life, with the mission of changing that behavior, by standing up for yourself and controlling your path in life. You may go through several relationships, only to not stand up for yourself, due to a variety of reasons, until you finally gather your inner strength to fight for yourself and your rights. The faster you stop the cycle, no matter what the situation, the sooner you can cross that chore off your list, while you move a step closer to your goal of finding out who and what you truly are. As soon as you enter the birth canal, your memories of all your amazing skills, talents, and outstanding abilities are erased, shutting your memories off from your conscious self, as a human being. Even though you are super-human in strength, fortitude, and cleverness, until you connect with your inner, subconscious self, you won't ever be aware of how truly amazing you are! Without connecting to your inner "Self", you won't have that deep level of consciousness, to show you how to activate your strengths and abilities. This is why your memories aren't readily available to you upon birth. If you knew how to use your abilities while you were young, you wouldn't want to take part in a challenge to learn something you already know. Having all the answers, you would not need the lessons. This way, all souls start on the same level playing field at birth. However, there are instances, where a young soul born in the flesh, is very aware of their potential, as not all their memories were erased, so they could jump over some of the hurdles in life's lessons and get to their mission at an earlier age. When a tiny child picks up an instrument and starts playing like they have done it before, they have! Many times, when a soul loves to do a certain thing, it will keep coming back again and again, to perform it while on earth. That's why God allows some Souls to reincarnate with their special talent memory, still Intact, allowing that soul to come into his/her talents at a very young age. Additionally, there are other allowances made for a soul that is reincarnating to perform a pivotal role in history to aid humanity, and that soul would also be "Spiritually

Awake" upon birth. The child will show extraordinary intelligence or skills because their life plan will need those abilities, soon after birth. Each case is different, as each soul is different and each lesson is different. Very old, recycled souls, who have already passed their learning eons ago, may choose to enter life on earth in the third dimension, just to have an easy life of leisure and enjoyment. Therefore, they will be Spiritually evolved right after birth and be able to access all their immense knowledge and skills, like the power to manifest wealth and also their healing powers of using white light therapy. These souls usually stand out because they have self-possessed powers that are like a beacon for other younger souls. Such beings give off a "Holy" glow and they are calm, yet strong, kind, and gentle. They have tamed their egos and are operating on multiple levels at the same time. Some become Gurus or powerful leaders in Spirituality or activists for human rights, animal rights, and saving planet earth. Once you pass a lesson, you no longer have to focus on that negative experience and you are free to focus on other issues you need to complete. If a soul is unable to move forward by completing a task, unfortunately for them, they must reincarnate again, until they pass that test. The moral of that story is to learn to find your voice, and your inner strength, applying those to your challenges as soon as you can, so you can put that behind you and move one step closer to perfecting your Spirit. You want to obtain a higher rank in the game, each time you incarnate, so you save yourself from suffering more incarnations.

TRICKSTERS

Back home in the Celestial realm, you are at ease and confident. Egos are non-existent in the higher frequency of the Holy dimension. Mutual respect for all beings is a cornerstone for being a part of this higher dimension. Gravity doesn't exist either, so flying or hovering around is a normal function, much like astral travel to other realms, dimensions, and planets becomes the norm. By now, much of this must sound a lot like life on earth. When you are born, you go to nursery school, pre-K, grade school, high school, and then college. Each year, your brain is engaged with a new and tougher curriculum. If you don't study hard and apply yourself, you won't pass and you'll have to repeat that grade you failed. See, just like it is in the Spirit realm! When all the lessons have been learned, one isn't required to incarnate again unless one chose to. Sometimes, an older soul will choose to volunteer to be the mother or father of a younger soul, so they will get good guidance and support, while in that incarnation on earth. A movie studio operates along the same lines as the Spirit realm. In our Divine home, everyone has "Star Power". Souls consist of electromagnetic energy of white light and pure loving conciseness. Your white light energy is as powerful as a "Real" Star! Your consciousness is what lets you think, feel and make decisions. You are all "Earthbound Angels" and your Spirit essence is capable of changing shape as well as projecting itself into other realms as well as interstellar, intergalactic, and inter-dimensional travel, without you ever leaving your body. You can also access the Multiverse any time you choose to. When you learn to meditate, you will begin seeing images, feeling people's emotions, and astral traveling to anywhere you can think of. It is in that state, where your Spirit Guides will show you pictures or images of things to come, things that help you understand what's going on behind the scenes. By meditating, you're ringing the bell that tells Spirit you are open to making contact. It takes some practice but keep a journal and jot down things you see or feel while meditating, that way you can see if there are any connections to what you're experiencing that day or that week. Soon, you will hear their words in your mind and the more you practice the faster and clearer their voices will sound. It is recommended to do this if you're in a safe environment and comfortable, so you won't feel scared. You can also get a lightweight chain from a necklace and hang a pendant or charm on it. Placing your elbow on the table, let the chain dangle from around your pointy finger. Ask out loud for a positive Spirit Guide, to please answer some questions for you. Only ask questions that have Yes, No, or Maybe answers. Tell the Spirit, that if they make the pendant swing to you and away from you, that means "Yes". If the Spirit makes the pendant swing from side to side, that means "No". If the Spirit makes the pendant swing around in a circle, that means, "Maybe". Because lower frequency entities can access this technique, it's very important to use protection first before even attempting this. The same goes for an Ouija board, ask out loud for only positive answers from positive beings to engage with you. When Jem first tried the chain and pendant technique, she asked a friend to sit across from her at the table, then she told them to ask a question in their mind, Not out loud, that they already knew the answer to. This way if they asked if they had a dog, and it said "No", when they do own a dog, you know it isn't a Spirit that was truthful or benevolent and she would stop for a while, then do it again later, until she found a Spirit that answered each question they asked only in their mind, correctly. Showing her client that there was no way she could try to swing the chain herself to cheat. It's a great way to start opening a dialogue with your Spirit Guides. Don't forget to Thank the Spirit that helps you, it strengthens the bond between you and they will step in and answer your questions, effectively blocking out all low-level Tricksters from working through you, until you get better and better at it and you no longer need the chain/pendant to communicate with them. Please always remember to ask Jesus/God/Angels/Source and the Masters to protect you with white light before you even start meditating, for your protection. If you ever get a creepy or negative feeling, stop what you're doing, get your "Sage", smudge stick, and light it as you let the smoke cleanse the area of any negativity. Sometimes it's good to sage your home once a week, just to have peace of mind.

TWIN FLAMES

When you choose to incarnate on earth, your human body of flesh could never hold, your entire "Star Being" inside you, as its full, true power and light, would pop out of every pore in your body and you would glow! Also, your soul is eternal and resides in Heaven, therefore before you enter life on earth, you remove a cotton ball size chunk of your being and place it in your sternum, upon birth. Don't let the size fool you, it's all you need during your tour of duty on earth. It contains the same powers and skills you already possessed before your incarnation and it's coded with all your special abilities, powers, traits, and knowledge in your DNA. The plan is to find out how to harness that Star power for yourself, so you can do amazing things during your incarnation and get the most out of your lifetime on earth. Every soul comes to earth with at least one Spirit guide, one to three personal Angels, and two totem animals in spirit. You chose your own Spirit guide in the pre-planning phase before birth. It's usually a member of your Star family. Star Families are made up of clusters of star seeds and Stardust, that floated out into space, grouped. They are never separated because the group came into existence together and is considered a bonded and divine family. Some people have big families because their cluster holds many star seeds, while others may have smaller families due to the small grouping of star seeds. Star seeds that were formed fused are what people call, "Twin Flames" and will usually incarnate as twins in a human form on earth. Twin flames may choose to be man/woman, man/man, or woman/woman, depending on their individual missions or joint mission. If one marries another person in that lifetime, they don't get jealous as they know their twin flame loves them the very most. Twin Flames could choose to be siblings, parents, relatives, or friends, the possibilities are exciting to them. When twin flames meet it's epic! It's as if they see themselves in the other person and it makes each of them feel "whole" again! Some individuals who put a bigger chunk of their essence in their human body will have a very special mission of causing great change on earth or they will play a pivotal role in the positive advancement of humanity and its collective consciousness. These special beings are wired directly into the matrix of very high frequencies and they have knowledge that is very futuristic and often considered so advanced as to be Divine in content or as witchcraft, by nonbelievers. Humans fear and ridicule what they don't understand. Each century on earth, a handful of these Highly Spiritual beings are sprinkled over planet earth, during that one-hundred-year period. This is all done for the benefit of mankind and it is not considered cheating, more like a gift from God/Jesus/Source. Here are just a few of those special beings, Nicola Tesla, Dr. Martin Luther King, Elvis Presley, Abraham Lincoln, John F. Kennedy, Mother Theresa, the Dali Lama, Buddha, and many others who radically changed the very fabric of humanity in an amazingly positive and beneficial way.

SMUDGE STICK

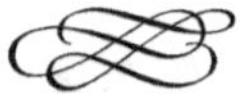

Spirit Guides work directly with you for your entire stay on earth. Most people will never be aware that they have a personal Spirit guide and Guardian Angels and often they will go their entire life feeling alone or forgotten by God. Since it was "You" that decided who would be your main guide, most likely you picked someone very close to you, someone you trust with your life. You chose someone you love and appreciate and trust to watch over you. You know they want the very best for you and won't betray you or let you down. Your only job is to let them into your life, Spiritually, consciously, and mentally. Once you acknowledge they exist, the rest will develop on their own, as you become more open to new experiences and you develop a stronger bond with them. Your subconscious is fully aware of their presence, only your ego and old, past beliefs are standing in your way of connecting with your True self. The more you communicate with them through speaking to them, during meditation, using cards, or while channeling, the easier your life will flow and the more grounded, loved, and appreciated you will feel. You will never feel alone again and it's an amazing feeling! Meditation is a great way to calm your mind and learn how to put strong, white light protection all around you, your nest, and your whole area, to keep dark, negative energies away from you. If possible, always use a "Smudge Stick" of sage, by lighting it and allowing its smoke to drift up inside your dwelling, as you move from room to room, letting it cleanse your space. Leave one window or door open and start on one side of the door or window, making your way through the house, until you end back to the other side of where you started, then close the door/window. It's important to walk around in a circle inside your house, going in one direction, till you end up where you started. This helps corral any negative energies and entities and shove them out the door or window. Some people use chants while smudging, asking God/Jesus/Source to remove all negativity from their abode. Do what feels right and comfortable for you.

I wish I had known of this method when we lived in that haunted house when I was a kid. It would have helped rid my bedroom of that creepy ghost! There wasn't a lot of Psychic information back in the early nineteen seventies. Trial and error worked for me. Having both parents that were not only educators, they also practiced meditation and channeling higher realm beings of light. Even now, I'm still learning, refining, and fine-tuning my abilities and methods. After all, we are all in constant motion and our cells are changing as do our bodies and mind. Meditation, even for fifteen or twenty minutes can help you get closer to your Spirit guides, by letting them know you are relaxed and breathing calmly. While your eyes are closed, let your mind wander, wherever it wants to and keep a journal of the visions if you see any, as well as write down your dreams before you get out of bed because you lose seventy percent of the dream after just five minutes of being awake. Dreams are a superb way to work out your problems, and worries and to release fear and doubt. See what your dreams are telling you. Many a nugget of wisdom and truth Is hidden in what seems like a zany, wild movie while you're sleeping!

ROBERT THE ANGEL

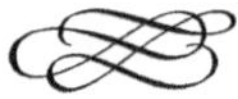

Besides Spirit guides, there are also "Over Souls". These Guides are like the overseers of the Spirit Guides and they work in tandem with them to help their human charges. When a human is going through a lot of tough or bad situations, the Over-Soul sends in extra Spirit Guides to help that person get through their state of affairs easier. Sometimes to help them learn a new skill or trade, the Over-Soul will send a Guide who has knowledge, skills, and experience in that topic, so they help the human learn it faster by whispering tips and ideas for shortcuts. Most times human beings think they just thought of it themselves but more often than not, it's their Spirit Guides that are placing the revelations in their consciousness. Once you trust in your Guide, the faster you catch on to the best way to communicate with them. The Over Souls also direct Angels, to a human that needs extra love and care, especially if they lost a loved one or are suffering from a long-standing illness, disease, or addiction. All of these actions are happening simultaneously all over the planet. Imagine how Spirituality advanced you have to be, to keep this whole production running for billions of humans over thousands of years! Without your Star families and the Spiritual realm, life on earth would be horrendous, as demonic, nefarious, and evil forces would take over and it would be a bloodbath of chaos. Without God/Jesus/Source and the Holy white light power, humans would suffer terrible atrocities and have no joy, pleasure, or love for life. Depending on your Soul's life path and where you are with being open to believing in things you can't see, some of you already know of this right now. Know that your Guide is a very close and personal friend or family member of yours. They know more about you right now than you do because your memory was wiped. You would never have picked a bad soul to watch over you, especially while you're in such a vulnerable position. Your powers and bodies are also restricted by a lack of memory and gravity. This way, unless you learn to communicate with your Spirit guide, you will take twice as long to complete each task. Think of it like hiking up a mountain. Would you just gear up, grab a compass and go off into the wilderness alone and wing it or would you rather have a trusted Guide that knows the perils and pitfalls with you, to lead the way and watch your back, warn you of danger, and show you the shortcuts? I thought so...I promise, you will never feel alone, once you can feel your Guide's strong presence and hear them speak. Everyone is capable of harnessing that skill, absolutely everyone!

JEM

It's the most amazing skill I possess. To have daily conversations with Archangel Michael and my personal "God Squad", consisting of, Ina, who's my soul sister, an Angel named Robert, who dictated books worth of knowledge and he speaks to me anytime I need him, Dante, who gives very accurate psychic readings to those in need of clarity, Saint Sebastian who has contributed a collection of details about how the Holy Realm operates, Nathen who provides tremendous insight and comfort to me, last but definitely not least, Napoleon, who has a voice that sounds like God and who woke me from my psychic slumber! What these Divine beings have done for me besides saving my life numerous times, is to patiently encourage me, counsel me through all my traumatic life situations, warn me of danger, and give me sound advice and comforting vibrations. Hearing their voices makes me feel like they are standing right next to me! I'm never lonely or scared, I feel their loving presence and it calms me, soothes my aching Soul. They have kept me anchored to this life and I am beyond blessed and honored to be a part of their team and to pass on all their Divine teachings with compassion and unconditional Love for humanity. My dad and mom, now in Spirit, are my constant companions from their celestial home and I feel even closer to them now that they are in the Spirit Realm because I can "Feel" their essence inside me and all around me and in everything I do. They have had time to watch how my life has been, so now they understand why I was so hyper and driven. It also gave them a chance to reflect on how their parenting affected me. I'm so proud of both of them for being so loving, open, and honest with me and my siblings. Cheers, Ken and Mel, you did a stellar job! God Bless You! A very special shout-out to all my Interstellar and Intergalactic Beings of Light families! Thank You for All Your Help And Hard Work!! I Love You All

A huge Thank You to the Middle Earth Beings of Light..the Agarthans! Love U

Thank you all so very much for your protection, guidance, and support through all my many missions, not only here on earth, but throughout the galaxies and dimensions. God Bless you for everything. I'm forever grateful for all the Angels, especially my personal Angels. Bless you Archangel Michael. Bless You

Archangel Jophiel, Bless You Archangel Raguel, who hover over me like expectant mothers, saving my beacon and my sanity! I love you all! I treasure each one of you! Thank You-Thank You-Thank You!

See You Soon…Jem

ROBERT THE ANGEL

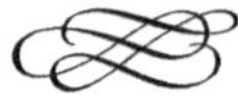

You must solve the mystery of your existence in each lifetime, using your mind, heart, body, spirit, and intuition. You are part of the Matrix of humanity and every soul is valuable, hence the importance of using your intuition, as it will guide you throughout all of your mortal lives. It's one of your superpowers, once you start trusting your instincts. Unfortunately, as the years have sped by, man has made many advancements in technology, so the need to rely on your intuition has almost been bred out of you. Cave men and women relied solely on their inner alarm system for everything, from what plants were safe to eat, to which ones were poisonous or medicinal and to alert them when a dangerous predator was near. They also knew to follow the tides, the rivers, the stars, the game trails, and the game. They lived in total harmony and oneness with their environment. Balance was always organically maintained in every way. They only killed what they needed and they made use of one hundred percent of it, showing their respect to the animal mother earth and God. With the introduction of the computer and the internet, young people today have lost their way and are disconnected from any spiritual path entirely. Spirit guides find it very hard to connect to today's youth, as they are now driven by electronic devices and new technologies instead of following their hearts and minds. The youth of today is so addicted and dependent on technology, it's as if they can't breathe without it. Having no guidance, they wander through life, tethered to their cell phones as if it's an umbilical cord keeping them alive. They are not grounded in any faith-based thoughts of a higher power. They are worshipping technologies instead of the true Masters of Faith. Most millennials don't attend church and find the teachings outdated and not worthy of their attention, so they lack the basic foundation for any spiritual ideology. For this reason, many of God's foot soldiers on earth have been tasked with waking up as many individuals as possible, as the current climate on earth is extremely volatile and dangerous. Psychics, Healers, and Empaths are aiding humanity by sharing their skills and knowledge with everyone that will listen but they are facing ridicule, hate, and disbelief from the masses. We are currently engaged in a battle of "Good versus Evil" and with the Demonic worshipping at an all-time high, we must wake up more souls to join this team seven, seven, seven, God's team. We are not saying people should go to church, instead, we just want humans to get in touch with their spiritual side, that way they can learn to manifest their desires and protect themselves from being used by those who have selfish and unhealthy agendas. Those who care zero for your well-being, your health, or your happiness. Even if a person doesn't believe in a higher power, there is no disputing the fact that evil forces are manipulating every government across the globe, with empty promises from those holding the puppet strings. Do you believe the Devil has any good intentions toward you? Does joining the Evil forces result in happiness and contentment? Joining team six, six, six, may give you fame, money, and clout but the price you pay when your times are up, means an eternity in Hell. God/Jesus/Source, wants to keep you safe and for you to live your very best life. Demonic forces only use souls for their negative agendas, while beings of white light are healers, and their agenda is positively focused on every soul's salvation, enlightenment, and harmony. Our sole mission is to help all of humanity see spirituality, in a fresh and current way, through modern technologies and to create an environment of no stress, more abundance, better health, and happiness for all.

Would you rather live in a world filled with hate, crime, poverty, disease, and misery, or would living in a frequency of love, compassion, good health, and abundance for all, be more to your liking? This is so doable and very easy. If you want an easier, more fulfilling, and content life, all you need to do is let the higher power who created you, into your daily life. Share your dreams and visions with your Angels, Guides, Jesus, and God, so they can assist you in how to obtain them through manifestation. If each person just announced out loud, that they want to be free, happy, and prosper, then you could, as a population, enter into a higher frequency and rise above all of that negativity and noise. You have all the power to make these positive changes within you but you have been programmed to accept all the lies and evil ideals, instead of thinking for yourselves. Right now, millions of folks have awakened and they see how their government is Not working for the betterment of the people. Humanity as a whole has been duped into thinking, "Well that's just the way it is, I can't do anything to change it". Bull-crap! You are powerful beings from the stars and each one of you is capable of outstanding things, together we will crush their evil movement and vanquish them entirely from your planet earth. All it takes is for you to stand up and say.. "This is unacceptable"! Don't be a victim, be a Voice! Once the tide turns through prayers and belief, your reality will open up and show you the kind of world where everyone lives in peace, love, and prosperity. In the higher frequency of the fifth dimension, only loving and benevolent vibrations can exist. Zero negativity is allowed and cruelty, crime, and greed are nonexistent and a thing of the past. This "Shift" in consciousness from the third dimension to the fifth dimension is called "The Great Awakening Of Souls" and it's going to happen whether you are on board or not. God/Jesus/Source, wants you to rise to this higher, cleaner frequency, as you are a beloved being from the realm of the Divine dimension, a child of God. If you pass up on this platinum opportunity, you, unfortunately, will be left behind in the third dimension, to suffer unimaginable pain and loss by those demonic entities that crave control and complete compliance from you. You will become a slave of Satan if you don't attempt to break free of the false reality and narrative that's holding you back from connecting to the Real you! We can't impress upon you just how dire this situation is because most folks won't believe this is a reality they could soon face. Already you should be noticing how those in power manipulate you to participate, even against your own beliefs. If everyone knows that they are being lied to and led astray, then once you stop believing in the lies and see the actions for what they truly are, you can break away from their deceptions. Once people's eyes are open to reality, they will never stand for being imprisoned on earth in their environment. Spiritual knowledge is the key to humanity's survival and fundamental for success in a life of the flesh. This is a time like no other on earth, everything is moving forward in a negative manner and folks are just following along, silent and asleep. It's time to make changes within yourselves and to take a stand for humanity and its future generations. This kind of knowledge must be filtered down through a Psychic who is Spirituality Advanced, so they can aid those who need help in understanding how all these works. The average person who has little or no spiritual knowledge lacks the time to research all the ways to get in touch with their higher powers or the powers of the Source. With so many life-altering events happening across the globe, time is of the essence and everyone must do their part. We don't expect you to enlist in an army and go to war, we are already in a war of ideals and principles. We can use words, followed by actions, like stopping buying into their twisted narrative, and instead, use kindness, compassion, and non judgment as our weapons. Being nice doesn't cost a thing. Being compassionate and loving is your greatest weapon against those pushing you toward any negative energies and agendas.

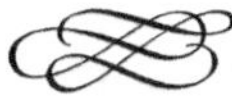

SPORTS CAR

If you put out positive thoughts and loving vibrations, you can halt the negative movement and help yourselves become one with the universe. When you are in balance with the earth and elements, tasks become easier, life itself is more fun and spontaneous. A feeling of peace and inner confidence will bloom when given a little attention and focus. Like, how well a plant grows when given some sun and water. Think of it as feeding your Spiritualist self! A feeling of calm control will emanate from your entire being, now that you are aligned with your mind, body, and soul. Compare it to driving an expensive sports car. You can feel your power, (Spirit), and you handle the curves with speed and agility (Body), You are in total control as if you and the car are one, (Mind). Now you are operating on all cylinders-Mind-Body-Spirit and you are in complete balance with your Being and your environment. That is the exhilaration of being aligned with your "Inner Self", that carefree feeling and confidence that is your birthright. God/Jesus/Source, wants Everyone to drive their own sports car! You were born with that right, the right to live free and in harmony with nature and your fellow man. Unless someone shows you how to Align yourself with your body, mind, and spirit, you will continue to drive a clunker of a car that breaks down, needs repairs, and is undependable, leaving you alone and stranded. This is very doable folks, your Spirit Guides want to help you in any way they can, so please try to have an open mind. That's the first step to taking control of your life and your surroundings. Your Guides know tricks and shortcuts, to a happy and healthy life, as they are your "Life Coaches". They can warn you of danger, help steer you in the right direction as well as just be great listeners when you're upset or are facing a stressful situation. Once you trust in yourself, then you are ready to trust in your Guides. Your destiny is calling......Please pick up!

The great debate over which came first, the chicken or the egg?

The debate over God or Science still rages today on earth. Scientists insist that only through the use of scientific methods and experiments, can we solve life's riddles. Their work and their discoveries have merit, however, they are only judging the mysteries of life, through their microscopes and their trial and era experiments. They are wearing blinders when it comes to all things supernatural. Refusing to believe in anything they can't label or explain away using their scientific knowledge. They may be smart when it comes to their field of study, but they are missing the big picture. Compared to beings of light from the seventh or eleventh dimension, they are just little boys with silly egos! Even the top scholars in every field of scientific study, cannot even fathom how lame their advancements are compared to those Supreme beings of light! It is like trying to explain our realm to toddlers. We can manipulate weather, asteroids, volcanoes, and time, instantaneously manifest anything we want, travel through time and space with just a thought, and project ourselves to other dimensions, realms, and multiverses. Being Masters of everything, we are responsible for the enlightenment and also humanity's evolution, both physically and Spiritually. Without the Spiritual frequencies and entities of the conscious white light and of the entirety of "All That Is", it would take one hundred thousand years on the 3D earth to catch up to the technologies we have possessed for eons. With your handheld internet devices, you can create worlds of wonder and fantasy, using editing tools, filters, and other high-tech abilities. Your phone enables you to talk with friends and family who are far away, as well as take pictures that capture your life's events and moments. You are the creators of your environment while using those devices, without them, you would be lonely, separated, and bored. Well, it's the same for the Creator of our universe! He created Man and Woman after he created planets and suns and moons to sustain those beings. He's been doing this on many other planets and in other dimensions that are far superior in their Spiritual Enlightenment as well as with their technologies. Scientists on earth think they are "God's" because they figured out some theories, made some advancements and cures, or developed electricity, telephones, cars, trains, and planes but without Belief in a Higher Power, they lack the open minds that are capable of discovering truly outstanding breakthroughs! They hold themselves back by denying God's existence and "His" Incredible natural powers of love and healing light. There would be nothing to study in science if "All That Is" never created the "Souls of Light". Their fragile egos keep them tethered to the third dimension of conciseness. For science to take a great leap into the future, they must first admit that there is way more to life, than just what you see under a microscope or a telescope. Science has its uses but Spirituality holds All The Keys to abundance, manifestation, a constant creation, and the secrets of life itself. Physicists and scientists haven't unlocked all the doors to our higher technologies and perhaps they never will in your lifetime. It's so complex and futuristic that there aren't even any words to explain it all in its entirety.

When one looks around at the tremendous diversity on planet earth, you have to wonder in amazement at its ingenious flow of give and take, Its synchronicity. All around you living and breathing organisms are thriving and plants and animals and aquatic beings are flourishing under the laws of nature itself. Predator or prey, each one is equipped with its special skill for obtaining food and also for escaping becoming food itself. Thus, creating natural order for the benefit of all species on land and in water. "All That Is" spoke to his advisors and they came up with a plan. They enlisted the aid of their benevolent Entities of Light, to design and develop prototypes of mammals, reptiles, birds, insects, sea creatures, and fish. The plan was to give each creature special features, designed for their environment, as well as camouflage and other ways to protect them and help them flourish. The porcupine is slow and lumbering, making it easy prey for predators, so quills were added so they could protect themselves from attack. Jellyfish are slow-moving in the water, therefore they were equipped with tentacles that sting and disable their prey and also protect them from being an easy meal. The Beings of Light had so much fun in this endeavor and it almost became a contest to see who could come up with the wildest creatures of all. That's why you see such divine colors of birds, fish, reptiles, and amazing animals all over planet earth! After the creations were tested and approved, they were placed on earth by interstellar and intergalactic beings, who set them up in their intended surroundings and environments, to breed and thrive. Every being, big and small has a very Spiritual Nature. They don't have emotions like revenge or hate. They operate by their instincts and intuition to hide them and keep them safe. That's why they know when bad weather or danger is coming before people do. God made sure they were strongly connected to "His Light". Even predators rely on their intuition and instincts to navigate life and to find food and shelter. Only the highest level of intelligent conscious matter could create such unbelievable and amazing details you see in everything under your sun. That is why we are reaching out to humanity now, it is never too late to make as many positive changes in your life as you can. How you think, how you treat yourself and others, and how you treat mother earth. Every positive effort to do the right thing will be recorded and counted as a point for your Karmic record. It's never too late to show how much you appreciate all you have and be thankful for everything and everyone. Express gratitude and thanks to God/Jesus/Source for all they have done for you. Your Soul will feel lighter, freer, and at peace. A calm will fill every fiber of your being and you will be stepping closer to reconnecting with the Spirit Realm and your Angels and Spirit Guides. You will be welcomed as We Love You and are so excited to be with you again in the fifth dimension of Love and Light!

Many Blessings to You All..

Archangel Michael

THE GREAT AWAKENING OF SOULS

Folks would learn to appreciate the animals more if they had to hunt down or raise their meat, poultry, and fish. Doing things is so easy these days that folks don't even have to venture outside of their homes if they don't want to. They can sit on their couch and order food, gadgets, services, and everything under the sun. Twenty-four, seven, three hundred and sixty-five days a year. It may be easier but the trade-off is that it isn't always better! People today are missing out on life, its richness, its flavor, and its depth. You are all just living in a bubble of emotions that cycle around in the earth's atmosphere. The collective energies of fear, depression, worry, anxiety, and anger, affect every human, even those that are upbeat. A person might wake up in a great mood, looking forward to whatever their day brings but after the frustration of sitting in traffic, waiting in line to get a coffee, listening to coworkers gossip about others, and getting annoyed by a multitude of other things, you're ready to punch something by the end of the day. In part, some of that negative energy was already in the atmosphere all around you, and if you're a sensitive person, you will be affected by the angry moods and negativity of others. Ever since Covid was released in twenty-twenty, the reality of daily life has had to shift tremendously, in just a few short months. Did you ever imagine you would be working from home instead of at the office? That schools, churches, businesses, malls, and restaurants would be closed or out of business? Dads and Mom didn't have to stay home before Covid and try to teach their children from the kitchen table. Everything takes longer, and costs more, while nothing changes to make it better. Religions are dying and are being replaced by new technologies, gadgets, and automation. Spiritually has pockets of devotees, however, the vast majority of folks are struggling and depressed over gas prices and inflation. Mother Earth is dying, right under your feet, while everyone is floundering around, unsure of what is true and what is fake. People are too focused on what words should or shouldn't be used, instead of trying to help change the world for the better. Don't get me wrong, there are good, loving, hard working folks out there and some humans who are doing all they can to help but all the energies of life on planet earth have become extremely unbalanced. Chaos is rearing its angry head. Fear and anxiety are at an all-time high, as things are spiraling out of control. Everyone on earth can see how insane things are, not just for themselves but for everyone on the planet. You are all being corralled into a pen of misery and slavery. Once folks start to question their reality, a crack in the dam, that's keeping humans from realizing their true powers and potential here on earth, will burst open and coat the entire earth with total love and compassion, from a higher frequency of conciseness. The more people give off positive vibrations of white light and prayers, they are helping humanity to rise up to a higher dimensional frequency, which will then create the ascension shift. It will be like a shock wave, of cosmic energy and higher vibration. It has more power than one hundred thousand nuclear bombs, but it's a benevolent evolution of a much higher frequency, for the entire atmosphere surrounding the planet earth and its inhabitants. This process is called, the **"Great Awakening Of Souls,"** an event that's currently being followed by many intergalactic federations, from various star systems across the galaxies. Nothing like this has ever occurred in the history of the universe! It's a social shift of consciousness, for billions of earth-bound souls. Never before, has a planet been given a frequency upgrade from the third dimension to the fifth dimension, especially because it would take at least three hundred years to gradually raise the vibrations over time. We are currently in the process of doing a three-hundred-year upgrade, in only three to five years! The powers that "Be", have had to rush this event, due to the war in Ukraine and the global elite, whose mission is to take total control over the whole planet with their One World Order, which will be the end of humanity's life as you know it. Governments are too war-hungry and the earth needs help, not more death, and destruction. The "Great Awakening Of Souls", was planned a very long time ago, that's why many benevolent beings from the higher dimensions, have been trying to help all they can to raise your vibrational frequencies. They can't do it for you, but they are working through our Psychics and Spiritually awakened humans, that are, and have been, in communication with us for many years. Though they have faced ridicule, persecution, and a lot of hardships. These highly evolved souls selflessly volunteered to be a part of this endeavor to aid humanity, before they incarnated into a human form on earth. Now it's finally about to unfold, like a glorious rainbow of radiant and holy, supernatural lights! A tremendous wave will blanket mother earth and the loving warmth and healing light, will envelop everything with a feeling of peace and serenity, so strong, that many will fall to their knees and cry. Those who are nonbelievers in a "Higher Power ", will feel crushed by darkness, so vile and empty, that they could go mad. Being cut off from the source of "All That Is", the Creator and God, the faithless are now unable to function in this new, higher, lighter, and faster vibration. They can't feel the loving energy because their souls are not tuned into the higher frequency of pure, unconditional love and healing conciseness. Those negative beings and evil entities, will perish, by spontaneous combustion or be forced to remain behind in the third dimension. Planet earth is already being infused with the stronger energies of the fifth dimension, that's why your planet's been experiencing such drastic and catastrophic weather and other natural disasters. With planet earth being bombarded by the five-D frequency, humanity must prepare for the coming shift of this Holy Energy. In the very first few hours of the shift, everyone will be Spiritually lifted by an intense, healing, white light and they will remain in that state for approximately five hours. A feeling of "Leveling Off", will fill everyone until they reach a gradual state of self-control and awareness that permeates their soul. Then you will obtain a feeling of wellness, love, and harmony with all things. There are a lot more details about every phase of the Shift but we are using simple terms, to help you grasp an understanding of the event itself. When you know what to expect, you will be grateful for this knowledge, not just for you and your families but also to teach others what you have learned. You will all gain strength in numbers. The more humans that are open-minded and curious about Supernatural events, the less fear and anxiety people will have because they were told what to expect and what to look out for, in advance. Think of it like a hurricane warning, it gives you time to gas up your vehicles, stock up on food and essentials, and shore up your property and your homes and businesses. Humanity as a whole, should come together, as fast as possible and form their neighborhood watch groups for safety in numbers. You have all probably taken note of the staggering amount of people dying left and right. Many souls chose to exit this life because they didn't want to be a part of the Ascension process and go through this unprecedented event. Sheep, birds, goats, and other animals are forming "Death Marches", by walking around and around in a circle that spirals outward until they die of exhaustion. There may be riots, looting, armed robberies, and a lot of whacked-out people that don't understand what's happening to them and everything around them. Imagine if you were to wake up one morning to find that almost half of the entire population on earth has simply vanished! Those left behind will feel intense fear and anxiety. There will be groups of God's foot soldiers doing all they can to convince those left behind, to turn their life over to Jesus, so they can also rise to the fifth dimension. The third dimension is a lower frequency that supports, not just positive energy but also negative energies and it has been corrupted by Demonic entities. Right under your noses, evil is doing its best to rule your world and put a stop to Christianity or any talk or worship of Jesus or God. The fifth dimension is a faster, lighter, cleaner, more harmonious vibration of unconditional love and compassion. Zero negativity exists in five-D, meaning, it's like living in Heaven while on earth! New technologies, like Holographic healing beds and advanced techniques in growing food and creating cheap energy and abundance for all, will be introduced to everyone that rises into the five-D frequency. No more starvation, no more diseases, no more crime and corruption, and no more paying electricity bills! There will be much chaos and many natural and unpredictable weather events and also panic and crime will be at staggering levels before the total Shift to the fifth dimension. Every human is at their level of openness and Spirituality, so some will rise in the first wave of the shift. Others who are less Spiritual will need more time to catch up to the others. The less judgmental you are, the more loving and compassionate you are, and the quicker you will leave the third dimension and enter the fifth dimension. First, you must choose either God's positive love frequency or the Devil, a lower frequency of negativity. Remember, both Jesus and the Devil know what's truly in your heart, you can't fake it just to make it to be welcomed in Heaven. The Devil will gladly take you if it is evil in your heart and soul. It is of great importance to build strong family, friends, and neighborhood connections, making everyone feel safer, and being with those who believe as you do and who are trustworthy. The term, "no man is an island", fits this unusual situation, and the time to get right with whatever Faith you believe in is Now! I know many of you right now are wondering, what all this has to do with Alzheimer's. Everything on earth is connected to everything throughout the universe and to all of the realms, dimensions, multiverses, and universes. Every choice you make has an impact that affects everything and everyone. When folks start working together, great changes can come about, just by everyone being positive, compassionate, and loving towards each other.

Rising to the fifth dimension is God's way of saving the believers, the loving and compassionate souls like Noah did with the Ark! He has not forsaken you, "He's" already here!

Thank you for giving us a chance to speak with you. We Love and Appreciate Every Soul and Their Journey. Please know that there are Legions of Benevolent Beings that are doing all they can to protect you and keep you safe during these tumultuous times.

Be Brave, Be Kind To Yourselves, and You Will Soon Be Living in Heaven On Earth! We Love You Dearly.

Angel Robert.

EPILOGUE

It's hard to say when our time to leave this earth will be or to predict how we will go. My Mother's been in the Dementia ward for five years now, and with each visit, there is less and less of her there, mentally and physically. It brings to mind an hourglass, the sands sifting down slowly. As a grown woman with kids of my own, you'd think I'd be tougher, but somehow watching her blowing away little by little, day by day, I'm overcome with a deep sense of loss and sadness. The helplessness and devastation choked me as if I had swallowed a bullfrog that won't go down. If I'm this devastated and overwhelmed, I can't even begin to imagine how my father, who's been married to her for sixty-two years, must feel.

My Mom's general health is good, and I catch glimpses of her amazing personality when it shines through in sudden bursts that startle you like fireworks, flooding your mind with precious memories that are long lost to her by the ravages of her disease. I know my true Mom, the smart, tough, talented, driven chief, cook, and bottle washer is still in there, buried under leaves of confusion. When I'm with her, I take her by the hand and do a little dance, then ball my eyes out on the way home. To all of you who are in my shoes, it's with firm resolve that I say, May God Bless Us All so that we can ride out this storm called Alzheimer's, each in our own family dingy, hanging on for dear life, all the while praying that one day a cure will come.

ABOUT THE AUTHOR

Jem considers herself to be a "Sirius Gypsy" whose head is always in the galaxies. Her dedication to helping humanity and animals has been the driving force throughout her unusual life.

She loves being a "Voice" for the Divine Beings Of Light and those who cannot speak. She resides in the "City of Angels" and loves every minute of whatever life throws her way!